ABOUT THIS PUBLICATION

FOR SERVICE ASSISTANCE

Customer Service
1.704.898.0770

North Carolina General Statues is published by The Muliti-Media Group of Greater Charlotte in Charlotte, North Carolina. Copyright 2015 by the Multi-Media Group of Greater Charlotte. This book or parts thereof may not be reproduced in any form, stored in a retrieval system, or transmitted in any form by any means—electronic, mechanical, photocopy, recording or otherwise—without prior written permission of the publisher, except as provided by United States of America copyright law.

The records required by U.S. Code 2257(a) through (c) and the pertinent regulations 28 C.F.R. Cli. 1, Part 75 with respect to this publication and all materials associated with such records are maintained by The Multi-Media Group of Greater Charlotte, Publisher and available for review by Attorney General.

www.visionbooks.org

Copyright © 2015 by MMGGC
All rights reserved!

TID: 5061514
ISBN (10) digit: 1502913682
ISBN (13) digit: 978-1502913685

123-4-56789-01239-Paperback
123-4-56789-01239-Hardback

First Edition

090520140547

Printed in the United States of America

2015 EDITION

North Carolina Criminal Law And Procedure-Pamphlet # 40

Printed In conjunction with the Administration of the Courts

North Carolina Criminal Law and Procedure
Pamphlet Reference Guide

Chapters	Pamphlet
Chapter 1 Civil Procedure	1
Chapter 1 Civil Procedure (Continue)	2
Chapter 1A Rules of Civil Procedure	2
Chapter 1B Contribution.	2
Chapter 1C Enforcement of Judgments.	2
Chapter 1D Punitive Damages.	2
Chapter 1E Eastern Band of Cherokee Indians.	2
Chapter 1F North Carolina Uniform Interstate Depositions and Discovery Act.	2
Chapter 2 - Clerk of Superior Court [Repealed and Transferred.]	3
Chapter 3 - Commissioners of Affidavits and Deeds [Repealed.]	3
Chapter 4 - Common Law	3
Chapter 5 - Contempt [Repealed.]	3
Chapter 5A - Contempt	3
Chapter 6 - Liability for Court Costs	3
Chapter 7 - Courts [Repealed and Transferred.]	3
Chapter 7A – Judicial Department	3
Chapter 7A – Continuation (Judicial Department)	4
Chapter 7A – Continuation (Judicial Department)	5
Chapter 7B - Juvenile Code	5
Chapter 8 - Evidence	6
Chapter 8A - Interpreters for Deaf Persons [Recodified.]	6
Chapter 8B - Interpreters for Deaf Persons	6
Chapter 8C - Evidence Code	6
Chapter 9 - Jurors	6
Chapter 10 - Notaries [Repealed.]	6
Chapter 10A - Notaries [Recodified.]	6
Chapter 10B - Notaries	6
Chapter 11 - Oaths	6
Chapter 12 - Statutory Construction	6
Chapter 13 - Citizenship Restored	6
Chapter 14 - Criminal Law	7
Chapter 14 –Criminal Law (Continuation)	8
Chapter 15 - Criminal Procedure	9
Chapter 15A - Criminal Procedure Act (Continuation)	10
Chapter 15A - Criminal Procedure Act (Continuation)	11
Chapter 15B - Victims Compensation	11
Chapter 15C - Address Confidentiality Program	11
Chapter 16 - Gaming Contracts and Futures	11
Chapter 17 - Habeas Corpus	11

Chapter 17A - Law-Enforcement Officers [Recodified.]	11
Chapter 17B - North Carolina Criminal Justice Education and Training System [Recodified.] Chapter 17C - North Carolina Criminal Justice Education and Training Standards Commission	11
	11
Chapter 17D - North Carolina Justice Academy	11
Chapter 17E - North Carolina Sheriffs' Education and Training Standards Commission	11
Chapter 18 - Regulation of Intoxicating Liquors [Repealed.]	12
Chapter 18A - Regulation of Intoxicating Liquors [Repealed.]	12
Chapter 18B - Regulation of Alcoholic Beverages	12
Chapter 18C - North Carolina State Lottery	12
Chapter 19 - Offenses against Public Morals	12
Chapter 19A - Protection of Animals	12
Chapter 20 - Motor Vehicles	13
Chapter 20 - Motor Vehicles (Continuation)	14
Chapter 20 - Motor Vehicles (Continuation)	15
Chapter 20 - Motor Vehicles (Continuation)	16
Chapter 21 - Bills of Lading	17
Chapter 22 - Contracts Requiring Writing	17
Chapter 22A - Signatures	17
Chapter 22B - Contracts Against Public Policy	17
Chapter 22C - Payments to Subcontractors	17
Chapter 23 - Debtor and Creditor.	17
Chapter 24 – Interest	17
Chapter 25 – Uniform Commercial Code	18
Chapter 25 – Uniform Commercial Code (Continuation)	19
Chapter 25A – Retail Installment Sales Act	20
Chapter 25B - Credit	20
Chapter 25C - Sales of Artwork	20
Chapter 26 - Suretyship	20
Chapter 27 - Warehouse Receipts [Repealed.]	20
Chapter 28 - Administration [Repealed.]	20
Chapter 28A - Administration of Decedents' Estates	20
Chapter 28B - Estates of Absentees in Military Service	20
Chapter 28C - Estates of Missing Persons	20
Chapter 29 - Intestate Succession	21
Chapter 30 - Surviving Spouses	21
Chapter 31 - Wills	21
Chapter 31A - Acts Barring Property Rights	21
Chapter 31B - Renunciation of Property and Renunciation of Fiduciary Powers Act	21
Chapter 31C - Uniform Disposition of Community Property Rights at Death Act	21
Chapter 32 - Fiduciaries	21
Chapter 32A - Powers of Attorney	21
Chapter 33 - Guardian and Ward [Repealed and Recodified.]	21

Chapter 33A - North Carolina Uniform Transfers to Minors Act	21
Chapter 33B - North Carolina Uniform Custodial Trust Act	21
Chapter 34 - Veterans' Guardianship Act	22
Chapter 35 - Sterilization Procedures	22
Chapter 35A - Incompetency and Guardianship	22
Chapter 36 - Trusts and Trustees [Repealed.]	22
Chapter 36A - Trusts and Trustees	22
Chapter 36B - Uniform Management of Institutional Funds Act [Repealed.]	22
Chapter 36C - North Carolina Uniform Trust Code	22
Chapter 36D - North Carolina Community Third Party Trusts, Pooled Trusts	23
Chapter 36E - Uniform Prudent Management of Institutional Funds Act	23
Chapter 37 - Allocation of Principal and Income [Repealed.]	23
Chapter 37A - Uniform Principal and Income Act	23
Chapter 38 - Boundaries	23
Chapter 38A - Landowner Liability	23
Chapter 39 - Conveyances	23
Chapter 39A - Transfer Fee Covenants Prohibited	23
Chapter 40 - Eminent Domain [Repealed.]	23
Chapter 40A - Eminent Domain	23
Chapter 41 - Estates	23
Chapter 41A - State Fair Housing Act	23
Chapter 42 - Landlord and Tenant	23
Chapter 42A - Vacation Rental Act	23
Chapter 43 - Land Registration	23
Chapter 44 - Liens	24
Chapter 44A - Statutory Liens and Charges	24
Chapter 45 - Mortgages and Deeds of Trust	24
Chapter 45A - Good Funds Settlement Act	24
Chapter 46 - Partition	24
Chapter 47 - Probate and Registration	25
Chapter 47A - Unit Ownership	25
Chapter 47B - Real Property Marketable Title Act	25
Chapter 47C - North Carolina Condominium Act	25
Chapter 47D - Notice of Settlement Act [Expired.]	25
Chapter 47E - Residential Property Disclosure Act	25
Chapter 47F - North Carolina Planned Community Act	25
Chapter 47G - Option to Purchase Contracts	25
Chapter 47H - Contracts for Deed	25
Chapter 48 - Adoptions +	26
Chapter 48A - Minors	26
Chapter 49 - Bastardy	26
Chapter 49A - Rights of Children	26
Chapter 50 - Divorce and Alimony	26
Chapter 50A - Uniform Child-Custody Jurisdiction and	

Enforcement Act	26
Chapter 50B - Domestic Violence	26
Chapter 50C - Civil No-Contact Orders	26
Chapter 51 - Marriage	26
Chapter 52 - Powers and Liabilities of Married Persons	27
Chapter 52A - Uniform Reciprocal Enforcement of Support Act [Repealed.]	27
Chapter 52B - Uniform Premarital Agreement Act	27
Chapter 52C - Uniform Interstate Family Support Act	27
Chapter 53 - Banks	27
Chapter 53A - Business Development Corporations and North Carolina Capital Resource Corporations	28
Chapter 53B - Financial Privacy Act	28
Chapter 54 - Cooperative Organizations	28
Chapter 54A - Capital Stock Savings and Loan Associations [Repealed.]	28
Chapter 54B - Savings and Loan Associations	29
Chapter 54C - Savings Banks	29
Chapter 55 - North Carolina Business Corporation Act	30
Chapter 55A - North Carolina Nonprofit Corporation Act	31
Chapter 55B - Professional Corporation Act	31
Chapter 55C - Foreign Trade Zones	31
Chapter 55D - Filings, Names, and Registered Agents for Corporations, Nonprofit Corporations, and Partnerships	31
Chapter 56 - Electric, Telegraph and Power Companies [Repealed.]	31
Chapter 57 - Hospital, Medical and Dental Service Corporations [Recodified.]	31
Chapter 57A - Health Maintenance Organization Act [Recodified.]	31
Chapter 57B - Health Maintenance Organization Act [Recodified.]	31
Chapter 57C - North Carolina Limited Liability Company Act.	31
Chapter 58 - Insurance.	32
Chapter 58 - Insurance (Continuation)	33
Chapter 58 - Insurance (Continuation)	34
Chapter 58 - Insurance (Continuation)	35
Chapter 58 - Insurance (Continuation)	36
Chapter 58 - Insurance (Continuation)	37
Chapter 58 - Insurance (Continuation)	38
Chapter 58A - North Carolina Health Insurance Trust Commission [Recodified.]	38
Chapter 59 - Partnership.	39
Chapter 59B - Uniform Unincorporated Nonprofit Association Act.	39
Chapter 60 - Railroads and Other Carriers [Repealed and Transferred.]	39
Chapter 61 - Religious Societies	39
Chapter 62 - Public Utilities	39

Chapter 62 - Public Utilities (Continuation)	40
Chapter 62A - Public Safety Telephone Service And Wireless Telephone Service	40
Chapter 63 - Aeronautics	40
Chapter 63A - North Carolina Global TransPark Authority	40
Chapter 64 - Aliens	40
Chapter 65 – Cemeteries	40
Chapter 66 - Commerce and Business	41
Chapter 67 - Dogs	41
Chapter 68 - Fences and Stock Law	41
Chapter 69 - Fire Protection	41
Chapter 70 - Indian Antiquities, Archaeological Resources and Unmarked Human Skeletal Remains Protection	42
Chapter 71 - Indians [Repealed.]	42
Chapter 71A - Indians	42
Chapter 72 - Inns, Hotels and Restaurants	42
Chapter 73 - Mills	42
Chapter 74 - Mines and Quarries	42
Chapter 74A - Company Police [Repealed.]	42
Chapter 74B - Private Protective Services Act [Repealed.]	42
Chapter 74C - Private Protective Services	42
Chapter 74D - Alarm Systems	42
Chapter 74E - Company Police Act	42
Chapter 74F - Locksmith Licensing Act	42
Chapter 74G - Campus Police Act	42
Chapter 75 - Monopolies, Trusts and Consumer Protection	42
Chapter 75A - Boating and Water Safety	43
Chapter 75B - Discrimination in Business	43
Chapter 75C - Motion Picture Fair Competition Act	43
Chapter 75D - Racketeer Influenced and Corrupt Organizations	43
Chapter 75E - Unlawful Activities in Connection With Certain Corporate Transactions	43
Chapter 76 - Navigation	43
Chapter 76A - Navigation and Pilotage Commissions	43
Chapter 77 - Rivers, Creeks, and Coastal Waters	43
Chapter 78 - Securities Law [Repealed.]	43
Chapter 78A - North Carolina Securities Act	43
Chapter 78B - Tender Offer Disclosure Act [Repealed.]	43
Chapter 78C - Investment Advisers	43
Chapter 78D - Commodities Act	43
Chapter 79 - Strays [Repealed.]	43
Chapter 80 - Trademarks, Brands, etc.	44
Chapter 81 - Weights and Measures [Recodified.]	44
Chapter 81A - Weights and Measures Act of 1975.	44
Chapter 82 - Wrecks [Repealed.]	44
Chapter 83 - Architects [Recodified.]	44

Chapter 83A - Architects	44
Chapter 84 - Attorneys-at-Law	44
Chapter 84A - Foreign Legal Consultants	44
Chapter 85 - Auctions and Auctioneers [Repealed.]	44
Chapter 85A - Bail Bondsmen and Runners [Recodified.]	44
Chapter 85B - Auctions and Auctioneers	44
Chapter 85C - Bail Bondsmen and Runners [Recodified.]	44
Chapter 86 - Barbers [Recodified.]	44
Chapter 86A - Barbers	44
Chapter 87 - Contractors	44
Chapter 88 - Cosmetic Art [Repealed.]	44
Chapter 88A - Electrolysis Practice Act	44
Chapter 88B - Cosmetic Art	45
Chapter 89 - Engineering and Land Surveying [Recodified.]	45
Chapter 89A - Landscape Architects	45
Chapter 89B - Foresters	45
Chapter 89C - Engineering and Land Surveying	45
Chapter 89D - Landscape Contractors	45
Chapter 89E - Geologists Licensing Act	45
Chapter 89F - North Carolina Soil Scientist Licensing Act	45
Chapter 89G - Irrigation Contractors	45
Chapter 90 - Medicine and Allied Occupations	45
Chapter 90 - Medicine and Allied Occupations (Continuation)	46
Chapter 90 - Medicine and Allied Occupations (Continuation)	47
Chapter 90 - Medicine and Allied Occupations (Continuation)	48
Chapter 90A - Sanitarians and Water and Wastewater Treatment Facility Operators	48
Chapter 90B - Social Worker Certification and Licensure Act	48
Chapter 90C - North Carolina Recreational Therapy Licensure Act	48
Chapter 90D - Interpreters and Transliterators	48
Chapter 91 - Pawnbrokers [Repealed.]	48
Chapter 91A - Pawnbrokers Modernization Act of 1989	48
Chapter 92 - Photographers [Deleted.]	48
Chapter 93 - Certified Public Accountants	48
Chapter 93A - Real Estate License Law	49
Chapter 93B - Occupational Licensing Boards	49
Chapter 93C - Watchmakers [Repealed.]	49
Chapter 93D - North Carolina State Hearing Aid Dealers and Fitters Board.	49
Chapter 93E - North Carolina Appraisers Act	49
Chapter 94 - Apprenticeship	49
Chapter 95 - Department of Labor and Labor Regulations	49
Chapter 95 - Department of Labor and Labor Regulations (Continuation)	50
Chapter 96 - Employment Security	50
Chapter 97 - Workers' Compensation Act	50
Chapter 97 - Workers' Compensation Act (Continuation)	51

Chapter 98 - Burnt and Lost Records	51
Chapter 99 - Libel and Slander	51
Chapter 99A - Civil Remedies for Criminal Actions	51
Chapter 99B - Products Liability	51
Chapter 99C - Actions Relating to Winter Sports Safety and Accidents	51
Chapter 99D - Civil Rights	51
Chapter 99E - Special Liability Provisions	51
Chapter 100 - Monuments, Memorials and Parks	51
Chapter 101 - Names of Persons	51
Chapter 102 - Official Survey Base	51
Chapter 103 - Sundays, Holidays and Special Days	51
Chapter 104 - United States Lands	51
Chapter 104A - Degrees of Kinship	51
Chapter 104B - Hurricanes or Other Acts of Nature	51
Chapter 104C - Atomic Energy, Radioactivity and Ionizing Radiation [Repealed and Recodified.]	51
Chapter 104D - Southern States Energy Compact	51
Chapter 104E - North Carolina Radiation Protection Act	51
Chapter 104F - Southeast Interstate Low-Level Radioactive Waste Management Compact [Repealed]	51
Chapter 104G - North Carolina Low-Level Radioactive Waste Management Authority Act of 1987 [Repealed]	51
Chapter 105 - Taxation	51
Chapter 105 - Taxation (Continuation)	52
Chapter 105 - Taxation (Continuation)	53
Chapter 105 - Taxation (Continuation)	54
Chapter 105A - Setoff Debt Collection Act	55
Chapter 105B - Defaulted Student Loan Recovery Act	55
Chapter 106 - Agriculture	55
Chapter 106 - Agriculture (Continue)	56
Chapter 106 - Agriculture (Continue)	57
Chapter 107 - Agricultural Development Districts [Repealed.]	57
Chapter 108 - Social Services [Repealed and Recodified.]	57
Chapter 108A - Social Services	57
Chapter 108B - Community Action Programs	58
Chapter 108C Medicaid and Health Choice Provider Requirements.	58
Chapter 108D Medicaid Managed Care for Behavioral Health Services.	58
Chapter 109 - Bonds [Recodified.]	58
Chapter 110 - Child Welfare	58
Chapter 111 - Aid to the Blind	58
Chapter 112 - Confederate Homes and Pensions [Repealed.]	58
Chapter 113 - Conservation and Development	58
Chapter 113 - Conservation and Development (Continuation)	59

Chapter 113A - Pollution Control and Environment	59
Chapter 113A - Pollution Control and Environment (Continuation)	60
Chapter 113B - North Carolina Energy Policy Act of 1975	60
Chapter 114 - Department of Justice	60
Chapter 115 - Elementary and Secondary Education [Repealed.]	60
Chapter 115A - Community Colleges, Technical Institutes, and Industrial Education Centers [Repealed.]	60
Chapter 115B - Tuition and Fee Waivers	60
Chapter 115C - Elementary and Secondary Education	60
Chapter 115C - Elementary and Secondary Education (Continuation)	61
Chapter 115C - Elementary and Secondary Education (Continuation)	62
Chapter 115C - Elementary and Secondary Education (Continuation)	63
Chapter 115D - Community Colleges	63
Chapter 115E - Private Educational Facilities Finance Act [Recodified]	63
Chapter 116 - Higher Education	63
Chapter 116 - Higher Education (Continuation)	63
Chapter 116A - Escheats and Abandoned Property [Repealed.]	64
Chapter 116B - Escheats and Abandoned Property	64
Chapter 116C - Continuum of Education Programs	64
Chapter 116D - Higher Education Bonds	64
Chapter 117 - Electrification	64
Chapter 118 - Firemen's and Rescue Squad Workers' Relief and Pension Funds [Recodified.]	64
Chapter 118A - Firemen's Death Benefit Act [Repealed.]	64
Chapter 118B - Members of a Rescue Squad Death Benefit Act [Repealed.]	64
Chapter 119 - Gasoline and Oil Inspection and Regulation	64
Chapter 120 - General Assembly	65
Chapter 120 - General Assembly (Continuation)	66
Chapter 120 - General Assembly (Continuation)	67
Chapter 120C - Lobbying	67
Chapter 121 - Archives and History	67
Chapter 122 - Hospitals for the Mentally Disordered [Repealed.]	67
Chapter 122A - North Carolina Housing Finance Agency	67
Chapter 122B - North Carolina Agricultural Facilities Finance Act [Repealed.]	67
Chapter 122C - Mental Health, Developmental Disabilities, and Substance Abuse Act of 1985	67
Chapter 122C - Mental Health, Developmental Disabilities, and Substance Abuse Act of 1985 (Continuation)	68
Chapter 122D - North Carolina Agricultural Finance Act	68

Chapter 122E - North Carolina Housing Trust and Oil Overcharge Act	68
Chapter 123 - Impeachment	69
Chapter 123A - Industrial Development [Repealed.]	69
Chapter 124 - Internal Improvements	69
Chapter 125 - Libraries	69
Chapter 126 - State Personnel System	69
Chapter 127 - Militia [Repealed.]	69
Chapter 127A - Militia	69
Chapter 127B - Military Affairs	69
Chapter 127C - Advisory Commission on Military Affairs	69
Chapter 128 - Offices and Public Officers	69
Chapter 128 - Offices and Public Officers (Continuation)	70
Chapter 129 - Public Buildings and Grounds	70
Chapter 130 - Public Health [Repealed.]	70
Chapter 130A - Public Health	70
Chapter 130A - Public Health (Continuation)	71
Chapter 130A - Public Health (Continuation)	72
Chapter 130B - Hazardous Waste Management Commission [Repealed.]	72
Chapter 131 - Public Hospitals [Repealed.]	72
Chapter 131A - Health Care Facilities Finance Act	72
Chapter 131B - Licensing of Ambulatory Surgical Facilities [Repealed.]	72
Chapter 131C - Charitable Solicitation Licensure Act [Repealed.]	72
Chapter 131D - Inspection and Licensing of Facilities	72
Chapter 131E - Health Care Facilities and Services	72
Chapter 131E - Health Care Facilities and Services (Continuation)	73
Chapter 131F - Solicitation of Contributions	73
Chapter 132 - Public Records	73
Chapter 133 - Public Works	74
Chapter 134 - Youth Development [Recodified.]	74
Chapter 134A - Youth Services [Repealed.]	74
Chapter 135 - Retirement System for Teachers and State Employees; Social Security; Health Insurance Program for Children	74
Chapter 135 - Retirement System for Teachers and State Employees; Social Security; Health Insurance Program for Children	75
Chapter 136 - Transportation	75
Chapter 136 - Transportation (Continuation)	76
Chapter 137 - Rural Rehabilitation [Repealed.]	76
Chapter 138 - Salaries, Fees and Allowances	76
Chapter 138A - State Government Ethics Act	76
Chapter 139 - Soil and Water Conservation Districts	76

Chapter 140 - State Art Museum; Symphony and Art Societies	76
Chapter 140A - State Awards System	76
Chapter 141 - State Boundaries	76
Chapter 142 - State Debt	76
Chapter 143 - State Departments, Institutions, and Commissions	77
Chapter 143 - State Departments, Institutions, and Commissions (Continuation)	78
Chapter 143 - State Departments, Institutions, and Commissions (Continuation)	79
Chapter 143 - State Departments, Institutions, and Commissions (Continuation)	80
Chapter 143A - State Government Reorganization	80
Chapter 143B - Executive Organization Act of 1973	80
Chapter 143B - Executive Organization Act of 1973 (Continuation)	81
Chapter 143B - Executive Organization Act of 1973 (Continuation)	82
Chapter 143C - State Budget Act	83
Chapter 143D - The State Governmental Accountability and Internal Control Act	83
Chapter 144 - State Flag, Official Governmental Flags, Motto, and Colors	83
Chapter 145 - State Symbols and Other Official Adoptions.	83
Chapter 146 - State Lands	83
Chapter 147 - State Officers	83
Chapter 148 - State Prison System	84
Chapter 149 - State Song and Toast	84
Chapter 150 - Uniform Revocation of Licenses [Repealed.]	84
Chapter 150A - Administrative Procedure Act [Recodified.]	84
Chapter 150B - Administrative Procedure Act	84
Chapter 151 - Constables [Repealed.]	84
Chapter 152 - Coroners	84
Chapter 152A - County Medical Examiner [Repealed.]	84
Chapter 152A - County Medical Examiner [Repealed.] (Continuation)	85
Chapter 153 - Counties and County Commissioners [Repealed.]	85
Chapter 153A - Counties	85
Chapter 153B - Mountain Resources Planning Act	85
Chapter 153C - Uwharrie Regional Resources Act	85
Chapter 154 - County Surveyor [Repealed.]	85
Chapter 155 - County Treasurer [Repealed.]	85
Chapter 156 - Drainage	85
Chapter 156 – Drainage (Continuation)	86

Chapter 157 - Housing Authorities and Projects	86
Chapter 157A - Historic Properties Commissions [Transferred.]	86
Chapter 158 - Local Development	86
Chapter 159 - Local Government Finance	86
Chapter 159 - Local Government Finance (Continuation)	87
Chapter 159A - Pollution Abatement and Industrial Facilities Financing Act [Unconstitutional.]	87
Chapter 159B - Joint Municipal Electric Power and Energy Act	87
Chapter 159C - Industrial and Pollution Control Facilities Financing Act	87
Chapter 159D - The North Carolina Capital Facilities Financing Act	87
Chapter 159E - Registered Public Obligations Act	87
Chapter 159F - North Carolina Energy Development Authority [Repealed.]	87
Chapter 159G - Water Infrastructure	87
Chapter 159H - [Reserved.]	87
Chapter 159I - Solid Waste Management Loan Program and Local Government Special Obligation Bonds	87
Chapter 160 - Municipal Corporations [Repealed And Transferred.]	87
Chapter 160A - Cities and Towns	88
Chapter 160A - Cities and Towns (Continuation)	89
Chapter 160B - Consolidated City-County Act	89
Chapter 160C - Baseball Park Districts [Repealed.]	90
Chapter 161 - Register of Deeds	90
Chapter 162 - Sheriff	90
Chapter 162A - Water and Sewer Systems	90
Chapter 162B Continuity of Local Government in Emergency.	90
Chapter 163 Elections and Election Laws.	90
Chapter 163 Elections and Election Laws. (Continuation)	91
Chapter 164 Concerning the General Statutes of North Carolina.	92
Chapter 165 Veterans.	92
Chapter 166 Civil Preparedness Agencies [Repealed.]	92
Chapter 166A North Carolina Emergency Management Act.	92
Chapter 167 State Civil Air Patrol [Repealed.]	92
Chapter 168 Persons with Disabilities.	92
Chapter 168A Persons With Disabilities Protection Act.	92

§ 62-146. Rates and service of motor common carriers of property.

(a) It shall be the duty of every common carrier of household goods by motor vehicle to provide safe and adequate service, equipment, and facilities for transportation in intrastate commerce and to establish, observe and enforce just and reasonable regulations and practices relating thereto, and, in the case of household goods carriers, relating to the manner and method of presenting, marking, packing and delivering property for transportation in intrastate commerce.

(b) Except under special conditions and for good cause shown, a common carrier by motor vehicle authorized to transport general commodities over regular routes shall establish reasonable through routes and joint rates, charges, and classifications with other such common carriers by motor vehicle; and such common carrier may establish, with the prior approval of the Commission, such routes, joint rates, charges and classifications with any irregular route common carrier by motor vehicle, or any common carrier by rail, express, or water.

(c) Repealed by Session Laws 1985, c. 676, s. 15.

(d) In case of joint rates between common carriers of property, it shall be the duty of the carriers parties thereto to establish just and reasonable regulations and practices in connection therewith, and just, reasonable, and equitable divisions thereof as between the carriers participating therein, which shall not unduly prefer or prejudice any of such participating carriers. Upon investigation and for good cause, the Commission may, in its discretion, prohibit the establishment of joint rates or service.

(e) Any person may make complaint in writing to the Commission that any rate, classification, rule, regulations, or practice in effect or proposed to be put into effect, is or will be in violation of this Article. Whenever, after hearing, upon complaint or in an investigation or its own initiative, the Commission shall be of the opinion that any individual or joint rate demanded, charged, or collected by any common carrier or carriers by motor vehicle, or by any such common carrier or carriers in conjunction with any other common carrier or carriers, for transportation of household goods in intrastate commerce, or any classification, rule, regulation, or practice whatsoever of such carrier or carriers affecting such rate or the value of the service thereunder, is or will be unjust or unreasonable or unjustly discriminatory or unduly preferential or unduly prejudicial, it shall determine and prescribe the lawful rate or the minimum or maximum, or the minimum and maximum rate thereafter to be observed, or the lawful classification, rule, regulation, or practice thereafter to be made effective.

(f)   Whenever, after hearing upon complaint or upon its own initiative, the Commission is of the opinion that the divisions of joint rates applicable to the transportation of household goods in intrastate commerce between a common carrier by motor vehicle and another carrier are or will be unjust, unreasonable, inequitable, or unduly preferential or prejudicial as between the carriers parties thereto (whether agreed upon by such carriers or otherwise established), the Commission shall by order prescribe the just, reasonable, and equitable division thereof to be received by the several carriers; and in cases where the joint rate or charge was established pursuant to a finding or order of the Commission and the divisions thereof are found by it to have been unjust, unreasonable, or inequitable or unduly preferential or prejudicial, the Commission may also by order determine what would have been the just, reasonable, and equitable divisions thereof to be received by the several carriers and require adjustment to be made in accordance therewith. The order of the Commission may require the adjustment of divisions between the carriers in accordance with the order from the date of filing the complaint or entry of order of investigation or such other dates subsequent thereto as the Commission finds justified, and in the case of joint rates prescribed by the Commission, the order as to divisions may be made effective as a part of the original order.

(g)   In any proceeding to determine the justness or reasonableness of any rate of any common carrier of household goods by motor vehicle, there shall not be taken into consideration or allowed as evidence any elements of value of the property of such carrier, good will, earning power, or the certificate under which such carrier is operating, and such rates shall be fixed and approved, subject to the provisions of subsection (h) hereof, on the basis of the operating ratios of such carriers, being the ratio of their operating expenses to their operating revenues, at a ratio to be determined by the Commission; and in applying for and receiving a certificate under this Chapter any such carrier shall be deemed to have agreed to the provisions of this paragraph, on its own behalf and on behalf of every transferee of such certificate or of any part thereof.

(h)   In the exercise of its power to prescribe just and reasonable rates and charges for the transportation of household goods in intrastate commerce by common carriers by motor vehicle, and classifications, regulations, and practices relating thereto, the Commission shall give due consideration, among other factors, to the inherent advantages of transportation by such carriers; to the effect of rates upon movement of traffic by the carrier or carriers for which rates are prescribed; to the need in the public interest of adequate and efficient transportation service by such carriers at the lowest cost consistent with the furnishing of such service; and to the need of revenues sufficient to enable such carriers under honest, economical, and efficient management to provide such service.

(i) Nothing in this section shall be held to extinguish any remedy or right of action not inconsistent herewith. This section shall be in addition to other provisions of this Chapter which relate to public utilities generally, except that in cases of conflict between such other provisions and this section, this section shall prevail for motor carriers. (1947, c. 1008, s. 23; 1949, c. 1132, s. 22; 1963, c. 1165, s. 1; 1985, c. 676, s. 15(5); 1995, c. 523, s. 9.)

§ 62-146.1. Rates and service of bus companies.

(a) It shall be the duty of every bus company to provide safe and adequate service, equipment and facilities for transportation of passengers in intrastate commerce and to establish, observe and enforce just and reasonable regulations and practices.

(b) The Commission by its rules and regulations may require the interlining of passengers by bus companies operating in intrastate commerce in this State where the point of destination of the passenger is not served by the originating carrier. In these cases it shall be the duty of every bus company to establish reasonable through rates with other bus companies; to establish, observe and enforce just and reasonable individual and joint rates, fares and charges and just and reasonable regulations and practices relating to the charges and to the issuance, form and substance of tickets and the carrying of personal and excess baggage.

(c) In case of joint rates between bus companies, it shall be the duty of the bus companies to establish just and reasonable regulations and practices in connection with the joint rates and just, reasonable and equitable divisions between the participating companies, which shall not unduly prefer or prejudice any of the participating companies.

(d) A bus company providing fixed route service may file with the Commission a petition for new or revised rates, fares or charges. Unless the Commission orders otherwise, no bus company shall make any changes in its rates, fares and charges, which have been established under this Chapter, except after 30 days' notice to the Commission. The notice shall plainly state the changes proposed to be made in the rates then in force, and the time when the changed rates will go into effect. The bus company shall also give notice, which may include notice by publication, of the proposed changes to other interested persons that the Commission may direct. All proposed changes shall be shown by filing new schedules, or shall be plainly indicated upon schedules filed with the Commission and in force at the time and kept open to public inspection by the bus company. The Commission, for good cause shown in writing, may allow changes in rates without requiring the 30 days' notice, under any conditions as it prescribes. All changes shall be immediately indicated by the bus company on its schedules.

(e)   Whenever there is filed with the Commission by any bus company any schedule stating a new or revised rate, fare or charge, the Commission may, either upon complaint or upon its own initiative, after reasonable notice, hold a hearing to determine if the proposed new or revised rates, fares or charges are just and reasonable. Pending the hearing and a decision, the Commission, upon filing with the proposed schedule and delivering to the affected bus company a statement in writing of its reasons, may, at any time before they become effective, suspend the operation of the rate or rates, for a period not to exceed 120 days from the filing of the petition. If the proceeding has not been concluded and a final order made within the period of suspension, the proposed change of rate shall go into effect at the end of the 120-day period.

(f)   In any proceeding to determine the justness or reasonableness of any rates, fares or charges of a bus company, the Commission shall authorize revenue levels that are adequate under honest, economical, and efficient management to cover total operating expenses, including the operation of leased equipment and depreciation, plus a reasonable profit. The standards and procedures adopted by the Commission under this subsection shall allow the bus company to achieve revenue levels that will provide a flow of net income, plus depreciation, adequate to support prudent capital outlays, assure the repayment of a reasonable level of debt, permit the raising of needed equity capital, attract and retain capital and amounts adequate to provide a sound passenger bus transportation system in this State, and take into account reasonable estimated or foreseeable future costs.

(g)   Notwithstanding any provision of this section, the Commission may not investigate, suspend, review or revoke the operation of proposed new or revised rates, fares or charges if the proposed new or revised rates, fares or charges do not exceed the standard rates, fares or charges then in effect by the petitioning bus company for comparable interstate transportation of passengers.

(h) Any person may make complaint in writing to the Commission that any rate, fare, charge, classification, rule, regulation, or practice in effect, or proposed to be put in effect, is or will be in violation of this Chapter. Whenever, after holding a hearing, upon complaint, in an investigation, or upon its own initiative, the Commission finds that any individual or joint rate demanded, charged, or collected by any bus company for transportation of passengers in intrastate commerce, or any classification, rule, regulation or practice of the bus company affecting the rate or the value of the service provided, is or will be unjust or unreasonable or unjustly discriminatory or unduly preferential or unduly prejudicial or constitute an unfair or destructive competitive practice, or otherwise contravenes the policies declared in this Chapter, or is in contravention of any provision of this Chapter, the Commission shall determine and prescribe the lawful rate, or the lawful classification, rule, regulation or practice to be put into effect.

(i) For purposes of this Chapter, rates, fares and charges established pursuant to this section shall be deemed fair, just and reasonable.

(j) Notwithstanding any other provision of this Chapter, the rates, fares and charges established for charter service by a bus company authorized and engaged in charter operations in this State shall be exempt from regulation by the Commission. A bus company authorized and engaged in charter operations shall file with the Commission a current statement of its rates, fares and charges as required by the Commission. (1985, c. 676, s. 15(6).)

§ 62-147: Repealed by Session Laws 1995, c. 523, s. 10.

§ 62-148. Rates on leased or controlled utility.

If any public utility operating in the State other than a motor carrier is owned, controlled or operated by lease or other agreement by any other public utility doing business in the State, its rates may, in the discretion of the Commission, be determined for such public utility by the rates prescribed for the public utility which owns, controls or operates it. (Ex. Sess. 1908, c. 144, s. 2; C.S., s. 3490; 1963, c. 1165, s. 1.)

§ 62-149. Unused tickets to be redeemed.

Whenever any ticket is sold and is not wholly used by the purchaser, it shall be the duty of the carrier selling such ticket to redeem it or the unused portion thereof at the price paid for it, or in such manner and at such price as the Commission shall prescribe by regulation. (1891, c. 290; 1893, c. 249; 1895, c. 83, ss. 2, 3; 1897, c. 418; Rev., s. 2627; C.S., s. 3503; 1963, c. 1165, s. 1.)

§ 62-150. Ticket may be refused intoxicated person; penalty for prohibited entry.

The ticket agent of any common carrier of passengers shall at all times have power to refuse to sell a ticket to any person applying for the same who may at the time be intoxicated. The driver or other person in charge of any conveyance for the use of the traveling public shall at all times have power to prevent any intoxicated person from entering such conveyance. If any intoxicated person, after being forbidden by the driver or other person having charge of any such conveyance for the use of the traveling public, shall enter such conveyance, he shall be guilty of a Class 1 misdemeanor. (1885, c. 358, ss. 1, 2, 3; Rev., ss. 2625, 2626, 3757; C.S., s. 3504; 1963, c. 1165, s. 1; 1993, c. 539, s. 478; 1994, Ex. Sess., c. 24, s. 14(c); 1998-128, s. 5.)

§ 62-151. Passenger refusing to pay fare or violating rules may be ejected.

If any passenger shall refuse to pay his fare, or be or become intoxicated, or violate the rules of a common carrier, it shall be lawful for the driver of the bus or other conveyance, and servants of the carrier, on stopping the conveyance, to put him and his baggage out of the conveyance, using no unnecessary force. (1871-2, c. 138, s. 34; Code, s. 1962; Rev., s. 2629; C.S., s. 3507; 1949, c. 1132, s. 30; 1953, c. 1140, s. 4; 1957, c. 1152, s. 16; 1961, c. 472, s. 11; 1963, c. 1165, s. 1; 1998-128, s. 6.)

§ 62-152: Repealed by Session Laws 1998-128, s. 13.

§ 62-152.1. Uniform rates; joint rate agreements among carriers.

(a)   Definitions. - As used in this section, unless the context otherwise requires, the term:

(1)   "Carrier" means any common carrier as defined in G.S. 62-3(6).

(2)   For purposes of this section, carriers by motor vehicles are carriers of the same class, carriers by pipeline are carriers of the same class, carriers by water are carriers of the same class, carriers by air are carriers of the same class, and freight forwarders are carriers of the same class.

(3)   The term "antitrust laws" means the provisions of Chapter 75 of the General Statutes (N.C.G.S. 75-1, et seq.), relating to combinations in restraint of trade.

(b)   For the purpose of achieving a stable rate structure it shall be the policy of this State to fix uniform rates for the same or similar services by carriers of the same class. In order to realize and effectuate this policy and regulatory goal any carrier subject to regulation by this Commission and party to an agreement between or among two or more carriers relating to rates, fares, classifications, divisions, allowances or charges (including charges between carriers and compensation paid or received for the use of facilities and equipment), or rules and regulations pertaining thereto, or procedures for the joint consideration, initiation or establishment thereof, may, under such rules and regulations as the Commission may prescribe, apply to the Commission for approval of the agreement, and the Commission shall by order approve any such agreement (if approval thereof is not prohibited by subsection (d) or (e) of this section) if it finds that, by reason of furtherance of the transportation policy and goal declared in this section and in G.S. 62-2 or G.S. 62-259 as may be pertinent, the relief provided in subsection (h) shall apply with respect to the making and carrying out of such agreement; otherwise, the application shall be denied. The approval of the Commission shall be granted only upon such terms and conditions as the Commission may prescribe as necessary to enable it to grant its approval in accordance with the standard above set forth in this subsection.

(c) Each conference, bureau, committee, or other organization established or continued pursuant to any agreement approved by the Commission under this section shall maintain such accounts, records, files and memoranda and shall submit to the Commission such information and reports as may be prescribed by the Commission, and all the accounts, records, files and memoranda shall be subject to inspection by the Commission or its duly authorized representatives.

(d) The Commission shall not approve under this section any agreement between or among carriers of different classes unless it finds that the agreement is of the character described in subsection (b) of this section and is limited to matters relating to transportation under joint rates or over through routes.

(e) The Commission shall not approve under this section any agreement which establishes a procedure for the determination of any matter through joint consideration unless it finds that under the agreement there is accorded to each party the free and unrestrained right to take independent action after any determination arrived at through such procedure.

(f) The Commission is authorized, upon complaint or upon its own initiative without complaint, to investigate and determine whether any agreement previously approved by it under this section, or terms and conditions upon which the approval was granted is not or are not in conformity with the standards set forth in subsection (b) of this section, or whether any such terms and conditions are not necessary for the purposes of conformity with such standards, and, after such investigation, the Commission shall by order terminate or modify its approval of such agreement if it finds such action necessary to insure conformity with such standards, and shall modify the terms and conditions upon which such approval was granted to the extent it finds necessary to insure conformity with such standards or to the extent to which it finds such terms and conditions not necessary to insure such conformity. The effective date of any order terminating or modifying approval, or modifying terms and conditions, shall be postponed for such period as the Commission determines to be reasonably necessary to avoid undue hardships.

(g) No order shall be entered under this section except after interested parties have been afforded reasonable notice and opportunity for hearing.

(h) Parties to any agreement approved by the Commission under this section and other parties are, if the approval of such agreement is not prohibited by subsection (d) or (e) of this section, hereby relieved from the operation of the antitrust laws with respect to the making of such agreement, and with respect to the carrying out of such agreement in conformity with the terms and conditions prescribed by the Commission.

(i) Any action of the Commission under this section in approving an agreement, or in denying an application for such approval, or in terminating or modifying its approval of an agreement, or prescribing the terms and conditions upon which its approval is to be granted, or in modifying such terms and conditions, shall be construed as having effect solely with reference to the applicability of the relief provisions of subsection (h) of this section. (1977, c. 219, s. 1; 1998-128, s. 7.)

§ 62-152.2. Standard transportation practices.

(a) For the purposes of this section, "standard transportation practices" means:

(1) Uniform cargo liability rules.

(2) Uniform bills of lading or receipts for property being transported.

(3) Uniform cargo credit rules.

(4) Antitrust immunity for joint line rates or routes, classification, and mileage guides.

(b) A person otherwise exempt from regulation by the Commission under Public Law 103-305 may file an application with the Commission to participate in one or more standard transportation practices under rules set out by the Commission. (1995, c. 523, s. 10.1.)

§ 62-153. Contracts of public utilities with certain companies and for services.

(a) All public utilities shall file with the Commission copies of contracts with any affiliated or subsidiary holding, managing, operating, constructing, engineering, financing or purchasing company or agency, and when requested by the Commission, copies of contracts with any person selling service of any kind. The Commission may disapprove, after hearing, any such contract if it is found to be unjust or unreasonable, and made for the purpose or with the effect of concealing, transferring or dissipating the earnings of the public utility. Such contracts so disapproved by the Commission shall be void and shall not be carried out by the public utility which is a party thereto, nor shall any payments be made thereunder. Provided, however, that in the case of motor carriers of passengers this subsection shall apply only to such contracts as the Commission shall request such carriers to file.

(b) No public utility shall pay any fees, commissions or compensation of any description whatsoever to any affiliated or subsidiary holding, managing, operating, constructing, engineering, financing or purchasing company or agency for services rendered or to be rendered without first filing copies of all proposed agreements and contracts with the Commission and obtaining its approval. Provided, however, that this subsection shall not apply to motor carriers of passengers. (1931, c. 455; 1933, c. 134, s. 8; c. 307, s. 17; 1941, c. 97; 1963, c. 1165, s. 1.)

§ 62-154. Surplus power rates.

The Commission is authorized to investigate the sale of surplus electric power and the rates made for such energy, and to prescribe reasonable rules and rates for such sales. (1963, c. 1165, s. 1.)

§ 62-155. Electric power rates to promote conservation.

(a) It is the policy of the State to conserve energy through efficient utilization of all resources.

(b) If the Utilities Commission after study determines that conservation of electricity and economy of operation for the public utility will be furthered thereby, it shall direct each electric public utility to notify its customers by the most economical means available of the anticipated periods in the near future when its generating capacity is likely to be near peak demand and urge its customers to refrain from using electricity at these peak times of the day. In addition, each public utility shall, insofar as practicable, investigate, develop, and put into service, with approval of the Commission, procedures and devices that will temporarily curtail or cut off certain types of appliances or equipment for short periods of time whenever an unusual peak demand threatens to overload its system.

(c) The Commission itself shall inform the general public as to the necessity for controlling demands for electricity at peak periods and shall require the several electric public utilities to carry out its program of information and education in any reasonable manner.

(d) The Commission shall study the feasibility of and, if found to be practicable, just and reasonable, make plans for the public utilities to bill customers by a system of nondiscriminatory peak pricing, with incentive rates for off-peak use of electricity charging more for peak periods than for off-peak periods to reflect the higher cost of providing electric service during periods of peak demand on the utility system. No order regarding such rates shall be issued by the Commission without a prior public hearing, whether in a single electric utility company rate case or in general orders relating to two or more or all electric utilities.

(e) No Class A electric public utility shall apply for any rate change unless it files at the time of the application a report of the probable effect of the proposed rates on peak demand on it and its estimate of the kilowatt hours of electricity that will be used by its customers during the ensuing one year and five years from the time such rates are proposed to become effective. (1975, c. 780, s. 2.)

§ 62-156. Power sales by small power producers to public utilities.

(a) In the event that a small power producer and an electric utility are unable to mutually agree to a contract for the sale of electricity or to a price for the electricity purchased by the electric utility, the commission shall require the utility to purchase the power, under rates and terms established as provided in subsection (b) of this section.

(b) No later than March 1, 1981, and at least every two years thereafter, the commission shall determine the rates to be paid by electric utilities for power purchased from small power producers, according to the following standards:

(1) Term of Contract. - Long-term contracts for the purchase of electricity by the utility from small power producers shall be encouraged in order to enhance the economic feasibility of small power production facilities.

(2) Avoided Cost of Energy to the Utility. - The rates paid by a utility to a small power producer shall not exceed, over the term of the purchase power contract, the incremental cost to the electric utility of the electric energy which, but for the purchase from a small power producer, the utility would generate or purchase from another source. A determination of the avoided energy costs to the utility shall include a consideration of the following factors over the term of the power contracts: the expected costs of the additional or existing generating capacity which could be displaced, the expected cost of fuel and other operating expenses of electric energy production which a utility would otherwise incur in generating or purchasing power from another source, and the expected security of the supply of fuel for the utilities' alternative power sources.

(3) Availability and Reliability of Power. - The rates to be paid by electric utilities for power purchased from a small power producer shall be established with consideration of the reliability and availability of the power. (1979, 2nd Sess., c. 1219, s. 2.)

§ 62-157. Telecommunications relay service.

(a) Finding. - The General Assembly finds and declares that it is in the public interest to provide access to public telecommunications services for hearing impaired or speech impaired persons, including those who also have vision impairment, and that a statewide telecommunications relay service for telephone service should be established.

(a1) Definitions. - For purposes of this section:

(1) "CMRS" is as defined in G.S. 62A-40.

(2) "CMRS connection" is as defined in G.S. 62A-40.

(3) "CMRS provider" is as defined in G.S. 62A-40.

(4) "Exchange access facility" means the access from a particular telephone subscriber's premises to the telephone system of a local exchange

telephone company, and includes local exchange company-provided access lines, private branch exchange trunks, and centrex network access registers, all as defined by tariffs of telephone companies as approved by the Commission.

(5) "Local service provider" means a local exchange company, competing local provider, or telephone membership corporation.

(b) Authority to Require Surcharge. - The Commission shall require local service providers to impose a monthly surcharge on all residential and business local exchange access facilities to fund a statewide telecommunications relay service by which hearing impaired or speech impaired persons, including those who also have vision impairment, may communicate with others by telephone. This surcharge, however, may not be imposed on participants in the Subscriber Line Charge Waiver Program or the Link-up Carolina Program established by the Commission. This surcharge, and long distance revenues collected under subsection (f) of this section, are not includable in gross receipts subject to the franchise tax levied under G.S. 105-120 or the sales tax levied under G.S. 105-164.4.

(c) Specification of Surcharge. - The Department of Health and Human Services shall initiate a telecommunications relay service by filing a petition with the Commission requesting the service and detailing initial projected required funding. The Commission shall, after giving notice and an opportunity to be heard to other interested parties, set the initial monthly surcharge based upon the amount of funding necessary to implement and operate the service, including a reasonable margin for a reserve. The surcharge shall be identified on customer bills as a special surcharge for provision of a telecommunications relay service for hearing impaired and speech impaired persons. The Commission may, upon petition of any interested party, and after giving notice and an opportunity to be heard to other interested parties, revise the surcharge from time to time if the funding requirements change. In no event shall the surcharge exceed twenty-five cents (25¢) per month for each exchange access facility.

(d) Funds to Be Deposited in Special Account. - The local service providers shall collect the surcharge from their customers and deposit the moneys collected with the State Treasurer, who shall maintain the funds in an interest-bearing, nonreverting account. After consulting with the State Treasurer, the Commission shall direct how and when the local service providers shall deposit these moneys. Revenues from this fund shall be available only to the Department of Health and Human Services to administer the statewide telecommunications relay service program, including its establishment, operation, and promotion. The Commission may allow the Department of Health and Human Services to use up to four cents (4¢) per access line per month of the surcharge for the purpose of providing telecommunications devices for hearing impaired or speech impaired persons, including those who also have vision impairment, through a distribution program. The Commission shall prepare such guidelines for the distribution program as it deems appropriate and in the public interest. Both the Commission and the Public Staff may audit all aspects of the telecommunications relay service program, including the distribution programs, as they do with any public utility subject to the provisions of this Chapter. Equipment paid for with surcharge revenues, as allowed by the Commission, may be distributed only by the Department of Health and Human Services.

(d1) The Department of Health and Human Services shall utilize revenues from the wireless surcharge collected under subsection (i) of this section to support the Division of Services for the Deaf and the Hard of Hearing, in accordance with G.S. 143B-216.33, G.S. 143B-216.34, and Chapter 8B of the General Statutes.

(e) Administration of Service. - The Department of Health and Human Services shall administer the statewide telecommunications relay service program, including its establishment, operation, and promotion. The Department may contract out the provision of this service for four-year periods to one or more service providers, using the provisions of G.S. 143-129. The Department shall administer all programs and services, including the Regional Resource Centers within the Division of Services for the Deaf and the Hard of Hearing in accordance with G.S. 143B-216.33, G.S. 143B-216.34, and Chapter 8B of the General Statutes.

(f) Charge to Users. - The users of the telecommunications relay service shall be charged their approved long distance and local rates for telephone services (including the surcharge required by this section), but no additional charges may be imposed for the use of the relay service. The local service providers shall collect revenues from the users of the relay service for long distance services provided through the relay service. These revenues shall be deposited in the special fund established in subsection (d) of this section in a manner determined by the Commission after consulting with the State Treasurer. Local service providers shall be compensated for collection, inquiry, and other administrative services provided by said companies, subject to the approval of the Commission.

(g)   Reporting Requirement. - The Commission shall, after consulting with the Department of Health and Human Services, develop a format and filing schedule for a comprehensive financial and operational report on the telecommunications relay service program. The Department of Health and Human Services shall thereafter prepare and file these reports as required by the Commission with the Commission and the Public Staff. The Department shall also be required to report to the Revenue Laws Study Committee.

(h)   Power to Regulate. - The Commission shall have the same power to regulate the operation of the telecommunications relay service program as it has to regulate any public utility subject to the provisions of this Chapter.

(i)   Wireless Surcharge. - A CMRS provider, as part of its monthly billing process, must collect the same surcharge imposed on each exchange access facility under this section for each CMRS connection. A CMRS provider may deduct a one percent (1%) administrative fee from the total amount of surcharge collected. A CMRS provider shall remit the surcharge collected, less the administrative fee, to the 911 Board in the same manner and with the same frequency as the local service providers remit the surcharge to the State Treasurer. The 911 Board shall remit the funds collected from the surcharge to the special account created under subsection (d) of this section. (1989, c. 599; 1997-443, s. 11A.118(a); 1999-402, s. 1; 2003-341, s. 1; 2007-383, s. 4; 2009-451, s. 10.56(c), (d); 2012-142, s. 10.24(a), (b).)

§ 62-158. Natural gas expansion.

(a)   In order to facilitate the construction of facilities in and the extension of natural gas service to unserved areas, the Commission may, after a hearing, order a natural gas local distribution company to create a special natural gas expansion fund to be used by that company to construct natural gas facilities in areas within the company's franchised territory that otherwise would not be feasible for the company to construct. The fund shall be supervised and administered by the Commission. Any applicable taxes shall be paid out of the fund.

(b)   Sources of funding for a natural gas local distribution company's expansion fund may, pursuant to the order of the Commission, after hearing, include:

(1) Refunds to a local distribution company from the company's suppliers of natural gas and transportation services pursuant to refund orders or requirements of the Federal Energy Regulatory Commission;

(2) Expansion surcharges by the local distribution company charged to customers purchasing natural gas or transportation services throughout that company's franchised territory; provided, however, in determining the amount of any surcharge the Commission shall take into account the prices of alternative sources of energy and the need to remain competitive with those alternative sources, and the need to maintain just and reasonable rates for natural gas and transportation services for all customers served by the company; provided further that the expansion surcharge shall not be greater than fifteen cents (15¢) per dekatherm; and

(3) Other sources of funding approved by the Commission.

(c) The application of all such funds to expansion projects shall be pursuant to the order of the Commission. The Commission shall ensure that all projects to which expansion funds are applied are consistent with the intent of this section and G.S. 62-2(9). In determining economic feasibility, the Commission shall employ the net present value method of analysis on a project specific basis. Only those projects with a negative net present value shall be determined to be economically infeasible for the company to construct. In no event shall the Commission authorize a distribution from the fund of an amount greater than the negative net present value of any proposed project as determined by the Commission. If at any time a project is determined by the Commission to have become economically feasible, the Commission may require the company to remit to the expansion fund or to customers appropriate portions of the distributions from the fund related to the project, and the Commission may order such funds to be returned with interest in a reasonable amount to be determined by the Commission. Utility plant acquired with expansion funds shall be included in the local distribution company's rate base at zero cost except to the extent such funds have been remitted by the company pursuant to order of the Commission.

(d) The Commission, after hearing, may adopt rules to implement this section, including rules for the establishment of expansion funds, for the use of such funds, for the remittance to the expansion fund or to customers of supplier and transporter refunds and expansion surcharges or other funds that were sources of the expansion fund, and for appropriate accounting, reporting and ratemaking treatment. The Commission and Public Staff shall report to the Joint Legislative Commission on Governmental Operations on the operation of any expansion funds in conjunction with the reports required under G.S. 62-36A. (1991, c. 598, s. 2; 2011-291, s. 2.15.)

§ 62-159. Additional funding for natural gas expansion.

(a)   In order to facilitate the construction of facilities in and the extension of natural gas service to unserved areas, the Commission may provide funding through appropriations from the General Assembly or the proceeds of general obligation bonds as provided in this section to either (i) an existing natural gas local distribution company; (ii) a person awarded a new franchise; or (iii) a gas district for the construction of natural gas facilities that it otherwise would not be economically feasible for the company, person, or gas district to construct.

(b)   The use of funds provided under this section shall be pursuant to an order of the Commission after a public hearing. The Commission shall ensure that all projects for which funds are provided under this section are consistent with the intent of this section and G.S. 62-2(9). In determining whether to approve the use of funds for a particular project pursuant to this section, the Commission shall consider the scope of a proposed project, including the number of unserved counties and the number of anticipated customers that would be served, the total cost of the project, the extent to which the project is considered feasible, and other relevant factors affecting the public interest. In determining economic feasibility, the Commission shall employ the net present value method of analysis on a project specific basis. Only those projects with a negative net present value shall be determined to be economically infeasible for the company, person, or gas district to construct. In no event shall the Commission provide funding under this section of an amount greater than the negative net present value of any proposed project as determined by the Commission. If at any time a project is determined by the Commission to have become economically feasible, the Commission shall require the recipient of funding to remit to the Commission appropriate funds related to the project, and the Commission may order those funds to be returned with interest in a reasonable amount to be determined by the Commission. Funds returned, together with interest, shall be deposited with the State Treasurer to be used for other expansion projects pursuant to the provisions of this section. Utility plant acquired with expansion funds shall be included in the local distribution company's rate base at zero cost except to the extent such funds have been remitted by the company pursuant to order of the Commission. In the event a gas district wishes to sell or otherwise dispose of facilities financed with funds received under this section, it must first notify the Commission which shall determine the method of repayment or accounting for those funds.

(c)   To the extent that one or more of the counties included in a proposed project to be funded pursuant to this section are counties affected by the loss of exclusive franchise rights provided for in G.S. 62-36A(b), the Commission may conclude that the public interest requires that the person obtaining the franchise or funding pursuant to this section be given an exclusive franchise and that the existing franchise be canceled. Any new exclusive franchise granted under this subsection shall be subject to the provisions of G.S. 62-36A(b). This subsection does not apply to gas districts formed under Article 28 of Chapter 160A of the General Statutes.

(d)   The Commission, after hearing, shall adopt rules to implement this section as soon as practicable. The Commission and Public Staff shall report to the Joint Legislative Commission on Governmental Operations on the use of funding provided under this section in conjunction with the reports required under G.S. 62-36A. (1998-132, s. 17; 1999-456, s. 17; 2011-291, s. 2.16.)

§ 62-159.1. Debt collection practices.

(a)   A public utility, electric membership corporation, and telephone membership corporation shall not do any of the following in its debt collection practices:

(1)   Suspend or disconnect service to a customer because of a past-due and unpaid balance for service incurred by another person who resides with the customer after service has been provided to the customer's household, unless one or more of the following apply:

a.   The customer and the person were members of the same household at a different location when the unpaid balance for service was incurred.

b.   The person was a member of the customer's current household when the service was established, and the person had an unpaid balance for service at that time.

c. The person is or becomes responsible for the bill for the service to the customer.

(2) Require that in order to continue service, a customer must agree to be liable for the delinquent account of any other person who will reside in the customer's household after the customer receives the service, unless one or more of the following apply:

a. The customer and the person were members of the same household at a different location when the unpaid balance for service was incurred.

b. The person was a member of the customer's current household when the service was established, and the person had an unpaid balance for service at that time.

(b) Notwithstanding the provisions of subsection (a) of this section, if a customer misrepresents his or her identity in a written or verbal agreement for service or receives service using another person's identity, the public utility, electric membership corporation, and telephone membership corporation shall have the power to collect a delinquent account using any remedy provided by law for collecting and enforcing private debts from that customer. (2009-302, s. 1.)

§ 62-159.2. Reserved for future codification purposes.

§ 62-159.3. Reserved for future codification purposes.

§ 62-159.4. Reserved for future codification purposes.

§ 62-159.5. Reserved for future codification purposes.

Article 8.

Securities Regulation.

§ 62-160. Permission to pledge assets.

No public utility shall pledge its faith, credit, moneys or property for the benefit of any holder of its preferred or common stocks or bonds, nor for any other business interest with which it may be affiliated through agents or holding companies or otherwise by the authority of the action of its stockholders, directors, or contract or other agents, the compliance or result of which would in any manner deplete, reduce, conceal, abstract or dissipate the earnings or assets thereof, decrease or increase its liabilities or assets, without first making application to the Commission and by order obtain its permission so to do. (1933, c. 307, s. 17; 1963, c. 1165, s. 1.)

§ 62-161. Assumption of certain liabilities and obligations to be approved by Commission; refinancing of public utility securities.

(a) No public utility shall issue any securities, or assume any liability or obligation as lessor, lessee, guarantor, indorser, surety, or otherwise, in respect to the securities of any other person unless and until, and then only to the extent that, upon application by such utility, and after investigation by the Commission of the purposes and uses of the proposed issue, and the proceeds thereof, or of the proposed assumption of obligation or liability in respect of the securities of any other person, the Commission by order authorizes such issue or assumption.

(b) The Commission shall make such order only if it finds that such issue or assumption is (i) for some lawful object within the corporate purposes of the public utility, (ii) is compatible with the public interest, (iii) is necessary or appropriate for or consistent with the proper performance by such utility of its service to the public and will not impair its ability to perform that service, and (iv) is reasonably necessary and appropriate for such purpose.

(c)   Any such order of the Commission shall specify the purposes for which any such securities or the proceeds thereof may be used by the public utility making such application.

(d)   If a public utility shall apply to the Commission for the refinancing of its outstanding shares of stock by exchanging or redeeming such outstanding shares, the exchange or redemption of such shares of any dividend rate or rates, class or classes, may be made in whole or in part, in the manner and to the extent approved by the Commission, notwithstanding any provisions of law applicable to corporations in general: Provided, that the proposed transactions are found by the Commission to be in the public interest and in the interest of consumers and investors, and provided that any redemption shall be at a price or prices, not less than par, and at a time or times, stated or provided for in the utility's charter or stock certificates. (1933, c. 307, s. 18; 1945, c. 656; 1963, c. 1165, s. 1.)

§ 62-162. Commission may approve in whole or in part or refuse approval.

The Commission, by its order, may grant or deny the application provided for in the preceding section [G.S. 62-161] as made, or may grant it in part or deny it in part or may grant it with such modification and upon such terms and conditions as the Commission may deem necessary or appropriate in the premises and may, from time to time, for good cause shown, make such supplemental orders in the premises as it may deem necessary or appropriate and may, by any such supplemental order, modify the provisions of any previous order as to the particular purposes, uses, and extent to which or the conditions under which any securities so authorized or the proceeds thereof may be applied; subject always to the requirements of the foregoing section [G.S. 62-161]. (1933, c. 307, s. 19; 1963, c. 1165, s. 1.)

§ 62-163. Contents of application for permission.

Every application for authority for such issue or assumption shall be made in such form and contain such matters as the Commission may prescribe. Every such application and every certificate of notification hereinafter provided for shall be made under oath, signed and filed on behalf of the public utility by its president, a vice-president, auditor, comptroller, or other executive officer duly designated for that purpose by such utility. (1933, c. 307, s. 20; 1963, c. 1165, s. 1.)

§ 62-164. Applications to receive immediate attention; continuances.

All applications for the issuance of securities or assumption of liability or obligation shall be placed at the head of the Commission's docket and disposed of promptly, and all such applications shall be disposed of in 30 days after the same are filed with the Commission, unless it is necessary for good cause to continue the same for a longer period for consideration. Whenever such application is continued beyond 30 days after the time it is filed, the order making such continuance must state fully the facts necessitating such continuance. (1933, c. 307, s. 21; 1963, c. 1165, s. 1.)

§ 62-165. Notifying Commission as to disposition of securities.

Whenever any securities set forth and described in any such application for authority or certificate of notification as pledged or held unencumbered in the treasury of the utility shall, subsequent to the filing of such application or certificate, be sold, pledged, repledged, or otherwise disposed of, by the utility, such utility shall, within 10 days after such sale, pledge, repledge, or other disposition, file with the Commission a certificate of notification to that effect, setting forth therein all such facts as may be required by the Commission. (1933, c. 307, s. 22; 1963, c. 1165, s. 1.)

§ 62-166. No guarantee on part of State.

Nothing herein shall be construed to imply any guarantee or obligation as to such securities on the part of the State of North Carolina. (1933, c. 307, s. 23; 1963, c. 1165, s. 1.)

§ 62-167. Article not applicable to note issues and renewals; notice to Commission.

The provisions of the foregoing sections shall not apply to notes issued by a utility for proper purposes and not in violation of law, payable at a period of not more than two years from the date thereof, and shall not apply to like notes issued by a utility payable at a period of not more than two years from date thereof, to pay, retire, discharge, or refund in whole or in part any such note or notes, and shall not apply to renewals thereof from time to time not exceeding in the aggregate six years from the date of the issue of the original note or notes so renewed or refunded. No such notes payable at a period of not more than two years from the date thereof, shall, in whole or in part, directly or indirectly, be paid, retired, discharged or refunded by any issue of securities or another kind of any term or character or from the proceeds thereof without the approval of the Commission. Within 10 days after the making of any such notes, so payable at periods of not more than two years from the date thereof, the utility issuing the same shall file with the Commission a certificate of notification, in such form as may be determined and prescribed by the Commission. (1933, c. 307, ss. 24, 25; 1963, c. 1165, s. 1.)

§ 62-168. Not applicable to debentures of court receivers.

Nothing contained in this Article shall limit the power of any court having jurisdiction to authorize or cause receiver's certificates or debentures to be issued according to the rules and practice obtained in receivership proceedings in courts of equity. (1933, c. 307, s. 25; 1963, c. 1165, s. 1.)

§ 62-169. Periodical or special reports.

The Commission shall require periodical or special reports from each public utility issuing any security, including such notes payable at periods of not more than two years from the date thereof, which shall show, in such detail as the Commission may require, the disposition made of such securities and the application of the proceeds. (1933, c. 307, s. 26; 1963, c. 1165, s. 1.)

§ 62-170. Failure to obtain approval not to invalidate securities or obligations; noncompliance with Article, etc.

(a) Securities issued and obligations and liabilities assumed by a public utility, for which the authorization of the Commission is required, shall not be invalidated because issued or assumed without such authorization therefor having first been obtained or because issued or assumed contrary to any term or condition of such order of authorization as modified by any order supplemental thereto entered prior to such issuance or assumption.

(b) Securities issued or obligations or liabilities assumed in accordance with all the terms and conditions of the order of authorization therefor shall not be affected by a failure to comply with any provision of this Article or rule or regulation of the Commission relating to procedure and other matters preceding the entry of such order of authorization or order supplemental thereto.

(c) A copy of any order made and entered by the Commission and certified by a clerk of the Commission approving the issuance of any securities or the assumption of any obligation or liability by a public utility shall be sufficient evidence of full and complete compliance by the applicant for such approval with all procedural and other matters required precedent to the entry of such order.

(d) Any public utility which willfully issues any such securities, or assumes any such obligation or liability, or makes any sale or other disposition of securities, or applies any securities or the proceeds thereof to purposes other than the purposes specified in an order of the Commission with respect thereto, contrary to the provisions of this Article, shall be liable to a penalty of not more than ten thousand dollars ($10,000), but such utility is only required to specify in general terms the purpose for which any securities are to be issued, or for which any obligation or liability is to be assumed, and the order of the Commission with respect thereto shall likewise be in general terms. (1933, c. 307, s. 27; 1963, c. 1165, s. 1.)

§ 62-171. Commission may act jointly with agency of another state where public utility operates.

If a commission or other agency or agencies is empowered by another state to regulate and control the amount and character of securities to be issued by any public utility within such other state, then the Utilities Commission of the State of North Carolina shall have the power to agree with such commission or other agency or agencies of such other state on the issue of stocks, bonds, notes or other evidences of indebtedness by a public utility owning or operating a public utility both in such state and in this State, and shall have the power to approve such issue jointly with such commission or other agency or agencies and to issue joint certificate of such approval: Provided, however, that no such joint approval shall be required in order to express the consent to an approval of such issue by the State of North Carolina if said issue is separately approved by the Utilities Commission of the State of North Carolina. (1933, c. 134, s. 8; c. 307, s. 28; 1941, c. 97; 1963, c. 1165, s. 1.)

§§ 62-172 through 62-179. Reserved for future codification purposes.

Article 9.

Acquisition and Condemnation of Property.

§ 62-180. Use of railroads and public highways.

Any person operating electric power, telegraph or telephone lines or authorized by law to establish such lines, has the right to construct, maintain and operate such lines along any railroad or public highway, but such lines shall be so constructed and maintained as not to obstruct or hinder unreasonably the usual travel on such railroad or highway. (1874-5, c. 203, s. 2; Code, s. 2007; 1899, c. 64, s. 1; 1903, c. 562; Rev., s. 1571; C.S., s. 1695; 1939, c. 228, s. 1; 1963, c. 1165, s. 1.)

§ 62-181. Electric and hydroelectric power companies may appropriate highways; conditions.

Every electric power or hydroelectric power corporation, person, firm or copartnership which may exercise the right of eminent domain under the Chapter Eminent Domain, where in the development of electric or hydroelectric power it shall become necessary to use or occupy any public highway, or any part of the same, after obtaining the consent of the public road authorities having supervision of such public highway, shall have power to appropriate said public highway for the development of electric or hydroelectric power: Provided, that said electric power or hydroelectric power corporation shall construct an equally good public highway, by a route to be selected by and subject to the approval and satisfaction of the public road authorities having supervision of such public highway: Provided further, that said company shall pay all damages to be assessed as provided by law, by the damming of water, the discontinuance of the road, and for the laying out of said new road. (1911, c. 114; C.S., s. 1696; 1939, c. 228, s. 2; 1963, c. 1165, s. 1.)

§ 62-182. Acquisition of right-of-way by contract.

Such telegraph, telephone, or electric power or lighting company has power to contract with any person or corporation, the owner of any lands or of any franchise or easement therein, over which its lines are proposed to be erected, for the right-of-way for planting, repairing and preservation of its poles or other property, and for the erection and occupation of offices at suitable distances for the public accommodation. This section shall not be construed as requiring electric power or lighting companies to erect offices for public accommodation. (1874-5, c. 203, s. 3; Code, s. 2008; 1899, c. 64; 1903, c. 562, ss. 1, 2; Rev., s. 1572; C.S., s. 1697; 1963, c. 1165, s. 1.)

§ 62-182.1. Access to dedicated public right-of-way.

When any map or plat of a subdivision, recorded as provided in G.S. 47-30 and G.S. 136-102.6, reflects the dedication of a public street or other public right-of-way, the dedicated public street or public right-of-way shall, upon recordation of the map or plat, become immediately available for use by any public utility, telephone membership corporation organized under G.S. 117-30, or cable television system to install, maintain, and operate lines, cables, or facilities for the provision of service to the public. No public utility, telephone membership corporation organized under G.S. 117-30, or cable television system shall place or erect any line, cable, or facility in, over, or upon a street or right-of-way in a subdivision that is intended to become a public street or public right-of-way, until a map or plat of the subdivision has been recorded as provided in G.S. 47-30 and G.S. 136-102.6, and except in accordance with procedures established by the Department of Transportation, Division of Highways, for accommodating utilities or cable television systems on highway rights-of-way. Upon recordation of a map or plat of a subdivision as provided in G.S. 47-30 and G.S. 136-102.6, no liability shall attach to the developer of the property as a result of any activity of a public utility, telephone membership corporation organized under G.S. 117-30, or cable television system occurring in the dedicated public street or public right-of-way. Nothing in this section shall relieve the developer of the property of responsibilities under G.S. 136-102.6. (2005-286, s. 1; 2006-259, s. 15.)

§ 62-183. Grant of eminent domain.

Such telegraph, telephone, electric power or lighting company shall be entitled, upon making just compensation therefor, to the right-of-way over the lands, privileges and easements of other persons and corporations, including rights-of-way for the construction, maintenance, and operation of pipelines for transporting fuel to their power plants; and to the right to erect poles and towers, to establish offices, and to take such lands as may be necessary for the establishment of their reservoirs, ponds, dams, works, railroads, or sidetracks, or powerhouses, with the right to divert the water from such ponds or reservoirs, and conduct the same by flume, ditch, conduit, waterway or pipeline, or in any other manner, to the point of use for the generation of power at its said powerhouses, returning said water to its proper channel after being so used. (1874-5, c. 203, s. 4; Code, s. 2009; 1899, c. 64; 1903, c. 562; Rev., s. 1573; 1907, c. 74; C.S., s. 1698; 1921, c. 115; 1923, c. 60; 1925, c. 175; 1957, c. 1046; 1963, c. 1165, s. 1; 1981, c. 919, s. 2.)

§ 62-184. Dwelling house of owner, etc., may be taken under certain cases.

The dwelling house, yard, kitchen, garden or burial ground of the owner may be taken under G.S. 62-183 when the company alleges, and upon the proceedings to condemn makes it appear to the satisfaction of the court, that it owns or otherwise controls not less than seventy-five percent (75%) of the fall of the river or stream on which it proposes to erect its works, from the location of its proposed dam to the head of its pond or reservoir; or when the Commission, upon the petition filed by the company, shall, after due inquiry, so authorize. Nothing in this section repeals any part or feature of any private charter, but any firm or corporation acting under a private charter may operate under or adopt any feature of this section. (1907, c. 74; 1917, c. 108; C.S., s. 1699; 1933, c. 134, ss. 7, 8; 1963, c. 1165, s. 1.)

§ 62-185. Exercise of right of eminent domain; parties' interests only taken; no survey required.

When such telegraph, telephone, electric power or lighting company fails on application therefor to secure by contract or agreement such right-of-way for the purposes aforesaid over the lands, privilege or easement of another person or corporation; it may condemn the said interest through the procedures of the Chapter entitled Eminent Domain.

Only the interest of such parties as are brought before the court shall be condemned in any such proceedings, and if the right-of-way of a railroad or railway company sought to be condemned extends into or through more counties than one, the whole right and controversy may be heard and determined in one county into or through which such right-of-way extends.

It is not necessary for the petitioner to make any survey of or over the right-of-way, nor to file any map or survey thereof, nor to file any certificate of the location of its line by its board of directors. (1874-5, c. 203, s. 5; Code, s. 2010; 1899, c. 64, s. 2; 1903, c. 562; Rev., s. 1574; C.S., s. 1700; 1963, c. 1165, s. 1; 1981, c. 919, s. 3.)

§ 62-186. Repealed by Session Laws 1981, c. 919, s. 4, effective January 1, 1982.

§ 62-187. Proceedings as under eminent domain.

The proceedings for the condemnation of lands, or any easement or interest therein, for the use of telegraph, telephone, electric power or lighting companies, the appraisal of the lands, or interest therein, the duty of the commissioners of appraisal, the right of either party to file exceptions, the report of commissioners, the mode and manner of appeal, the power and authority of the court or judge, the final judgment and the manner of its entry and enforcement, and the rights of the company pending the appeal, shall be as prescribed in Chapter 40A, the Chapter entitled Eminent Domain. (Code, s.

2012; 1899, c. 64; 1903, c. 562; Rev., s. 1576; C.S., s. 1702; 1963, c. 1165, s. 1; 1981, c. 919, s. 5.)

§ 62-188. Repealed by Session Laws 1981, c. 919, s. 6, effective January 1, 1982.

§ 62-189. Powers granted corporations under Chapter exercisable by persons, firms or copartnerships.

All the rights, powers and obligations given, extended to, or that may be exercised by any corporation or incorporated company under this Chapter shall be extended to and likewise be exercised and are hereby granted unto all persons, firms or copartnerships engaged in or authorized by law to engage in the business herein described. Such persons, firms, copartnerships and corporations engaging in such business shall be subject to the provisions and requirements of the public laws which are applicable to others engaged in the same kind of business. (1939, c. 228, s. 3; 1963, c. 1165, s. 1.)

§ 62-190. Right of eminent domain conferred upon pipeline companies; other rights.

(a)   Any pipeline company transporting or conveying natural gas, gasoline, crude oil, coal in suspension, or other fluid substances by pipeline for the public for compensation, and incorporated under the laws of the State, or foreign corporations domesticated under the laws of North Carolina, may exercise the right of eminent domain under the provisions of the Chapter, Eminent Domain, and for the purpose of constructing and maintaining its pipelines and other works shall have all the rights and powers given other corporations by this Chapter and acts amendatory thereof. Nothing herein shall prohibit any such pipeline company granted the right of eminent domain under the laws of this State from extending its pipelines from within this State into another state for the purpose of transporting natural gas or coal in suspension into this State, nor to prohibit any such pipeline company from conveying or transporting natural gas, gasoline, crude oil, coal in suspension, or other fluid substances from within this

State into another state. All such pipeline companies shall be deemed public utilities and shall be subject to regulation under the provisions of this Chapter.

(b)   Liquid pipeline right-of-way must be selected to avoid, as far as practicable, areas containing private dwellings, industrial buildings, and places of assembly.

No liquid pipeline may be located within 50 feet of any private dwelling, or any industrial building or place of public assembly in which persons work, congregate, or assemble, unless it is provided with at least 12 inches of cover in addition to that prescribed in Part 195, Title 49, Code of Federal Regulations.

Any liquid pipeline installed underground must have at least 12 inches of clearance between the outside of the pipe and the extremity of any other underground structure, except that for drainage tile the minimum clearance may be less than 12 inches but not less than two inches. However, where 12 inches of clearance is impracticable, the clearance may be reduced if adequate provisions are made for corrosion control. (1937, c. 280; 1951, c. 1002, s. 3; 1957, c. 1045, s. 2; 1963, c. 1165, s. 1; 1985, c. 696, s. 1; 1998-128, s. 8.)

§ 62-191. Flume companies exercising right of eminent domain become common carriers.

All flume companies availing themselves of the right of eminent domain under the provisions of the Chapter Eminent Domain shall become common carriers of freight, for the purpose for which they are adapted, and shall be under the direction, control and supervision of the Commission in the same manner and for the same purposes as is by law provided for other common carriers of freight. (1907, c. 39, s. 4; C.S., s. 3517; 1933, c. 134, s. 8; 1941, c. 97, § 5; 1963, c. 1165, s. 1.)

§ 62-192: Repealed by Session Laws 1998-128, s. 13.

§§ 62-193 through 62-199. Reserved for future codification purposes.

Article 10.

Transportation in General.

§ 62-200. Duty to transport household goods within a reasonable time.

(a)   It shall be unlawful for any common carrier of household goods doing business in this State to omit or neglect to transport within a reasonable time any goods, merchandise or other articles of value received by it for shipment and billed to or from any place in this State, unless otherwise agreed upon between the carrier and the shipper, or unless the same be burned, stolen or otherwise destroyed, or unless otherwise provided by the Commission.

(b)   Any common carrier violating any of the provisions of this section shall forfeit to the party aggrieved the sum of ten dollars ($10.00) for the first day and one dollar ($1.00) for each succeeding day of such unlawful detention or neglect, but the forfeiture shall not be collected for a period exceeding 30 days.

(c)   In reckoning what is a reasonable time for such transportation, it shall be considered that such common carrier has transported household goods within a reasonable time if it has done so in the ordinary time required for transporting such articles by similar carriers between the receiving and shipping stations. The Commission is authorized to establish reasonable times for transportation by the various modes of carriage which shall be held to be prima facie reasonable, and a failure to transport within such times shall be held prima facie unreasonable. This section shall be construed to refer not only to delay in starting the household goods from the station where they are received, but to require the delivery at their destination within the time specified: Provided, that if such delay shall be due to causes which could not in the exercise of ordinary care have been foreseen or which were unavoidable, then upon the establishment of these facts to the satisfaction of the court trying the cause, the defendant common carrier shall be relieved from any penalty for delay in the transportation of household goods, but it shall not be relieved from the costs of such action. In all actions to recover penalties against a common carrier under this section, the burden of proof shall be upon such carrier to show where the delay, if any, occurred. The penalties provided in this section shall be in addition to the damages recoverable for failure to transport within a reasonable time.

(d) This section shall not apply to motor carriers of passengers. (Code, s. 1964; 1899, c. 164, s. 2, subsecs. 2, 7; 1903, c. 444; c. 590, s. 3; c. 693; 1905, c. 545; Rev., ss. 1094, 2631, 2632; 1907, cc. 217, 461; C.S., ss. 1053, 3515, 3516; 1933, c. 134, s. 8; 1941, c. 97; 1963, c. 1165, s. 1; 1995, c. 523, s. 11; 1995 (Reg. Sess., 1996), c. 742, s. 33; 1998-128, s. 9.)

§ 62-201. Freight charges to be at legal rates; penalty for failure to deliver to consignee on tender of same.

All common carriers doing business in this State shall settle their freight charges according to the rate stipulated in the bill of lading, provided the rate therein stipulated be in conformity with the classifications and rates made and filed with the North Carolina Utilities Commission in the case of intrastate shipments, by which classifications and rates all consignees shall in all cases be entitled to settle freight charges with such carriers; and it shall be the duty of such common carriers to inform any consignee of the correct amount due for freight according to such classification and rates. Upon payment or tender of the amount due on any shipment which has arrived at its destination according to such classification and rates, such common carrier shall deliver the freight in question to the consignee. Any failure or refusal to comply with the provisions hereof shall subject such carrier so failing or refusing to liability for actual damages plus a penalty of fifty dollars ($50.00) for each such failure or refusal, to be recovered by any consignee aggrieved by a suit in a court of competent jurisdiction. Provided, however, that this section shall not apply to motor carriers of passengers. (1905, c. 330, s. 1; Rev., s. 2633; C.S., s. 3518; 1933, c. 134, s. 8; 1941, c. 97, s. 5; 1963, c. 1165, s. 1.)

§ 62-202. Baggage and freight to be carefully handled.

All common carriers shall handle with care all baggage and freight placed with them for transportation, and they shall be liable in damages for any and all injuries to the baggage or freight of persons from whom they have collected fare or charged freight while the same is under their control. Upon proof of injury to baggage or freight in the possession or under the control of any such carrier, it shall be presumed that the injury was caused by the negligence of the carrier.

This section shall not apply to motor carriers of passengers. (1897, c. 46; Rev., s. 2624; C.S., s. 3523; 1963, c. 1165, s. 1.)

§ 62-203. Claims for loss or damage to goods; filing and adjustment.

(a) Every common carrier receiving household goods for transportation in intrastate commerce shall issue a bill of lading therefor, and shall be liable to the lawful holder thereof for any loss, damage, or injury to such household goods caused by it, or by any carrier participating in the haul when transported on a through bill of lading, and any such carrier delivering said household goods so received and transported shall be liable to the lawful holder of said bill of lading or to any party entitled to recover thereon for such loss, damage, or injury, notwithstanding any contract or agreement to the contrary; provided, however, the Commission may, by regulation or order, authorize or require any such common carrier to establish and maintain rates related to the value of shipments declared in writing by the shipper, or agreed upon as the release value of such shipments, such declaration or agreement to have no effect other than to limit liability and recovery to an amount not exceeding the value so declared or released, in which case, any tariff filed pursuant to such regulation or order shall specifically refer thereto; provided further, that a rate shall be afforded the shipper covering the full value of the goods shipped; provided further, that nothing in this section shall deprive any lawful holder of such bill of lading of any remedy or right of action which such holder has under existing law; provided further, that the carrier issuing such bill of lading, or delivering such household goods so received and transported, shall be entitled to recover from the carrier on whose route the loss, damage, or injury shall have been sustained the amount it may be required to pay to the owners of such property.

(b) Every claim for loss of or damage to household goods while in possession of a common carrier shall be adjusted and paid within 90 days after the filing of such claim with the agent of such carrier at the point of destination of such shipment, or point of delivery to another common carrier, by the consignee or at the point of origin by the consignor, when it shall appear that the consignee was the owner of the shipment: Provided, that no such claim shall be filed until after the arrival of the shipment, or some part thereof, at the point of destination, or until after the lapse of a reasonable time for the arrival thereof.

(c) In every case such common carrier shall be liable for the amount of such loss or damage, together with interest thereon from the date of the filing of the claim therefor until the payment thereof. Failure to adjust and pay such claim within the periods respectively herein prescribed shall subject each common carrier so failing to a penalty of fifty dollars ($50.00) for each and every such failure, to be recovered by any consignee aggrieved (or consignor, when it shall appear that the consignor was the owner of the property at the time of shipment and at the time of suit, and is, therefore, the party aggrieved), in any court of competent jurisdiction: Provided, that unless such consignee or consignor recover in such action the full amount claimed, no penalty shall be recovered, but only the actual amount of the loss or damage, with interest as aforesaid; and that no penalty shall be recoverable under the provisions of this section where claims have been filed by both the consignor and consignee, unless the time herein provided has elapsed after the withdrawal of one of the claims.

(d)   A check shall be affixed to every parcel of baggage when taken for transportation by the agent or servant of a common carrier, if there is a handle, loop or fixture so that the same can be attached upon the parcel or baggage so offered for transportation, and a duplicate thereof given to the passenger or person delivering the same on his behalf. If such check be refused on demand, the common carrier shall pay to such passenger the sum of ten dollars ($10.00), to be recovered in a civil action; and further, no fare or toll shall be collected or received from such passenger, and if such passenger shall have paid his fare the same shall be refunded by the carrier.

(e)   If a passenger, whose bag has been checked, shall produce the check and his baggage shall not be delivered to him, he may by an action recover the value of such baggage.

(f)   Causes of action for the recovery of the possession of the property shipped, for loss or damage thereto, and for the penalties herein provided for, may be united in the same complaint.

(g)   This section shall not deprive any consignee or consignor of any other rights or remedies existing against common carriers in regard to freight charges or claims for loss or damage to freight, but shall be deemed and held as creating an additional liability upon such common carriers.

(h)   This section shall not apply to motor carriers of passengers and only subsection (a) of this section shall apply to motor carriers of property. (1871-2, c. 138, s. 36; Code, s. 1970; 1905, c. 330, ss. 2, 4, 5; Rev., ss. 2623, 2634, 2635; 1907, c. 983; 1911, c. 139; C.S., ss. 3510, 3524, 3525; 1947, c. 781; c. 1008, s. 27; 1963, c. 1165, s. 1; 1995, c. 523, s. 12.)

§ 62-204. Notice of claims, statute of limitations for loss, damage or injury to property.

Any claim for loss, damage or injury to property while in the possession of a common carrier shall be filed by the claimant with the carrier in writing within nine months after the same occurred, and the cause of action with respect thereto shall be deemed to have accrued at the expiration of 30 days after the date of such notice, and action for the recovery thereon may be commenced immediately thereafter or at any time within two years after notice in writing shall have been given to the claimant by the adverse party that the claim or any part thereof specified in such notice has been disallowed, and neither party shall by rule, regulation, contract, or otherwise, provide for a shorter time for filing such claims or for commencing actions thereon than the period set out in this section. Provided, however, that this section shall not apply to motor carriers of passengers. (1947, c. 1008, s. 21; 1963, c. 1165, s. 1.)

§ 62-205. Joinder of causes of action.

To expedite the settlement of claims between shippers and common carriers, a shipper may join in the same complaint against a common carrier any number of claims for overcharges, or a common carrier may join in the same complaint any number of claims against a shipper for undercharges, whether such claims arose at the same time or in the course of shipments at different times; provided, that each such claim shall be so identified that the same and the allegations with respect thereto may be distinguished from other claims so joined in the complaint, and in cases in which the right of subrogation may be invoked the judgment shall specify the amount of recovery, if any, on each such claim. For the purpose of jurisdiction under this section the aggregate amount set out in the complaint shall be deemed the sum in controversy. Provided, however, that this section shall not apply to motor carriers of passengers. (1947, c. 1008, s. 20; 1963, c. 1165, s. 1.)

§ 62-206. Carrier's right against prior carrier.

Any common carrier shall have all the rights and remedies herein provided for against a common carrier from which it received the household goods in question. Provided, however, that this section shall not apply to motor carriers of passengers. (1905, c. 330, s. 3; Rev., s. 2636; C.S., s. 3526; 1963, c. 1165, s. 1; 1995, c. 523, s. 13.)

§ 62-207: Repealed by Session Laws 1998-128, s. 13.

§ 62-208. Common carriers to settle promptly for cash-on-delivery shipments; penalty.

Every common carrier which shall fail to make settlement with the consignor of a cash-on-delivery shipment, either by payment of the moneys stipulated to be collected upon the delivery of the articles so shipped or by the return to such consignor of the article so shipped, within 20 days after demand made by the consignor and payment or tender of payment by him of the lawful charges for transportation, shall forfeit and pay to such consignor a penalty of twenty-five dollars ($25.00), where the value of the shipment is twenty-five dollars ($25.00) or less; and, where the value of the shipment is over twenty-five dollars ($25.00), a penalty equal to the value of the shipment; the penalty not to exceed fifty dollars ($50.00) in any case: Provided, no penalty shall be collectible where the shipment, through no act of negligence of the common carrier is burned, stolen or otherwise destroyed: Provided further, that the penalties here named shall be cumulative and shall not be in derogation of any right the consignor may have under any other provision of law to recover of the common carrier damages for the loss of any cash-on-delivery shipment or for negligent delay in handling the same. Provided, however, that this section shall not apply to motor carriers of passengers. (1909, c. 866; C.S., s. 3530; 1963, c. 1165, s. 1.)

§ 62-209. Sale of unclaimed baggage or household goods; notice; sale of rejected property; escheat.

(a) Any common carrier which has had in its possession on hand at any destination in this State any article whether baggage or household goods, for a period of 60 days from its arrival at destination, which said carrier cannot deliver because unclaimed, may at the expiration of said 60 days sell the same at public auction at any point where in the opinion of the carrier the best price can be obtained: Provided, however, that notice of such sale shall be mailed to the consignor and consignee, by registered or certified mail, if known to such carrier, not less than 15 days before such sale shall be made; or if the name and address of the consignor and consignee cannot with reasonable diligence be ascertained by such carrier, notice of the sale shall be published once a week for two consecutive weeks in some newspaper of general circulation published at the point of sale: Provided, that if there is no such paper published at such point, the publication may be made in any paper having a general circulation in the State: Provided further, however, that if the nondelivery of said article is due to the consignee's and consignor's rejection of it, then such article may be sold by the carrier at public or private sale, and at such time and place as will in the carrier's judgment net the best price, and this without further notice to either consignee or consignor, and without the necessity of publication.

(b)   Repealed by Session Laws 1995, c. 523, s. 14.

(c)   The common carrier shall keep a record of the articles sold and of the prices obtained therefor, and shall, after deducting all charges and the expenses of the sale, including advertisement, if advertised, pay the balance to the owner of such articles on demand therefor made at any time within five years from the date of the sale. If no person shall claim the surplus within five years, such surplus shall be paid to the Escheat Fund of the Department of State Treasurer.

(d)   This section shall not apply to motor carriers of passengers. (1871-2, c. 138, s. 50; Code, s. 1987; Rev., s. 2639; 1921, c. 124, ss. 1, 2, 3; C.S., s. 3534; 1963, c. 1165, s. 1; 1981, c. 531, s. 17; 1995, c. 523, s. 14.)

§ 62-210. Discrimination between connecting lines.

All common carriers subject to the provisions of this Chapter shall afford all reasonable, proper and equal facilities for the interchange of traffic between their respective lines and for the forwarding and delivering of passengers and freight to and from their several lines and those connecting therewith, and shall not discriminate in their rates, routes and charges against such connecting lines, and shall be required to make as close connection as practicable for the convenience of the traveling public. Common carriers shall obey all rules and regulations made by the Commission relating to trackage. Irregular route motor carriers shall interchange traffic only with the approval of the Commission. Provided, however, that this section shall not apply to motor carriers of passengers. (1899, c. 164, s. 21; Rev., s. 1088; C.S., s. 1107; 1933, c. 134, s. 8; 1935, c. 258; 1941, c. 97; 1963, c. 1165, s. 1.)

§ 62-211: Repealed by Session Laws 1995, c. 523, s. 15.

§ 62-212. Indemnity agreements in motor carrier transportation contracts.

(a) A provision, clause, covenant, or agreement contained in, collateral to, or affecting a motor carrier transportation contract that purports to indemnify, defend, or hold harmless, or has the effect of indemnifying, defending, or holding harmless the promisee from or against any liability for loss or damage resulting from the negligence or intentional acts or omission of the promisee is against the public policy of this State and is void and unenforceable.

(b) The following definitions apply in this section:

(1) Motor carrier transportation contract. - A contract, agreement, or understanding covering at least one of the following:

a. The transportation of property for compensation or hire by the motor carrier.

b. Entrance on property by the motor carrier for the purpose of loading, unloading, or transporting property for compensation or hire.

c. A service incidental to activity described in sub-subdivision a. or b. of this subdivision, including storage of property.

(2) Promisee. - The person with whom the motor carrier enters into a motor carrier transportation contract and any agents, employees, servants, or independent contractors who are directly responsible to that person, except for motor carriers party to a motor carrier transportation contract with the person, and the motor carrier's agents, employees, servants, or independent contractors directly responsible to the motor carrier.

(c) Nothing contained in this section affects a provision, clause, covenant, or agreement where the motor carrier indemnifies or holds harmless the contract's promisee against liability for damages to the extent that the damages were caused by and resulted from the negligence of the motor carrier, its agents, employees, servants, or independent contractors who are directly responsible to the motor carrier.

(d) Notwithstanding the other provisions contained in this section, the term "motor carrier transportation contract", as defined in this section, shall not include the Uniform Intermodal Interchange and Facilities Access Agreement administered by the Intermodal Association of North America, or other agreements providing for the interchange, use or possession of intermodal chassis, containers, trailers, or other intermodal equipment that contain substantially the same indemnity provision as the provision contained in the Uniform Intermodal Interchange and Facilities Access Agreement. (2005-185, s. 1; 2006-264, s. 45.5(a).)

§§ 62-213 through 62-219. Reserved for future codification purposes.

Article 11.

Railroads.

§ 62-220: Recodified as § 136-190 by Session Laws 1998-128, s. 14.

§§ 62-221 through 62-222: Repealed by Session Laws 1998-128, s. 13.

§§ 62-223 through 62-226: Recodified as §§ 136-191 through 136-194 by Session Laws 1998-128, s. 14.

§§ 62-227 through 62-234: Repealed by Session Laws 1998-128, s. 13.

§ 62-235: Repealed by Session Laws 1995 (Regular Session, 1996), c. 673, s. 3.

§ 62-236: Recodified as § 136-20.1 by Session Laws 1995 (Regular Session, 1996), c. 673, s. 5.

§ 62-237: Recodified as G.S. 136-195 by Session Laws 1998-128, s. 14, effective September 4, 1998.

§§ 62-238 through 62-239: Repealed by Session Laws 1998-128, s. 13.

§ 62-240: Recodified as § 136-196 by Session Laws 1998-128, s. 14.

§§ 62-241 through 62-247: Repealed by Session Laws 1998-128, s. 13.

§§ 62-248 through 62-258. Reserved for future codification purposes.

Article 12.

Motor Carriers.

§ 62-259. Additional declaration of policy for motor carriers.

In addition to the declaration of policy set forth in G.S. 62-2 of Article 1 of Chapter 62, it is declared the policy of the State of North Carolina to preserve and continue all motor carrier transportation services now afforded this State; and to provide fair and impartial regulations of motor carriers in the use of the public highways in such a manner as to promote, in the interest of the public, the inherent advantages of highway transportation; to promote and preserve adequate economical and efficient service to all the communities of the State by motor carriers; to encourage and promote harmony among all carriers and to prevent discrimination, undue preferences or advantages, or unfair or destructive competitive practices between all carriers; to foster a coordinated statewide motor carrier service; and to conform with the national transportation policy and the federal motor carriers acts insofar as the same may be practical and adequate for application to intrastate commerce. The provisions of this section and these policies are applicable to bus companies and their rates and services only to the extent with which they are consistent with the provisions of G.S. 62-259.1 and of the Bus Regulatory Reform Act of 1985. (1947, c. 1008, s. 1; 1949, c. 1132, s. 2; 1963, c. 1165, s. 1; 1985, c. 676, s. 16.)

§ 62-259.1. Specific declaration of policy for bus companies.

The transportation of passengers, their baggage and express, by bus companies has become increasingly subject to competition from other forms of transportation which are unregulated or only partially regulated as to rates and services. It is in the public interest and it is the policy of this State that bus companies be partially deregulated so that they may rely upon competitive market forces to determine the best quality, variety and price of bus services, thereby promoting the public health, safety and welfare by strengthening and increasing the viability of this necessary form of transportation. (1985, c. 676, s. 17.)

§ 62-260. Exemptions from regulations.

(a) Nothing in this Chapter shall be construed to include persons and vehicles engaged in one or more of the following services by motor vehicle if not engaged at the time in the transportation of other passengers or other property by motor vehicle for compensation:

(1) Transportation of passengers or household goods for or under the control of the State of North Carolina, or any political subdivision thereof, or any board, department or commission of the State, or any institution owned and supported by the State;

(2) Transportation of passengers by taxicabs when not carrying more than fifteen passengers or transportation by other motor vehicles performing bona fide taxicab service and not carrying more than fifteen passengers in a single vehicle at the same time when such taxicab or other vehicle performing bona fide taxicab service is not operated on a regular route or between termini; provided, no taxicab while operating over the regular route of a common carrier outside of a municipality and a residential and commercial zone adjacent thereto, as such zone may be determined by the Commission as provided in subdivision (8) of this subsection, shall solicit passengers along such route, but nothing herein shall be construed to prohibit a taxicab operator from picking up passengers along such route upon call, sign or signal from prospective passengers;

(3) Transportation by motor vehicles owned or operated by or on behalf of hotels while used exclusively for the transportation of hotel patronage between hotels and local railroad or other common carrier stations;

(4) Transportation of passengers to and from airports and passenger airline terminals when such transportation is incidental to transportation by aircraft;

(5) Transportation of passengers by trolley buses operated by electric power derived from a fixed overhead wire, furnishing local passenger transportation similar to street railway service;

(6) Transportation by motor vehicles used exclusively for the transportation of passengers to or from religious services or transportation of pupils and employees to and from private or parochial schools or transportation to and from functions for students and employees of private or parochial schools;

(7) Transportation of any bona fide employees to and from their place(s) of regular employment;

(8) Transportation of passengers when the movement is within a municipality exclusively, or within contiguous municipalities and within a residential and commercial zone adjacent to and a part of such municipality or

contiguous municipalities; provided, the Commission shall have power in its discretion, in any particular case, to fix the limits of any such zone;

(9) through (17) Repealed by Session Laws 1995, c. 523, s. 16.

(18) Charter parties, as defined by this subdivision when such charter party is sponsored or organized by, and used by, any organized senior citizen group whose members are sixty (60) years of age or older. Such charter party shall be subject to subsections (f) and (g) of this section. "Charter party", for the purpose of this subdivision, means a group of persons who, pursuant to a common purpose and under a single contract, and at a fixed charge for the vehicle, have acquired the exclusive use of a passenger-carrying motor vehicle to travel together as a group from a point of origin to a specified destination or for a particular itinerary, either agreed upon in advance or modified by the chartering group after having left the place of origin.

(b) The Commission shall have jurisdiction to fix rates of carriers of passengers operating as described in (5) and (8) of subsection (a) of this section in the manner provided in this Chapter, and shall have jurisdiction to hear and determine controversies with respect to extensions and services, and the Commission's rules of practice shall include appropriate provisions for bringing such controversies before the Commission and for the hearing and determination of the same; provided nothing in this paragraph shall include taxicabs.

(c) The Commission may conduct investigations to determine whether any person purporting to operate under the exemption provisions of this section is, in fact, so operating, and make such orders as it deems necessary to enforce compliance with this section.

(d) The venue for any action commenced to enforce compliance with the terms of this Article against any person purporting to operate under any of the exemptions provided in this section shall be in one of the counties of the superior court district or set of districts as defined in G.S. 7A-41.1 wherein the violation is alleged to have taken place and such person shall be entitled to trial by jury.

(e) None of the provisions of this section nor any of the provisions of this Chapter shall be construed so as to prohibit or regulate the transportation of property by any motor carrier when the movement is within a municipality or within contiguous municipalities and within a zone adjacent to and commercially a part of such municipality or contiguous municipalities, as defined by the Commission. The Commission shall have the power in its discretion, in any particular case, to fix the limits of any such zone. Nothing herein shall be construed as an abridgment of the police powers of any municipality over such operation wholly within any such municipality. Nothing in this Chapter shall be construed to prohibit or regulate the transportation of household effects of families from one residence to another by persons who do not hold themselves out as being, and are not generally engaged in the business of transporting such property for compensation.

(f) Notwithstanding the exemption for transportation of passengers and household goods provided under subsections (a) through (e) of this section, all motor carriers transporting passengers for compensation under said exemptions or under any special exemptions granted by the Utilities Commission under G.S. 62-261 shall be subject to the same requirements for security for protection of the public as are established for regulated motor common carriers by the rules of the Utilities Commission pursuant to G.S. 62-268, and all such motor carriers transporting for hire under said exemption provisions shall further be subject to the same requirements for safety of operation of said motor vehicles as are required of regulated motor common carriers under the provisions of Chapter 20 and the regulations of the Division adopted pursuant thereto. The Division is authorized to promulgate rules and regulations for the enforcement of said requirements in the case of all such exempt operations, and the officers and agents of the Division shall have full authority to inspect said exempt vehicles and to apply all enforcement regulations and penalties for violation of said security regulations and safety regulations as in the case of regulated motor carriers.

(g) The owners of all motor vehicles used in any transportation for compensation which is declared to be exempt under this section shall register such operation with the Division of Motor Vehicles and shall secure from the Division of Motor Vehicles a certificate of exemption. (1947, c. 1008, s. 4; 1949, c. 1132, s. 5; 1951, c. 987, s. 1; 1953, c. 1140, s. 2; 1955, c. 1194, ss. 1, 2; 1959, c. 102, c. 639, s. 15; 1963, c. 1165, c. 1; 1967, cc. 1135, 1203; 1969, c. 681; 1971, cc. 856, 1192; 1973, c. 175; 1977, c. 217; 1979, c. 204, s. 1; 1985, c. 454, ss. 9-11; 1987 (Reg. Sess., 1988), c. 1037, s. 94; 1995, c. 523, s. 16.)

§ 62-261. Additional powers and duties of Commission applicable to motor vehicles.

The Commission is hereby vested with the following powers and duties:

(1)   To supervise and regulate bus companies and to that end, the Commission may establish reasonable requirements with respect to continuous and adequate service, transportation of baggage, newspapers, mail and light express, uniform system of accounts, records and reports and preservation of records.

(2)   To supervise the operation and safety of passenger bus stations in any manner necessary to promote harmony among the carriers using such stations and efficiency of service to the traveling public.

(3)   Repealed by Session Laws 1985, c. 454, s. 12.

(4)   For the purpose of carrying out the provisions of this Article, the Utilities Commission may avail itself of the special information of the Board of Transportation in promulgating safety requirements and in considering applications for certificates or permits with particular reference to conditions of the public highway or highways involved, and the ability of the said public highway or highways to carry added traffic; and the Board of Transportation, upon request of the Utilities Commission, shall furnish such information.

(5)   The Commission may, without prior notice and hearing, make and enter any order, rule, regulation, or requirement, not affecting rates, upon unanimous finding by the Commission of the existence of an emergency and make such order, rule, regulation or requirement effective upon notice given to each affected motor carrier by registered mail, or by certified mail pending a hearing thereon as provided in this subdivision. It shall not be necessary for the Commission to give notice to the carriers affected or to hold a hearing prior to a revision in the rules regarding procedures to be followed in filing rates. Any such emergency order, rule, regulation or requirement shall be subject to continuation, modification, change, or revocation after notice and hearing and all such emergency orders, rules, regulations and requirements shall be supplanted and superseded by any final order, rule, regulation or requirement entered by the Commission.

(6)   The Commission shall regulate brokers and make and enforce reasonable requirements respecting their licenses, financial responsibility, accounts, records, reports, operations and practices.

(7)   Repealed by Session Laws 1985, c. 454, s. 12.

(8)   To determine, upon its own motion, or upon motion by a motor carrier, or any other party in interest, whether the transportation of household goods in intrastate commerce performed by any motor carrier or class of motor carriers lawfully engaged in operation in this State is in fact of such nature, character, or quantity as not substantially to affect or impair uniform regulation by the Commission of transportation by motor carriers engaged in intrastate commerce. Upon so finding, the Commission shall issue a certificate of exemption to such motor carrier or class of motor carriers which, during the period such certificate shall remain effective and unrevoked, shall exempt such carrier or class of motor carriers from compliance with the provisions of this Article, and shall attach to such certificate such reasonable terms and conditions as the public interest may require. At any time after the issuance of any such certificate of exemption, the Commission may by order revoke all or any part thereof, if it shall find that the transportation in intrastate commerce performed by the carrier or class of carriers designated in such certificate will be, or shall have become, or is reasonably likely to become, or such nature, character, or quantity as in fact substantially to affect or impair uniform regulation by the Commission of intrastate transportation by motor carriers in effectuating the policy declared in this Chapter. Upon revocation of any such certificate, the Commission shall restore to the carrier or carriers affected thereby, without further proceedings, the authority, if any, to operate in intrastate commerce held by such carrier or carriers at the time the certificate of exemption pertaining to such carrier or carriers became effective. No certificate of exemption shall be denied, and no order of revocation shall be issued, under this paragraph, except after reasonable opportunity for hearing to interested parties.

(9)   To inquire into the management of the business of motor carriers and into the management of business of persons controlling, controlled by or under common control with, motor carriers to the extent that such persons have a pecuniary interest in the business of one or more motor carriers, and the Commission shall keep itself informed as to the manner and method in which the same are conducted, and may obtain from such carriers and persons such information as the Commission deems necessary to carry out the provisions of this Article.

(10)   Repealed by Session Laws 1985, c. 454, s. 12.

(11)   The Commission may from time to time establish such just and reasonable classifications of groups of carriers included in the term "common

carrier by motor vehicle" as the special nature of the service performed by such carriers shall require; and such just and reasonable rules, regulations, and requirements, consistent with the provisions of this Article, to be observed by such carriers so classified or grouped, as the Commission deems necessary or desirable in the public interest. (1947, c. 1008, s. 5; 1949, c. 1132, s. 6; 1953, c. 1140, s. 5; 1957, c. 65, s. 11; c. 1152, s. 7; 1961, c. 472, s. 9; 1963, c. 1165, s. 1; 1969, c. 723, s. 2; c. 763; 1973, c. 507, s. 5; 1985, c. 454, s. 12; c. 676, s. 18; 1995, c. 523, s. 17.)

§ 62-262. Applications and hearings other than for bus companies.

(a) Except as otherwise provided in G.S. 62-260[,] G.S. 62-262.1 and 62-265, no person shall engage in the transportation of passengers or household goods in intrastate commerce unless such person shall have applied to and obtained from the Commission a certificate authorizing such operations, and it shall be unlawful for any person knowingly or wilfully to operate in intrastate commerce in any manner contrary to the provisions of this Article, or of the rules and regulations of the Commission. No certificate shall be amended so as to enlarge or in any manner extend the scope of operations of a motor carrier without complying with the provisions of this section.

(b) Upon the filing of an application for a certificate, the Commission shall, within a reasonable time, fix a time and place for hearing such application. The Commission shall from time to time prepare a truck calendar containing notice of such hearings, a copy of which shall be mailed to the applicant and to any other persons desiring it, upon payment of charges to be fixed by the Commission. The notice or calendar herein required shall be mailed at least 20 days prior to the date fixed for the hearing, but the failure of any person, other than applicant, to receive such notice or calendar shall not, for that reason, invalidate the action of the Commission in granting or denying the application.

(c) The Commission may, in its discretion, except where a regular calendar providing notice is issued, require the applicant to give notice of the time and place of such hearing together with a brief description of the purpose of said hearing and the exact route or routes and authority applied for, to be published not less than once each week for two successive weeks in one or more newspapers of general circulation in the territory proposed to be served. The Commission may in its discretion require the applicant to give such other and further notice in the form and manner prescribed by the Commission to the end that all interested parties and the general public may have full knowledge of such hearing and its purpose. If the Commission requires the applicant to give notice by publication, then a copy of such notice shall be immediately mailed by the applicant to the Commission, and upon receipt of same the chief clerk shall cause the copy of notice to be entered in the Commission's docket of pending proceedings. The applicant shall, prior to any hearing upon his application, be required to satisfy the Commission that such notice by publication has been duly made, and in addition to any other fees or costs required to be paid by the applicant, the applicant shall pay into the office of the Commission the cost of the notices herein required to be mailed by the Commission.

(d) Any motor carrier desiring to protest the granting of an application for a certificate, in whole, or in part, may become a party to such proceedings by filing with the Commission, not less than 10 days prior to the date fixed for the hearing, unless the time be extended by order of the Commission, its protest in writing under oath, containing a general statement of the grounds for such protest and the manner in which the protestant will be adversely affected by the granting of the application in whole or in part. Such protestant may also set forth in his protest its proposal, if any, to render either alone or in conjunction with other motor carriers, the service proposed by the applicant, either in whole or in part. Upon the filing of such protest it shall be the duty of the protestant to file three copies with the Commission, and the protestant shall certify that a copy of said protest has been delivered or mailed to the applicant or applicant's attorney. When no protest is filed with the Commission within the time herein limited, or as extended by order of the Commission, the Commission may proceed to decide the application on the basis of testimony taken at a hearing, or on the basis of information contained in the application and sworn affidavits, and make the necessary findings of fact and issue or decline to issue the certificate applied for without further notice. Persons other than motor carriers shall have the right to appear before the Commission and give evidence in favor of or against the granting of any application and with permission of the Commission may be accorded the right to examine and cross-examine witnesses.

(e) The burden of proof shall be upon the applicant for a certificate to show to the satisfaction of the Commission:

(1) That public convenience and necessity require the proposed service in addition to existing authorized transportation service, and

(2) That the applicant is fit, willing and able to properly perform the proposed service, and

(3) That the applicant is solvent and financially able to furnish adequate service on a continuing basis.

(f) to (h) Repealed by Session Laws 1985, c. 676, s. 19.

(i), (j) Repealed by Session Laws 1995, c. 523, s. 18.

(k) The Commission shall by general order, or rule, having regard for the public convenience and necessity, provide for the abandonment or permanent or temporary discontinuance of transportation service previously authorized in a certificate.

(l) The provisions of this section shall not be applicable to applications for certificates of authority by bus companies or related hearings. (1947, c. 1008, s. 11; 1949, c. 1132, s. 10; 1953, c. 825, s. 3; 1957, c. 1152, ss. 8, 9; 1959, c. 639, s. 11; 1963, c. 1165, s. 1; 1965, c. 214; 1981, c. 193, s. 4; 1985, c. 676, s. 19; 1995, c. 523, s. 18.)

§ 62-262.1. Certificates of authority for passenger operations by bus companies.

(a) Except as provided in G.S. 62-260, 62-262 and 62-265, no person shall engage in the transportation of passengers in intrastate commerce by motor vehicle without having applied for and obtained a certificate authorizing those operations from the Commission. It shall be unlawful for any person to knowingly or willfully operate in intrastate commerce in a manner contrary to the provisions of this Article or to the rules and regulations of the Commission. No certificate shall be amended to enlarge, or in any manner extend, the scope of operations of a bus company without complying with the provisions of this section.

(b) Any bus company desiring a certificate of authority to operate in intrastate commerce in this State over fixed routes, or to enlarge or in any manner extend the scope of its fixed route operations previously granted by the Commission, may do so by filing a verified application with the Commission and by paying the filing fee established by G.S. 62-300.

(c) The Commission shall issue a certificate of authority to an applicant for the transportation of passengers over a fixed route or to enlarge or extend authority previously granted, if the Commission finds that the applicant is fit, willing and able to provide the transportation to be authorized by the certificate and to comply with the provisions of this Chapter, unless the Commission finds, on the basis of evidence presented by any person objecting to the issuance of the certificate, that the transportation to be authorized is not consistent with the public interest.

(d) In making any findings relating to public interest under subsection (c) of this section, the Commission shall consider, to the extent applicable, (i) the transportation policy of this State as it relates to bus companies under G.S. 62-259.1 and this Chapter; (ii) the value of competition to the traveling and shipping public; (iii) the effect of issuance of the certificate on bus company service to small communities; and (iv) whether issuance of the certificate would impair the ability of any other fixed route carrier of passengers to provide a substantial portion of its fixed route passenger service, except that diversion of revenue or traffic from a fixed route carrier of passengers, alone, shall not be sufficient to support a finding that issuance of the certificate would impair the ability of the carrier to provide a substantial portion of its fixed route passenger service.

(e) Within 10 days after the filing of an application, the applicant shall provide notice to be given as required by Commission rule. If no protest, raising material issues of fact to the granting of the application, is filed with the Commission within 30 days after the notice is given, the Commission may, upon review of the record and without a hearing, issue its certificate of authority granting the requested operating authority, if it is satisfied that the applicant meets the requirements set forth in subsection (c) of this section.

(f) If protests are filed raising material issues of fact to the granting of the application, the Commission shall set the application for hearing, as soon as possible, and cause notice to be given as provided by its rules. At the hearing, the only issues for consideration are those set forth in subsections (c) and (d) of this section. The Commission shall issue its final order not later than 180 days after the application is filed.

(g) Any bus company authorized to transport passengers in intrastate commerce over fixed routes in this State and which in fact provides that service may, without filing a new application or paying further fees: (i) transport newspapers, express parcels or United States mail over the fixed routes on which it provides passenger transportation; (ii) provide charter operations to all points in the State; and (iii) transport charter passengers in the same motor vehicles with fixed route passengers.

(h) Any bus company seeking a certificate to engage solely in charter operations within the State, or to enlarge or in any manner extend the scope of its charter operations previously granted by the Commission, may obtain one by (i) filing a verified application for the authority with the Commission; (ii) paying the applicable filing fee as prescribed by G.S. 62-300; and (iii) demonstrating that it is fit, willing and able to perform the proposed charter operations.

(i) Within 10 days after filing of an application for charter operations, the applicant shall provide notice as required by Commission rule or regulation. If no protests to the granting of the application, raising material issues of fact, are received by the Commission within 30 days after the notice is given, the Commission shall issue its certificate granting the requested authority unless it determines that the applicant is unfit, unwilling or unable to perform the proposed operations. In the event of this determination, or if protests to the proposed operation raising material issues of fact are received, the Commission shall set the application for hearing, as soon as possible, and provide notice to be given as provided by its rules and shall issue its final order within 180 days after application is filed. At the hearing, the only issue for consideration shall be whether the applicant is fit, willing and able to perform the proposed charter operations and the issue of need shall not be considered. On the issue of its fitness, willingness and ability to perform the proposed charter operations, the applicant in its application and at any hearing shall present evidence from which the Commission may find that: (i) the applicant has sufficient assets to perform properly the proposed operations; (ii) the operation will be conducted only with properly qualified drivers; (iii) the applicant will maintain safe, clean and attractive buses and equipment; (iv) the applicant will maintain insurance for the protection of the public as provided in this Chapter; (v) the applicant has sufficient equipment to conduct the proposed operation; and (vi) the applicant will observe all applicable laws, rules and regulations of this State.

(j) Any bus company authorized and engaged solely in charter operations shall not be required to transport passengers over a fixed route in this State as an incidence to its charter operations. (1985, c. 676, s. 20.)

§ 62-262.2. Discontinuance or reduction in service.

(a) When a bus company proposes to discontinue service over any intrastate route or proposes to reduce its level of service to any points on a route to a level which is less than one trip per day (excluding Saturdays and Sundays), it shall petition the Commission for permission to do so. Within 10 days after the filing of a petition, the Commission shall require notice to be given.

(b) Any person or the Public Staff may object, to the Commission, to the granting of permission to any bus company to discontinue or reduce transportation under this section. If neither objects to the granting of permission to discontinue or reduce service under this section, within 30 days after the notice as required by subsection (a) of this section, the Commission may grant the permission based on the record and without hearing.

(c) If, within 30 days after the notice as required by subsection (a) of this section, any person or the Public Staff objects in writing to the Commission to granting of such permission, the Commission shall grant such permission unless the Commission finds as a fact, that the discontinuance or reduction in service is not consistent with the public interest or that continuing the transportation, without the proposed discontinuance or reduction, will not constitute an unreasonable burden on interstate commerce. In making a finding under this subsection, the Commission shall accord great weight to the extent to which the interstate and intrastate revenues from the transportation proposed to be reduced or discontinued are less than the variable costs of providing the transportation, including depreciation for revenue equipment. The Commission may also consider, to the extent applicable, all other factors which are to be considered by the Interstate Commerce Commission in a proceeding commenced under 49 U.S.C. § 10935. For the purposes of this section, the bus company filing a petition for permission to discontinue or reduce service shall have the burden of proving (i) the amount of its interstate and intrastate revenues received for transportation to, from or between, but not through, points on the involved intrastate route; and (ii) the system variable costs of providing the transportation.

(d) The Commission may make its determination with or without a public hearing. The Commission shall take final action upon the petition not later than 120 days after any written objections to the petition are filed.

(e) The provisions of G.S. 62-262(k) shall not be applicable to bus companies. (1985, c. 676, s. 21; 1989 (Reg. Sess., 1990), c. 1024, s. 15.)

§ 62-263. Application for broker's license.

(a)   No person shall engage in the business of a broker in intrastate operations within this State unless such person holds a broker's license issued by the Commission.

(b)   The Commission shall prescribe the form of application and such reasonable requirements and information as may in its judgment be necessary.

(c)   Upon the filing of an application for license the Commission may fix a time and place for the hearing of the application and require such notices, publications, or other service as it may prescribe by the general rule or regulation.

(d)   A license shall be issued to any qualified applicant therefor authorizing the whole or any part of the operations covered by the application if it is found that the applicant is fit, willing and able properly to perform the service proposed and to conform to the provisions of this Article and the requirements, rules and regulations of the Commission thereunder, and that the proposed service, to the extent to be authorized by the license, is or will be consistent with the public interest and policy declared herein.

(e)   The Commission shall have the same authority over persons operating under and holding a brokerage license as it has over motor carriers under this Article, and shall require a broker to furnish bond or other security approved by the Commission and sufficient for the protection of travelers by motor vehicle. (1949, c. 1132, s. 13; 1963, c. 1165, s. 1.)

§ 62-264: Repealed by Session Laws 1995, c. 523, s. 19.

§ 62-265. Emergency operating authority.

To meet unforeseen emergencies, the Commission may, upon its own initiative, or upon written request by any person, department or agency of the State, or of any county, city or town, with or without a hearing, grant appropriate authority to any owner of a duly licensed vehicle or vehicles, whether such owner holds a certificate or not, to transport passengers or household goods between such points, or within such area during the period of the emergency and to the extent necessary to relieve the same, as the Commission may fix in its order granting such authority; provided, that unless the emergency is declared by the General Assembly or under its authority, the Commission shall find from such request, or from its own knowledge or conditions, that a real emergency exists and that relief to the extent authorized in its order is immediate, pressing and necessary in the public interest, and that the carrier so authorized has the necessary equipment and is willing to perform the emergency service as prescribed by the order. In all cases, under this section, the Commission shall first afford the holders of certificates operating in the territory affected an opportunity to render the emergency service. Upon the termination of the emergency, the operating privileges so granted shall automatically expire and the Commission shall forthwith withdraw all operating privileges granted to any person under this section. (1947, c. 1008, s. 17; 1949, c. 1132, s. 17; 1963, c. 1165, s. 1; 1995, c. 523, s. 20.)

§ 62-266. Repealed by Session Laws 1985, c. 454, s. 13, effective June 24, 1985.

§ 62-267. Deviation from regular route operations.

(a)   A common carrier of passengers by motor vehicle operating under a certificate issued by the Commission may occasionally deviate from the routes over which it is authorized to operate under the certificate, under such general or special rules and regulations as the Commission may prescribe.

(b)   Repealed by Session Laws 1995, c. 523, s. 21.

(c)   In no event shall the operation of empty equipment by any carrier over any route or highway be construed as a violation of the rights of any carrier. (1947, c. 1008, s. 18; 1949, c. 1132, s. 18; 1963, c. 1165, s. 1; 1995, c. 523, s. 21.)

§ 62-268. Security for protection of public; liability insurance.

No certificate or broker's license shall be issued or remain in force until the applicant shall have procured and filed with the Division of Motor Vehicles such security bond, insurance or self-insurance for the protection of the public as the Commission shall by regulation require. The Commission shall require that every motor carrier for which a certificate or license is required by the provisions of this Chapter, shall maintain liability insurance or satisfactory surety of at least fifty thousand dollars ($50,000) because of bodily injury to or death of one person in any one accident and, subject to said limit for one person, one hundred thousand dollars ($100,000) because of bodily injury to or death of two or more persons in any one accident, and fifty thousand dollars ($50,000) because of injury to or destruction of property of others in any one accident; and the Commission may require any greater amount of insurance as may be necessary for the protection of the public. Notwithstanding any rule or regulation to the contrary, the Commission shall not require that any insurance procured and filed be provided in any single policy of insurance or through a single insurer, if the insurers involved are otherwise qualified. A motor carrier may satisfy the requirements of the Commission by procuring insurance with coverage and limits of liability required by the Commission in one or more policies of insurance issued by one or more insurers.

Notwithstanding any other provisions of this section or Chapter, bus companies shall file with the Commission proof of financial responsibility in the form of bonds, policies of insurance, or shall qualify as a self insurer, with minimum levels of financial responsibility as prescribed for motor carriers of passengers pursuant to the provisions of 49 U.S.C. § 31138. Provided, further, that no bus company operating solely within the State of North Carolina and which is exempt from regulation under the provisions of G.S. 62-260(a)(7) shall be required to file with the Commission proof of the financial responsibility in excess of one million five hundred thousand dollars ($1,500,000). (1947, c. 1008, s. 19; 1949, c. 1132, s. 19; 1963, c. 1165, s. 1; 1973, c. 1206; 1977, c. 920; 1985, c. 454, s. 14; c. 676, s. 22; 1987, c. 374; 1995, c. 523, s. 22; 1998-217, s. 8.)

§ 62-269. Accounts, records and reports.

The Commission may prescribe the forms of any and all accounts, records and memoranda to be kept by motor carriers, brokers, and lessors, including the accounts, records, and memoranda of the movement of traffic, as well as of the receipts and expenditures of moneys; and it shall be unlawful for such carriers, brokers, and lessors, to keep any accounts, records, and memoranda contrary to any rules, regulations, or orders of the Commission with respect thereto. The Commission may issue orders specifying such operating, accounting, or financial papers, records, books, blanks, stubs, correspondence, or documents of motor carriers, brokers, or lessors, as may after a reasonable time be destroyed, and prescribing the length of time they shall be preserved. The Commission or its duly authorized special agents, accountants, or examiners shall at all times have access to and authority, under its order, to inspect and examine any and all lands, buildings, or equipment of motor carriers, brokers, and lessors; and shall have authority to inspect and copy any and all accounts, books, records, memoranda, correspondence, and other documents of such carriers, brokers, and lessors, and such accounts, books, records, memoranda, correspondence, and other documents of any person controlling, controlled by, or under common control with any such carrier, as the Commission deems relevant to such person's relation to or transactions with such carrier. Motor carriers, brokers, lessors, and persons shall submit their accounts, books, records, memoranda, correspondence, and other documents for the inspection and copying authorized by this section, and motor carriers, brokers, and lessors, shall submit their lands, buildings, and equipment for examination and inspection, to any duly authorized special agent, accountant, auditor, inspector, or examiner of the Commission upon demand and the display of proper credentials. (1947, c. 1008, s. 28; 1949, c. 1132, s. 25; 1959, c. 639, ss. 5, 6, 9, 10; 1961, c. 472, s. 10; 1963, c. 1165, s. 1.)

§ 62-270. Orders, notices, and service of process.

It shall be the duty of every motor carrier operating under a certificate issued under the provisions of this Article to file with the Division of Motor Vehicles a designation in writing of the name and post-office address of a person upon whom service of notices or orders may be made under this Article. Such designation may from time to time be changed by like writing similarly filed. Service of notice or orders in proceedings under this Article may be made upon a motor carrier by personal service upon it or upon the person so designated by it, or by registered mail, return receipt requested, or by certified mail with return receipt requested, addressed to it or to such person at the address filed. In proceedings before the Commission involving the lawfulness of rates, charges, classifications, or practices, service of notice upon the person or agent who has filed a tariff or schedule in behalf of such carrier shall be deemed to be due and sufficient service upon the carrier. (1947, c. 1008, s. 29; 1949, c. 1132, s. 26; 1957, c. 1152, ss. 6, 11; 1963, c. 1165, s. 1; 1985, c. 454, s. 15; 1995, c. 523, s. 23.)

§ 62-271. Collection of rates and charges of motor carriers of household goods.

No common carriers of household goods by motor vehicle shall deliver or relinquish possession at destination of any freight transported by it in intrastate commerce until all tariff rates and charges thereon have been paid, except under such rules and regulations as the Commission may from time to time prescribe to govern the settlement of all such rates and charges, including rules and regulations for weekly or monthly settlement, and to prevent unjust discrimination or undue preference or prejudice; provided, that the provisions of this section shall not be construed to prohibit any such carrier from extending credit in connection with rates and charges on freight transported for the United States, for any department, bureau, or agency thereof, or for the State, or political subdivision thereof. Where any common carrier by motor vehicle is instructed by a shipper or consignor to deliver household goods transported by such carrier to a consignee other than the shipper or consignor, such consignee shall not be legally liable for transportation charges in respect of the transportation of such household goods (beyond those billed against him at the time of delivery for which he is otherwise liable) which may be found to be due after the household goods have been delivered to him, if the consignee (i) is an agent only and had no beneficial title in the household goods, and (ii) prior to delivery of the household goods has notified the delivering carrier in writing of the fact of such agency and absence of beneficial title, and, in the case of shipment reconsigned or diverted to a point other than that specified in the original bill of lading, has also notified the delivering carrier in writing of the name and address of the beneficial owner of the household goods. In such cases the shipper and consignor, or, in the case of a shipment so reconsigned or diverted, the beneficial owner shall be liable for such additional charges, irrespective of any provisions to the contrary in the bill of lading or in the contract under which the shipment was made. If the consignee has given to the carrier erroneous information as to who is the beneficial owner, such consignee shall himself be liable for such additional charges, notwithstanding the foregoing provisions of this section. On shipments reconsigned or diverted by an agent who has furnished the carrier with a notice of agency and the proper name and address of the beneficial owner, and where such shipments are refused or abandoned at ultimate destination, the said beneficial owner shall be liable for all legally applicable charges in connection therewith. (1947, c. 1008, s. 31; 1963, c. 1165, s. 1; 1995, c. 523, s. 24.)

§ 62-272. Allowance to shippers for transportation services.

If the owner of household goods transported under the provisions of this Article directly or indirectly renders any service connected with such transportation, or furnishes any instrumentality used therein, the charge and allowance therefor shall be published in the tariffs or schedules filed in the manner provided in this Article and shall be no more than is just and reasonable; and the Commission may, after hearing on a complaint or on its own initiative, determine what is a reasonable charge as the maximum to be paid by the carrier or carriers for the services so rendered or for the use of the instrumentality so furnished, and fix the same by appropriate order. (1947, c. 1008, s. 32; 1963, c. 1165, s. 1; 1995, c. 523, s. 25.)

§ 62-273. Embezzlement of C.O.D. shipments.

Household goods received by any motor carrier to be transported in intrastate commerce and delivered upon collection on such delivery and remittance to the shipper of the sum of money stated in the shipping instructions to be collected and remitted to the shipper, and the money collected upon delivery of such party, are hereby declared to be held in trust by any carrier having possession thereof or the carrier making the delivery or collection, and upon failure of any such carrier to account for the household goods so received, either to the shipper to whom the collection is payable or the carrier making delivery to any carrier handling the household goods or making the collection, within 15 days after demand in writing by the shipper, or carrier, or upon failure of the delivering carrier to remit the sum so directed to be collected and remitted to the shipper, within 15 days after collection is made, shall be prima facie evidence that the household goods so received, or the funds so received, have been wilfully converted by such carrier to its own use, and the carrier so offending shall be guilty of a Class H felony and such carrier may be indicted, tried, and punished in the county in which such shipment was delivered to the carrier or in any other county into or through which such shipment was transported by such carrier. (1947, c. 1008, s. 33; 1963, c. 1165, s. 1; 1993, c. 539, s. 1277; 1994, Ex. Sess., c. 24, s. 14(c); 1995, c. 523, s. 26.)

§ 62-273.1. Criminal history record checks of applicants for and current holders of certificate to transport household goods.

(a) The following definitions apply in this section:

(1) Applicant. - An individual, partnership, limited liability corporation, or corporation who applies for certification as a common carrier of household goods in the State of North Carolina.

(2) Certificate. - A certificate of exemption or a certificate of public convenience and necessity issued by the Utilities Commission to authorize the holder to engage in the intrastate transportation of household goods for compensation in the State of North Carolina.

(3) Criminal history. - A State or federal history of conviction of a crime, whether a misdemeanor or felony, that bears upon an applicant's or current holder's fitness to possess a certificate.

(4) Current holder. - An individual, partnership, limited liability corporation, or corporation who has been certified as a common carrier of household goods in the State of North Carolina.

(b) The Commission shall conduct a criminal history record check of applicants and current holders of a certificate to transport household goods. An applicant for or current holder of a certificate to transport household goods must furnish the Commission with a complete set of the applicant's fingerprints in a manner prescribed by the Commission. In those instances where the quality characteristic of an applicant's or current holder's fingerprints is determined to be too low or otherwise inadequate for processing by the FBI, the applicant or current holder shall comply with the Commission's criminal history record check requirement pursuant to the Commission's alternate name-based records check procedure.

(c) If the applicant's or current holder's verified criminal history record check reveals one or more convictions, the convictions shall not automatically constitute cause for denying an application or revoking a certificate. However, all of the following factors shall be considered by the Commission in determining whether the application should be denied or the certificate revoked:

(1)　The level and seriousness of the crime.

(2)　The date of the crime.

(3)　The age of the person at the time of the conviction.

(4)　The nature of the crime as it relates to the duties and responsibilities of a common carrier of household goods.

(5)　The employment history of the person after the date the crime was committed.

(6)　Any evidence of rehabilitation of the person after the date the crime was committed.

(d)　The Commission may deny an application or revoke a certificate if the applicant or current holder refuses to consent to a criminal history record check or use of fingerprints or other identifying information required by the State or National Repositories of Criminal Histories. (2012-9, s. 1.)

§ 62-274. Evidence; joinder of surety.

No report by any carrier of any accident arising in the course of the operations of such carrier, made pursuant to any requirement of the Commission, and no report by the Commission of any investigation of any such accident, shall be admitted as evidence, or used for any other purpose in any suit or action for damages growing out of any matter mentioned in such report or investigation; nor shall the discharge by any carrier of any truck driver or other employee after any such accident be offered or admitted in evidence for any purpose, in any suit or action against such carrier for damages arising out of any such accident; nor shall any insurance company or surety executing any insurance policy, bond, or other security for the protection of the public, as provided in G.S. 62-268, or as provided in G.S. 62-112, be joined with the assured carrier in any action or suit for damages, debt, or claim thereby secured; nor shall evidence of any such policy, bond, or other security be offered or received in any such action or suit against the carrier, but the surety or insurer shall be obligated within the amount of such policy, bond or other security to pay any final judgment against the carrier. (1947, c. 1008, s. 34; 1949, c. 1132, s. 31; 1963, c. 1165, s. 1.)

§ 62-275. Repealed by Session Laws 1985, c. 676, s. 23, effective July 10, 1985.

§ 62-276. Construction of Article.

Nothing herein contained shall be construed to relieve any motor carrier from any regulation otherwise imposed by law or lawful authority, and this Article shall not be construed to relieve any such motor carrier from any obligation or duty imposed by Chapter 20 of the General Statutes of North Carolina. (1949, c. 1132, s. 35; 1963, c. 1165, s. 1.)

§ 62-277. Repealed by Session Laws 1985, c. 454, s. 16, effective June 24, 1985.

§ 62-278. Revocation of license plates by Utilities Commission.

(a) The license plates of any carrier of persons or household goods by motor vehicle for compensation may be revoked and removed from the vehicles of any such carrier for wilful violation of any provision of this Chapter, or for the wilful violation of any lawful rule or regulation made and promulgated by the Utilities Commission. To that end the Commission shall have power upon complaint or upon its own motion, after notice and hearing, to order the license plates of any such offending carrier revoked and removed from the vehicles of such carrier for a period not exceeding 30 days, and it shall be the duty of the Department of Motor Vehicles to execute such orders made by the Utilities Commission upon receipt of a certified copy of the same.

(b)   This section shall be in addition to and independent of other provisions of law for the enforcement of the motor carrier laws of this State. (1951, c. 1120; 1963, c. 1165, s. 1; 1995, c. 523, s. 27.)

§ 62-279. Injunction for unlawful operations.

If any motor carrier, or any other person or corporation, shall operate a motor vehicle in violation of any provision of this Chapter applicable to motor carriers or motor vehicles generally, except as to the reasonableness of rates or charges and the discriminatory character thereof, or shall operate in violation of any rule, regulation, requirement or order of the Commission, or of any term or condition of any certificate, the Commission or any holder of a certificate duly issued by the Commission may apply to a superior court judge who has jurisdiction pursuant to G.S. 7A-47.1 or 7A-48 in the district or set of districts as defined in G.S. 7A-41.1 in which the motor carrier or other person or corporation so operates, for the enforcement of any provisions of this Article, or of any rule, regulation, requirement, order, term or condition of the Commission. Such court shall have jurisdiction to enforce obedience to this Article or to any rule, order, or decision of the Commission by a writ of injunction or other process, mandatory or otherwise, restraining such carrier, person or corporation, or its officers, agents, employees and representatives from further violation of this Article or of any rule, order, regulation, or decision of the Commission. (1947, c. 1008, s. 30; 1949, c. 1132, s. 30; 1953, c. 1140, s. 4; 1957, c. 1152, s. 16; 1961, c. 472, ss. 8, 11; 1963, c. 1165, s. 1; 1987 (Reg. Sess., 1988), c. 1037, s. 95; 1995, c. 523, s. 28.)

§ 62-280. Household goods carrier; marking or identification of vehicles.

(a)   No carrier of household goods shall operate any motor vehicle upon a highway, public street, or public vehicular area within the State in the transportation of household goods for compensation in violation of the provisions of G.S. 20-398.

(b)   The Utilities Commission may assess a civil penalty not in excess of five thousand dollars ($5,000) for the violation of subsection (a) of this section. The clear proceeds of any civil penalties collected pursuant to this subsection shall be remitted to the Civil Penalty and Forfeiture Fund in accordance with G.S. 115C-457.2. (2011-244, s. 2.)

§ 62-280.1. False representation of household goods carrier certificate unlawful.

(a) It is unlawful for a person not issued a certificate to operate as a carrier of household goods under the provisions of this Chapter to do any of the following:

(1) Orally, in writing, in print, or by sign, including the use of a vehicle placard, phone book, Internet, magazine, newspaper, billboard, or business card, or in any other manner, directly or by implication, represent that the person holds a certificate or is otherwise authorized to operate as a carrier of household goods in this State.

(2) Use in connection with the person's name or place of business any words, letters, abbreviations, or insignia indicating or implying that the person holds a certificate or is otherwise authorized to operate as a carrier of household goods in this State.

(b) Any person who violates subsection (a) of this section shall be guilty of a Class 3 misdemeanor and punished only by a fine of not more than five hundred dollars ($500.00) for the first offense and not more than two thousand dollars ($2,000) for any subsequent offense.

(c) The Utilities Commission may assess a civil penalty not in excess of five thousand dollars ($5,000) for the violation of subsection (a) of this section. The clear proceeds of any civil penalties collected pursuant to this subsection shall be remitted to the Civil Penalty and Forfeiture Fund in accordance with G.S. 115C-457.2. (2011-244, s. 2.)

§ 62-281. Repealed by Session Laws 1985, c. 454, s. 17, effective June 24, 1985.

§§ 62-282 through 62-289. Reserved for future codification purposes.

Article 12A.

Human Service Transportation.

§ 62-289.1. Short title.

This Article shall be known and may be cited as the "North Carolina Act to Remove Barriers to Coordinating Human Service and Volunteer Transportation". (1981, c. 792, s. 1.)

§ 62-289.2. Purpose.

In order to promote improved transportation for the elderly, handicapped and residents of rural areas and small towns through an expanded and coordinated transportation network, it is the intent of the General Assembly to recognize human service transportation and volunteer transportation as separate but contributing components of the North Carolina transportation system. Further, it is the intent of the General Assembly to remove barriers to low cost human service transportation. (1981, c. 792, s. 1.)

§ 62-289.3. Definitions.

As used in this Article:

(1) "Human service agency" means any charitable or governmental agency including, but not limited to: county departments of social services, area mental health, mental retardation or substance abuse authorities, local health departments, councils on aging, community action agencies, sheltered workshops, group homes and State residential institutions.

(2) "Human service transportation" means motor vehicle transportation provided on a nonprofit basis by a human service agency for the purpose of transporting clients or recipients in connection with programs sponsored by the agency. "Human service transportation" shall also mean motor vehicle transportation provided by for-profit persons under exclusive contract with a human service agency for the transportation of clients or recipients, and such provider shall also qualify as a human service agency for the purpose of motor vehicle registration during the term of the contract. The motor vehicle may be owned, leased, borrowed, or contracted for use by or from the human service agency.

(3) "Nonprofit" as applied to human service transportation means motor vehicle transportation provided at cost.

(4) "Person" means an individual, corporation, company, association, partnership or other legal entity.

(5) "Volunteer transportation" means motor vehicle transportation provided by any person under the direction, sponsorship, or supervision of a human service agency. The person may receive an allowance to defray the actual cost of operating the vehicle but shall not receive any other compensation. (1981, c. 792, s. 1; 1987, c. 407.)

§ 62-289.4. Classification of transportation.

The forms of transportation defined in G.S. 62-289.3(2) and (5) shall be classified as "human service transportation" and "volunteer transportation" for purposes of regulation, insurance, and general administration. (1981, c. 792, s. 1.)

§ 62-289.5. Inapplicable laws and regulations.

Human services transportation and volunteer transportation shall not be considered as for-hire transportation, commercial transportation or motor carriers, as defined by G.S. 62-3(17). Such transportation shall not be subject to regulation as motor carriers under G.S. 62-261. (1981, c. 792, s. 1.)

§ 62-289.6. Insurance for volunteers.

Human service agencies are authorized to purchase insurance to cover persons who provide volunteer transportation. (1981, c. 792, s. 1.)

§ 62-289.7. Municipal licenses and taxes.

No county, city, town, municipal corporation or other unit of local government may impose a special tax on or require a special license for human service transportation or volunteer transportation other than that customarily used or imposed on private passenger automobiles unless the tax or license is provided for by a statute, ordinance, or regulation specifically addressing human service transportation or volunteer transportation. (1981, c. 792, s. 1.)

Article 13.

Reorganization of Public Utilities.

§ 62-290. Corporations whose property and franchises sold under order of court or execution.

When the property and franchises of a public utility corporation are sold under a judgment or decree of a court of this State, or of the district court of the United States, or under execution, to satisfy a mortgage debt or other encumbrance thereon, such sale vests in the purchaser all the right, title, interest and property of the parties to the action in which such judgment or decree was made, to said property and franchises, subject to all the conditions, limitations and restrictions of the corporation; and the purchaser and his associates thereupon become a new corporation, by such name as they select, and they are the stockholders in the ratio of the purchase money by them contributed; and are entitled to all the rights and franchises and subject to all the conditions, limitations and penalties of the corporation whose property and franchises have been so sold. In the event of the sale of a railroad in foreclosure of a mortgage or deed of trust, whether under a decree of court or otherwise, the corporation created by or in consequence of the sale succeeds to all the franchises, rights and privileges of the original corporation only when the sale is of all the railroad owned by the company and described in the mortgage or deed of trust, and when the railroad is sold as an entirety. If a purchaser at any such sale is a corporation, such purchasing corporation shall succeed to all the properties, franchises, powers, rights, and privileges of the original corporation: Provided, that this shall not affect vested rights and shall not be construed to alter in any manner the public policy of the State now or hereafter established with reference to trusts and contracts in restraint of trade. (Code, ss. 697, 698; 1897, c. 305; 1901, c. 2, s. 99; Rev., s. 1238; 1913, c. 25, s. 1; 1919, c. 75; C.S., s. 1221; 1955, c. 1371, s. 2; 1963, c. 1165, s. 1.)

§ 62-291. New owners to meet and organize; special rule for railroads.

(a)   The persons for whom the property and franchises have been purchased pursuant to G.S. 62-290 shall meet within 30 days after the delivery of the conveyance made by virtue of said judgment or decree, and organize the new corporation, 10 days' written notice of the time and place of the meeting having been given to each of said persons. At this meeting they shall adopt a corporate name and seal, determine the amount of the capital stock of the corporation, and shall have power and authority to make and issue certificates of stock in shares of such amounts as they see fit. The corporation may then, or at any time thereafter, create and issue preferred stock to such an amount, and at such time, as they may deem necessary.

(b)   Whenever the purchaser of the real estate, track and fixtures of any railroad corporation which has heretofore been sold, or may hereafter be sold, by virtue of any mortgage executed by such corporation or execution issued upon any judgment or decree of any court, shall acquire title to the same in the manner prescribed by law, such purchaser may associate with him any number of persons, and make and acknowledge and file articles of association as prescribed by this Chapter. Such purchaser and his associates shall thereupon be a new corporation, with all the powers, privileges and franchises and subject to all of the provisions of this Chapter.

(c)   When any railroad corporation shall be dissolved, or its property sold and conveyed under any execution, deed of trust, mortgage or other conveyance, the owner or purchaser shall constitute a new corporation upon compliance with law. (1871-2, c. 138, s. 5; Code, ss. 1936, 2005; 1901, c. 2, ss.

100, 101, 102; Rev., ss. 1239, 1240, 2552, 2565; C.S., ss. 1222, 3462, 3463; 1955, c. 1371, s. 2; 1963, c. 1165, s. 1.)

§ 62-292. Certificate to be filed with Secretary of State.

It is the duty of the new corporation provided for by this Article, within one month after its organization, to make certificate thereof, under its common seal, attested by the signature of its president, specifying the date of the organization, the name adopted, the amount of capital stock, and the names of its president and directors, and transmit the certificate to the Secretary of State, to be filed and recorded in his office. A certified copy of this certificate so filed shall be recorded in the office of the clerk of the superior court of the county in which is located the principal office of the corporation, and is the charter and evidence of the corporate existence of the new corporation. (1901, c. 2, s. 103; Rev., s. 1241; C.S., s. 1223; 1955, c. 1371, s. 2; 1963, c. 1165, s. 1.)

§ 62-293. Effect on liens and other rights.

Nothing contained in this Article in any manner impairs the lien of a prior mortgage, or other encumbrance, upon the property or franchises conveyed under a sale pursuant to this Article when by the terms of the judgment or decree under which the sale was made, or by operation of law, the sale was made subject to the lien of any such prior mortgage or other encumbrance. No such sale and conveyance or organization of such new corporation in any way affects the rights of any person or body politic not a party to the action in which the judgment or decree was made, nor of any party except as determined by the judgment or decree. When a trustee has been made a party to such action and his cestui que trust, for reason satisfactory to the court, has not been made a party thereto, the rights and interest of the cestui que trust are concluded by the decree. (1901, c. 2, s. 103; Rev., s. 1241; C.S., s. 1224; 1955, c. 1371, s. 2; 1963, c. 1165, s. 1.)

§§ 62-294 through 62-299. Reserved for future codification purposes.

Article 14.

Fees and Charges.

§ 62-300. Particular fees and charges fixed; payment.

(a) The Commission shall receive and collect the following fees and charges in accordance with the classification of utilities as provided in rules and regulations of the Commission, and no others:

(1) Twenty-five dollars ($25.00) with each notice of appeal to the Court of Appeals or the Supreme Court, and with each notice of application for a writ of certiorari.

(2) With each application for a new certificate for motor carrier rights, the fee shall be two hundred fifty dollars ($250.00) when filed by Class 1 motor carriers, one hundred dollars ($100.00) when filed by Class 2 motor carriers, and twenty-five dollars ($25.00) when filed by Class 3 motor carriers, and twenty-five dollars ($25.00) as filing fee for any amendment thereto so as to extend or enlarge the scope of operations thereunder, and twenty-five dollars ($25.00) for each broker who applies for a brokerage license under the provisions of this Chapter.

(3) With each application for a general increase in rates, fares and charges and for each filing of a tariff which seeks general increases in rates, fares and charges, the fee will be five hundred dollars ($500.00) for Class A utilities and Class 1 motor carriers, two hundred fifty dollars ($250.00) for Class B utilities and Class 2 motor carriers, one hundred dollars ($100.00) for Class C utilities and twenty-five dollars ($25.00) for Class D utilities and Class 3 motor carriers; provided that in the case of an application or tariff for a general increase in rates filed by a tariff agent for more than one carrier, the applicable fee shall be the highest fee prescribed for any motor carrier included in the application or tariff. This fee shall not apply to applications for adjustments in particular rates, fares, or charges for the purpose of eliminating inequities, preferences or discriminations or to applications to adjust rates and charges based solely on the increased cost of fuel used in the generation or production of electric power.

(4) One hundred dollars ($100.00) with each application by motor carrier of passengers for the abandonment or permanent or temporary discontinuance of transportation service previously authorized in a certificate.

(4a) Repealed by Session Laws 1998-128, s. 10.

(5) With each application for a certificate of public convenience and necessity or for any amendment thereto so as to extend or enlarge the scope of operations thereunder, the fee shall be two hundred fifty dollars ($250.00) for Class A utilities, one hundred dollars ($100.00) for Class B utilities, and twenty-five dollars ($25.00) for Class C and D utilities and twenty-five dollars ($25.00) for any other person seeking a certificate of public convenience and necessity.

(5a) With each application by a bus company for an original certificate of authority or for any amendment thereto or to an existing certificate of public convenience and necessity so as to extend or enlarge the scope of operations thereunder the fee shall be two hundred fifty dollars ($250.00).

(6) With each application for approval of the issuance of securities or for the approval of any sale, lease, hypothecation, lien, or other transfer of any household goods or operating rights of any carrier or public utility over which the Commission has jurisdiction, the fee shall be two hundred fifty dollars ($250.00) for Class A utilities and Class 1 motor carriers, one hundred dollars ($100.00) for Class B utilities and Class 2 motor carriers, and twenty-five dollars ($25.00) for Class C and D utilities and Class 3 motor carriers; provided, that in the case of sales, leases and transfers between two or more carriers or utilities, the applicable fee shall be the highest fee prescribed for any party to the transaction.

(7) Ten dollars ($10.00) with each application, petition, or complaint not embraced in (2) through (6) of this section, wherein such application, petition, or complaint seeks affirmative relief against a carrier or public utility over which the Commission has jurisdiction. This fee shall not apply to applications for adjustments in particular rates, fares or charges for the purpose of eliminating inequities, preferences or discriminations; nor shall this fee apply to applications, petitions, or complaints made by any county, city or town; nor shall this fee apply to applications or petitions made by individuals seeking service or relief from a public utility.

(8) Repealed by Session Laws 1985, c. 454, s. 18.

(9) One dollar ($1.00) for each page (81/2 x 11 inches) of transcript of testimony, but not less than five dollars ($5.00) for any such transcript.

(10) Twenty cents (20¢) for each page of copies of papers, orders, certificates or other records, but not less than one dollar ($1.00) for any such order or record, plus five dollars ($5.00) for formal certification of any such paper, order or record.

(11), (12) Repealed by Session Laws 1985, c. 454, s. 18.

(13) Two hundred fifty dollars ($250.00) with each application for a certificate of public convenience and necessity to construct a transmission line.

(14) Twenty-five dollars ($25.00) with each filing by a person otherwise exempt from Commission regulation under Public Law 103-305 to participate in standard transportation practices as set out by the Commission.

(15) One hundred dollars ($100.00) for each application for exemption filed by nonprofit and consumer-owned water or sewer utilities pursuant to G.S. 62-110.5.

(b) All witness fees, officers' fees serving papers, and cost of serving notice by publication shall be paid by the party at whose instance or for whose benefit such fees and costs are incurred.

(c) No application, petition, complaint, notice of appeal, notice of application for writ of certiorari, or other document or paper, the filing of which requires the payment of a fee under this Article, shall be deemed filed until the fees herein required shall have been paid to the Commission.

(d) The fees and charges as set forth in subdivisions (1), (7), (9) and (10) of subsection (a) of this section shall not apply to the State of North Carolina or to any board, department, commission, institution or other agency of the State; and all applications, petitions or complaints submitted by the State of North Carolina or any board, department, commission, institution or other agency of the State shall be filed without the payment of the fees required by this section. All transcripts, papers, orders, certificates, or other records necessary to perfect an appeal, or to determine whether an appeal is to be taken, shall be furnished without charge to the Attorney General upon his request in cases in which the Attorney General appears in the public interest or as representing any board, department, commission, institution or other agency of the State.

(e) The provisions of this section shall apply with respect to the regulation of electric membership corporations as provided in G.S. 117-18.1. (1953, c. 825, s.

1; 1955, c. 64; 1957, c. 1152, s. 15; 1961, c. 472, ss. 2-4; 1963, c. 1165, s. 1; 1967, c. 1039; c. 1190, s. 7; 1969, c. 721, s. 2; 1971, c. 736, s. 2; 1975, c. 447, s. 1; 1977, c. 1003; 1977, 2nd Sess., c. 129, s. 32; 1979, c. 792; 1985, c. 311, ss. 1-4; c. 454, ss. 18, 19; c. 676, s. 24; 1991, c. 189, s. 2; 1995, c. 523, ss. 29, 32; 1997-437, s. 3; 1998-128, s. 10; 1999-180, s. 6.)

§ 62-301: Repealed by Session Laws 1989, c. 787, s. 2.

§ 62-302. Regulatory fee.

(a)   Fee Imposed. - It is the policy of the State of North Carolina to provide fair regulation of public utilities in the interest of the public, as provided in G.S. 62-2. The cost of regulating public utilities is a burden incident to the privilege of operating as a public utility. Therefore, for the purpose of defraying the cost of regulating public utilities, every public utility subject to the jurisdiction of the Commission shall pay a quarterly regulatory fee, in addition to all other fees and taxes, as provided in this section. The fees collected shall be used only to pay the expenses of the Commission and the Public Staff in regulating public utilities in the interest of the public.

It is also the policy of the State to provide limited oversight of certain electric membership corporations as provided in G.S. 62-53. Therefore, for the purpose of defraying the cost of providing the oversight authorized by G.S. 62-53 and G.S. 117-18.1, each fiscal year each electric membership corporation whose principal purpose is to furnish or cause to be furnished bulk electric supplies at wholesale as provided in G.S. 117-16 shall pay an annual fee as provided in this section.

(b)   Public Utility Rate. -

(1)   Repealed by Session Laws 2000-140, s. 56, effective July 21, 2000.

(2)   The public utility regulatory fee for each fiscal year shall be the greater of (i) a percentage rate, established by the General Assembly, of each public utility's North Carolina jurisdictional revenues for each quarter or (ii) six dollars and twenty-five cents ($6.25) each quarter.

When the Commission prepares its budget request for the upcoming fiscal year, the Commission shall propose a percentage rate of the public utility regulatory fee. For fiscal years beginning in an odd-numbered year, that proposed rate shall be included in the budget message the Governor submits to the General Assembly pursuant to G.S. 143C-3-5. For fiscal years beginning in an even-numbered year, that proposed rate shall be included in a special budget message the Governor shall submit to the General Assembly. The General Assembly shall set the percentage rate of the public utility regulatory fee by law.

The percentage rate may not exceed the amount necessary to generate funds sufficient to defray the estimated cost of the operations of the Commission and the Public Staff for the upcoming fiscal year, including a reasonable margin for a reserve fund. The amount of the reserve may not exceed the estimated cost of operating the Commission and the Public Staff for the upcoming fiscal year. In calculating the amount of the reserve, the General Assembly shall consider all relevant factors that may affect the cost of operating the Commission or the Public Staff or a possible unanticipated increase or decrease in North Carolina jurisdictional revenues.

(3) If the Commission, the Public Staff, or both experience a revenue shortfall, the Commission shall implement a temporary public utility regulatory fee surcharge to avert the deficiency that would otherwise occur. In no event may the total percentage rate of the public utility regulatory fee plus any surcharge established by the Commission exceed twenty-five hundredths percent (0.25%).

(4) As used in this section, the term "North Carolina jurisdictional revenues" means:

a. All revenues derived or realized from intrastate tariffs, rates, and charges approved or allowed by the Commission or collected pursuant to Commission order or rule, but not including tap-on fees or any other form of contributions in aid of construction.

b. All revenues derived from retail services no longer otherwise regulated by the operation of G.S. 62-133.5(h) or G.S. 62-133.5(m) for a local exchange company or competing local provider that has elected to be regulated under those subsections.

(b1) Electric Membership Corporation Rate. - The electric membership corporation regulatory fee for each fiscal year shall be a dollar amount as established by the General Assembly by law.

When the Commission prepares its budget request for the upcoming fiscal year, the Commission shall propose the amount of the electric membership corporation regulatory fee. For fiscal years beginning in an odd-numbered year, the proposed amount shall be included in the budget message the Governor submits to the General Assembly pursuant to G.S. 143C-3-5. For fiscal years beginning in an even-numbered year, the proposed amount shall be included in a special budget message the Governor shall submit to the General Assembly.

The amount of the electric membership corporation regulatory fee proposed by the Commission may not exceed the amount necessary to defray the estimated cost of the operations of the Commission and the Public Staff for the regulation of the electric membership corporations in the upcoming fiscal year, including a reasonable margin for a reserve fund. The amount of the reserve may not exceed the estimated cost of the Commission and the Public Staff for the regulation of the electric membership corporations for the upcoming fiscal year.

(c) When Due. - The electric membership corporation regulatory fee imposed under this section shall be paid in quarterly installments. The fee is due and payable to the Commission on or before the 15th day of the second month following the end of each quarter.

The public utility regulatory fee imposed under this section is due and payable to the Commission on or before the 15th day of the second month following the end of each quarter. Every public utility subject to the public utility regulatory fee shall, on or before the date the fee is due for each quarter, prepare and render a report on a form prescribed by the Commission. The report shall state the public utility's total North Carolina jurisdictional revenues for the preceding quarter and shall be accompanied by any supporting documentation that the Commission may by rule require. Receipts shall be reported on an accrual basis.

If a public utility's report for the first quarter of any fiscal year shows that application of the percentage rate would yield a quarterly fee of twenty-five dollars ($25.00) or less, the public utility shall pay an estimated fee for the entire fiscal year in the amount of twenty-five dollars ($25.00). If, after payment of the estimated fee, the public utility's subsequent returns show that application of the percentage rate would yield quarterly fees that total more than twenty-five dollars ($25.00) for the entire fiscal year, the public utility shall pay the cumulative amount of the fee resulting from application of the percentage rate, to the extent it exceeds the amount of fees, other than any surcharge, previously paid.

(d)   Use of Proceeds. - A special fund in the office of State Treasurer, the Utilities Commission and Public Staff Fund, is created. The fees collected pursuant to this section and all other funds received by the Commission or the Public Staff, except for the clear proceeds of civil penalties collected pursuant to G.S. 62-50(d) and the clear proceeds of funds forfeited pursuant to G.S. 62-310(a), shall be deposited in the Utilities Commission and Public Staff Fund. The Fund shall be placed in an interest bearing account and any interest or other income derived from the Fund shall be credited to the Fund. Moneys in the Fund shall only be spent pursuant to appropriation by the General Assembly.

The Utilities Commission and Public Staff Fund shall be subject to the provisions of the State Budget Act except that no unexpended surplus of the Fund shall revert to the General Fund. All funds credited to the Utilities Commission and Public Staff Fund shall be used only to pay the expenses of the Commission and the Public Staff in regulating public utilities in the interest of the public as provided by this Chapter and in regulating electric membership corporations as provided in G.S. 117-18.1.

The clear proceeds of civil penalties collected pursuant to G.S. 62-50(d) and the clear proceeds of funds forfeited pursuant to G.S. 62-310(a) shall be remitted to the Civil Penalty and Forfeiture Fund in accordance with G.S. 115C-457.2. (1989, c. 787, s. 1; 1998-215, s. 126; 1999-180, s. 5; 2000-140, s. 56; 2006-203, s. 18; 2009-238, s. 6; 2011-52, s. 2.)

§§ 62-303 through 62-309. Reserved for future codification purposes.

Article 15.

Penalties and Actions.

§ 62-310. Public utility violating any provision of Chapter, rules or orders; penalty; enforcement by injunction.

(a) Any public utility which violates any of the provisions of this Chapter or refuses to conform to or obey any rule, order or regulation of the Commission shall, in addition to the other penalties prescribed in this Chapter forfeit and pay a sum up to one thousand dollars ($1,000) for each offense, to be recovered in an action to be instituted in the Superior Court of Wake County, in the name of the State of North Carolina on the relation of the Utilities Commission; and each day such public utility continues to violate any provision of this Chapter or continues to refuse to obey or perform any rule, order or regulation prescribed by the Commission shall be a separate offense.

(b) If any person or corporation shall furnish water or sewer utility service in violation of any provision of this Chapter applicable to water or sewer utilities, except as to the reasonableness of rates or charges and the discriminatory character thereof, or shall provide such service in violation of any rule, regulation or order of the Commission, the Commission shall apply to a superior court judge who has jurisdiction pursuant to G.S. 7A-47.1 or 7A-48 in the district or set of districts as defined in G.S. 7A-41.1 in which the person or corporation so operates, for the enforcement of any provision of this Chapter or of any rule, regulation or order of the Commission. The court shall have jurisdiction to enforce obedience to this Chapter or to any rule, regulation or order of the Commission by appropriate writ, order or other process restraining such person, corporation, or their representatives from further violation of this Chapter or of any rule, regulation or order of the Commission. (1899, c. 164, s. 23; Rev., s. 1087; C.S., s. 1106; 1933, c. 134, s. 8; c. 307, ss. 36, 37; 1941, c. 97; 1963, c. 1165, s. 1; 1973, c. 1073; 1987 (Reg. Sess., 1988), c. 1037, s. 96.)

§ 62-311. Willful acts of employees deemed those of public utility.

The willful act of any officer, agent, or employee of a public utility, acting within the scope of his official duties of employment, shall, for the purpose of this Article, be deemed to be the willful act of the utility. (1933, c. 307, s. 29; 1963, c. 1165, s. 1.)

§ 62-312. Actions to recover penalties.

Except as otherwise provided in this Chapter, an action for the recovery of any penalty under this Chapter shall be instituted in Wake County, and shall be instituted in the name of the State of North Carolina on the relation of the Utilities Commission against the person incurring such penalty; or whenever such action is upon the complaint of any injured person, it shall be instituted in the name of the State of North Carolina on the relation of the Utilities Commission upon the complaint of such injured person against the person incurring such penalty. Such action may be instituted and prosecuted by the Attorney General, the district attorney of the Wake County Superior Court, or the injured person. The procedure in such actions, the right of appeal and the rules regulating appeals shall be the same as provided by law in other civil actions. (Code, s. 1976; 1885, c. 221; 1899, c. 164, ss. 8, 15; Rev., ss. 1092, 1113, 2647; C.S., ss. 1062, 1111, 3415; 1933, c. 134, s. 8; c. 307, s. 30; 1941, c. 97; 1963, c. 1165, s. 1; 1973, c. 47, s. 2.)

§ 62-313. Refusal to permit Commission to inspect records made misdemeanor.

Any public utility, its officers or agents in charge thereof, that fails or refuses upon the written demand of the Commission, or a majority of said Commission, and under the seal of the Commission, to permit the Commission, its authorized representatives or employees to examine and inspect its books, records, accounts and documents, or its plant, property, or facilities, as provided for by law, shall be guilty of a Class 3 misdemeanor. Each day of such failure or refusal shall constitute a separate offense and each such offense shall be punishable only by a fine of not less than five hundred dollars ($500.00) and not more than five thousand dollars ($5,000). (1963, c. 1165, s. 1; 1993, c. 539, s. 483; 1994, Ex. Sess., c. 24, s. 14(c).)

§ 62-314. Violating rules, with injury to others.

If any public utility doing business in this State by its agents or employees shall be guilty of the violation of the rules and regulations provided and prescribed by the Commission, and if after due notice of such violation given to the principal officer thereof, if residing in the State, or, if not, to the manager or superintendent or secretary or treasurer if residing in the State, or, if not, then to any local agent thereof, ample and full recompense for the wrong or injury done thereby to any person as may be directed by the Commission shall not be made within 30 days from the time of such notice, such public utility shall incur a penalty for each offense of five hundred dollars ($500.00). (1899, c. 164, s. 15; Rev., s. 1086; C.S., s. 1105; 1933, c. 134, s. 8; 1941, c. 97; 1963, c. 1165, s. 1.)

§ 62-315. Failure to make report; obstructing Commission.

Every officer, agent or employee of any public utility, who shall willfully neglect or refuse to make and furnish any report required by the Commission for the purposes of this Chapter, or who shall willfully or unlawfully hinder, delay or obstruct the Commission in the discharge of the duties hereby imposed upon it, shall forfeit and pay five hundred dollars ($500.00) for each offense, to be recovered in an action in the name of the State. A delay of 10 days to make and furnish such report shall raise the presumption that the same was willful. (1899, c. 164, s. 18; Rev., s. 1089; C.S., s. 1108; 1933, c. 134, s. 8; 1941, c. 97; 1963, c. 1165, s. 1.)

§ 62-316. Disclosure of information by employee of Commission unlawful.

It shall be unlawful for any agent or employees of the Commission knowingly and willfully to divulge any fact or information which may come to his knowledge during the course of any examination or inspection made under authority of this Chapter, except as he may be directed by the Commission or by a court or judge thereof. (1947, c. 1008, s. 30; 1949, c. 1132, s. 30; 1953, c. 1140, s. 4; 1957, c. 1152, s. 16; 1961, c. 472, ss. 8, 11; 1963, c. 1165, s. 1; 1971, c. 736, s. 1.)

§ 62-317. Remedies for injuries cumulative.

The remedies given by this Chapter to persons injured shall be regarded as cumulative to the remedies otherwise provided by law against public utilities. (1899, c. 164, s. 26; Rev., s. 1093; C.S., s. 1112; 1963, c. 1165, s. 1.)

§ 62-318. Allowing or accepting rebates a misdemeanor.

If any person shall participate in illegally pooling freights or shall directly or indirectly allow or accept rebates on freights, he shall be guilty of a Class 1 misdemeanor. (1879, c. 237, s. 2; Code, s. 1968; Rev., s. 3762; C.S., s. 3520; 1963, c. 1165, s. 1; 1993, c. 539, s. 484; 1994, Ex. Sess., c. 24, s. 14(c).)

§ 62-319. Riding on train unlawfully; venue.

If any person, with the intention of being transported free in violation of law, rides or attempts to ride on top of any car, coach, engine or tender, on any railroad in this State, or on the drawheads between cars, or under cars, on truss rods, or trucks, or in any freight car, or on a platform of any baggage car, express car or mail car on any train, he shall be guilty of a Class 3 misdemeanor. Any person charged with a violation of this section may be tried in any county in this State through which such train may pass carrying such person, or in any county in which such violation may have occurred or may be discovered. (1899, c. 625; 1905, c. 32; Rev., s. 3748; C.S., s. 3508; 1963, c. 1165, s. 1; 1993, c. 539, s. 485; 1994, Ex. Sess., c. 24, s. 14(c).)

§ 62-320: Repealed by Session Laws 1995, c. 523, s. 30.

§ 62-321. Penalty for nondelivery of intrastate telegraph message.

Any telegraph company doing business in this State that shall fail to transmit and deliver any intrastate message within a reasonable time shall forfeit and pay to anyone who may sue for same a penalty of twenty-five dollars ($25.00). Such penalty shall be in addition to any right of action that any person may have for the recovery of damages. Proof of the sending of any message from one point in this State to another point in this State shall be prima facie evidence that it is an intrastate message. (1919, c. 175; C.S., s. 1704; 1963, c. 1165, s. 1.)

§ 62-322. Unauthorized manufacture or sale of switch-lock keys a misdemeanor.

It shall be unlawful for any person to make, manufacture, sell or give away to any other person any duplicate key to any lock used by any railroad company in this State on its switches or switch tracks, except upon the written order of that officer of such railroad company whose duty it is to distribute and issue switch-lock keys to the employees of such railroad company. Any person violating the provisions of this section shall be guilty of a Class 1 misdemeanor. (1909, c. 795; C.S., s. 3477; 1963, c. 1165, s. 1; 1993, c. 539, s. 487; 1994, Ex. Sess., c. 24, s. 14(c).)

§ 62-323. Willful injury to property of public utility a misdemeanor.

If any person shall willfully do or cause to be done any act or acts whatever whereby any building, construction or work of any public utility, or any engine, machine or structure or any matter or thing appertaining to the same shall be stopped, obstructed, impaired, weakened, injured or destroyed, he shall be guilty of a Class 1 misdemeanor. (1871-2, c. 138, s. 39; Code, s. 1974; Rev., s. 3756; C.S., s. 3478; 1963, c. 1165, s. 1; 1993, c. 539, s. 488; 1994, Ex. Sess., c. 24, s. 14(c).)

§ 62-324. Disclosure of information as to shipments unlawful.

(a) It shall be unlawful for any common carrier engaged in intrastate commerce or any officer, receiver, trustee, lessee, agent, or employee of such carrier, or for any other person authorized by such carrier, to receive information, knowingly to disclose to, or permit to be acquired by any person other than the shipper or consignee without the consent of such shipper or consignee, any information concerning the nature, kind, quantity, destination, consignee, or routing of any property tendered or delivered to such common carrier for such transportation, which information may be used to the detriment or prejudice of such shipper or consignee, or which may improperly disclose his business transactions to a competitor; and it shall also be unlawful for any person to solicit or knowingly receive any such information which may be so used.

(b) Nothing in this section shall be construed to prevent the giving of such information in response to any legal process issued under the authority of any court, or any officer or agent of the State or of the government of the United

States, in the exercise of his power, or to any officer or other duly authorized person seeking such information for the prosecution of persons charged with or suspected of crimes or to another carrier, or its duly authorized agent, for the purpose of adjusting mutual traffic accounts in the ordinary course of business of such carriers. (1947, c. 1008, s. 30; 1961, c. 472, s. 8; 1963, c. 1165, s. 1.)

§ 62-325. Unlawful motor carrier operations.

(a) Any person, whether carrier, passenger, shipper, consignee, or any officer, employee, agent, or representative thereof, who shall knowingly offer, grant, or give or solicit, accept, or receive any rebate, concession, or discrimination in violation of any provision of this Chapter, or who by means of any false statement or representation, or by the use of any false or fictitious bill, bill of lading, receipt, voucher, roll, account, claim, certificate, affidavit, deposition, lease, or bill of sale, or by any other means or device, shall knowingly and willfully by any such means or otherwise fraudulently seek to evade or defeat regulations as in this Chapter provided for motor carriers, shall be deemed guilty of a Class 3 misdemeanor and upon conviction thereof only be fined not more than five hundred dollars ($500.00) for the first offense and not more than two thousand dollars ($2,000) for any subsequent offense.

(b) Any motor carrier, or other person, or any officer, agent, employee, or representative thereof, who shall willfully fail or refuse to make a report to the Commission as required by this Article, or other applicable law, or to make specific and full, true, and correct answer to any question within 30 days from the time it is lawfully required by the Commission so to do, or to keep accounts, records, and memoranda in the form and manner prescribed by the Commission, or shall knowingly and willfully falsify, destroy, mutilate, or alter any such report, account, record, or memorandum, or shall knowingly and willfully neglect or fail to make true and correct entries in such accounts, records, or memoranda of all facts and transactions appertaining to the business of the carrier, or person required under this Article to keep the same, or shall knowingly and willfully keep any accounts, records, or memoranda contrary to the rules, regulations, or orders of the Commission with respect thereto, shall be deemed guilty of a Class 3 misdemeanor and upon conviction thereof only be subject for each offense to a fine of not more than five thousand dollars ($5,000). As used in this subsection the words "kept" and "keep" shall be construed to mean made, prepared, or compiled, as well as retained. It shall be the duty of the Commission to prescribe and enforce such general rules and regulations as it may deem necessary to compel all motor carriers to keep accurate records of all revenue received by them to the end that any tax levied and assessed by the State of North Carolina upon revenues may be collected. Any agent or employee of a motor carrier who shall willfully and knowingly make a false report or record of fares, charges, or other revenue received by a carrier or collected in its behalf shall be guilty of a Class 1 misdemeanor.

(c) Any person who, at any bus terminal, solicits or otherwise attempts to induce any person to use some form of transportation for compensation other than that lawfully using said terminal premises by contract with the terminal operator or by valid order of the Commission shall be guilty of a Class 3 misdemeanor. (1947, c. 1008, s. 30; 1949, c. 1132, s. 30; 1953, c. 1140, s. 4; 1957, c. 1152, s. 16; 1961, c. 472, ss. 8, 11; 1963, c. 1165, s. 1; 1993, c. 539, s. 489; 1994, Ex. Sess., c. 24, s. 14(c).)

§ 62-326. Furnishing false information to the Commission; withholding information from the Commission.

(a) Every person, firm or corporation operating under the jurisdiction of the Utilities Commission or who is required by law to file reports with the Commission who shall knowingly or willfully file or give false information to the Utilities Commission in any report, reply, response, or other statement or document furnished to the Commission shall be guilty of a Class 1 misdemeanor.

(b) Every person, firm, or corporation operating under the jurisdiction of the Utilities Commission or who is required by law to file reports with the Commission who shall willfully withhold clearly specified and reasonably obtainable information from the Commission in any report, response, reply or statement filed with the Commission in the performance of the duties of the Commission or who shall fail or refuse to file any report, response, reply or statement required by the Commission in the performance of the duties of the Commission shall be guilty of a Class 1 misdemeanor. (1969, c. 765, s. 1; 1993, c. 539, s. 490; 1994, Ex. Sess., c. 24, s. 14(c).)

§ 62-327. Gifts to members of Commission, Commission employees, or public staff.

It shall be unlawful for any officer, agent, employee, or attorney of any public utility or any public utility holding company, subsidiary, or affiliated company, to knowingly offer or make to any member of the Commission, Commission staff, or public staff, any gift of money, property, or anything of value. It shall be unlawful for any member of the Commission, Commission staff, or public staff to knowingly accept any gift of money, property, or anything of value from any officer, agent, employee, or attorney of any public utility or any public utility holding company, subsidiary, or affiliated company; provided, however, that it shall not be unlawful for members of the Commission, Commission staff, or public staff to attend public breakfasts, lunches, dinners, or banquets sponsored by such entities. Any person violating this section shall be guilty of a Class 3 misdemeanor and may only be fined in the discretion of the court; provided, further, that any member of the Commission staff, or member of the public staff violating this section shall also be subject to dismissal for cause. (1977, c. 468, s. 16; 1993, c. 539, s. 491; 1994, Ex. Sess., c. 24, s. 14(c).)

§ 62-328. Unauthorized use of Citizens Band equipment.

(a) As used in this section, "Citizens Band radio equipment" means Citizens Band radio equipment authorized by the Federal Communications Commission.

(b) It shall be unlawful for any person willfully and knowingly to use Citizens Band radio equipment not authorized by the Federal Communications Commission. Unauthorized Citizens Band radio equipment includes the use of power amplifiers or equipment prohibited under applicable federal regulations.

(c) This section does not apply to any licensee that is exempted under the provisions of 47 U.S.C. § 302a(f)(2).

(d) Any person willfully and knowingly violating the provisions of this section shall be guilty of a Class 3 misdemeanor. (2004-72, s. 1.)

§ 62-329: Reserved for future codification.

§ 62-330: Reserved for future codification.

§ 62-331: Reserved for future codification.

§ 62-332: Reserved for future codification.

Article 16.

Security Provisions.

§ 62-333. Screening employment applications.

The Chief Personnel Officer, or that person's designee, of any public utility franchised to do business in North Carolina shall be permitted to obtain from the State Bureau of Investigation a confidential copy of criminal history record information for screening an applicant for employment with or an employee of a utility or utility contractor where the employment or job to be performed falls within a class or category of positions certified by the North Carolina Utilities Commission as permitting or requiring access to nuclear power facilities or access to or control over nuclear material.

The State Bureau of Investigation shall charge a reasonable fee to defray the administrative costs of providing criminal history record information for purposes of employment application screening. The State Bureau of Investigation is authorized to retain fees charged pursuant to this section and to expend those fees in accordance with the State Budget Act for the purpose of discharging its duties under this section. (1979, c. 796; 1979, 2nd Sess., c. 1212, s. 10; 2013-410, s. 6.1.)

§ 62-334: Reserved for future codification purposes.

§ 62-335: Reserved for future codification purposes.

§ 62-336: Reserved for future codification purposes.

§ 62-337: Reserved for future codification purposes.

§ 62-338: Reserved for future codification purposes.

§ 62-339: Reserved for future codification purposes.

§ 62-340: Reserved for future codification purposes.

§ 62-341: Reserved for future codification purposes.

§ 62-342: Reserved for future codification purposes.

§ 62-343: Reserved for future codification purposes.

§ 62-344: Reserved for future codification purposes.

§ 62-345: Reserved for future codification purposes.

§ 62-346: Reserved for future codification purposes.

§ 62-347: Reserved for future codification purposes.

§ 62-348: Reserved for future codification purposes.

§ 62-349: Reserved for future codification purposes.

Article 17.

Miscellaneous Provisions.

§ 62-350. (See Editor's note) Regulation of pole attachments.

(a)   A municipality, or a membership corporation organized under Chapter 117 of the General Statutes, that owns or controls poles, ducts, or conduits shall allow any communications service provider to utilize its poles, ducts, and conduits at just, reasonable, and nondiscriminatory rates, terms, and conditions adopted pursuant to negotiated or adjudicated agreements. A request to utilize poles, ducts, or conduits under this section may be denied only if there is insufficient capacity or for reasons of safety, reliability, and generally applicable engineering principles, and those limitations cannot be remedied by rearranging, expanding, or otherwise reengineering the facilities at the reasonable and actual cost of the municipality or membership corporation to be reimbursed by the communications service provider. In granting a request under this section, a municipality or membership corporation shall require the requesting entity to comply with applicable safety requirements, including the National Electrical

Safety Code and the applicable rules and regulations issued by the Occupational Safety and Health Administration.

(b) Following receipt of a request from a communications service provider, a municipality or membership corporation shall negotiate concerning the rates, terms, and conditions for the use of or attachment to the poles, ducts, or conduits that it owns or controls. Following a request from a party to an existing agreement made pursuant to the terms of the agreement or made within 120 days prior to or following the end of the term of the agreement, the communications service provider and the municipality or membership corporation which is a party to that agreement shall negotiate concerning the rates, terms, and conditions for the continued use of or attachment to the poles, ducts, or conduits owned or controlled by one of the parties to the agreement. The negotiations shall include matters customary to such negotiations, including a fair and reasonable rate for use of facilities, indemnification by the attaching entity for losses caused in connection with the attachments, and the removal, replacement, or repair of installed facilities for safety reasons. Upon request, a party shall state in writing its objections to any proposed rate, terms, and conditions of the other party.

(c) In the event the parties are unable to reach an agreement within 90 days of a request to negotiate pursuant to subsection (b) of this section, or if either party believes in good faith that an impasse has been reached prior to the expiration of the 90-day period, either party may bring an action in Business Court in accordance with the procedures for a mandatory business case set forth in G.S. 7A-45.4, and the Business Court shall have exclusive jurisdiction over such actions. The parties shall identify with specificity in their respective pleadings the issues in dispute, and the Business Court shall (i) establish a procedural schedule which, unless otherwise agreed by the parties, is intended to resolve the action within a time period not to exceed 180 days of the commencement of the action, (ii) resolve any dispute identified in the pleadings consistent with the public interest and necessity so as to derive just and reasonable rates, terms, and conditions, taking into consideration and applying such other factors or evidence that may be presented by a party, including without limitation the rules and regulations applicable to attachments by each type of communications service provider under section 224 of the Communications Act of 1934, as amended, and (iii) apply any new rate adopted as a result of the action retroactively to the date immediately following the expiration of the 90-day negotiating period or initiation of the lawsuit, whichever is earlier. If the new rate is for the continuation of an existing agreement, the new rate shall apply retroactively to the date immediately following the end of the existing agreement. Prior to commencing any action under this subsection, a party must pay any undisputed fees related to the use of poles, ducts, or conduits which are due and owing under a preexisting agreement with the municipality or membership corporation. In any action brought under this subsection, the court may resolve any existing disputes regarding fees alleged to be owing under a preexisting agreement or regarding safety compliance arising under subsection (d) of this section. The provisions of this section do not apply to an entity whose poles, ducts, and conduits are subject to regulation under section 224 of the Communications Act of 1934, as amended.

(d) In the absence of an agreement between an attaching party and the involved municipality or membership corporation that provides otherwise, the following shall apply:

(1) When the lines, equipment, or attachments of a communications service provider that are attached to the poles, ducts, or conduits of a municipality or membership corporation do not comply with applicable safety rules and regulations set forth in subsection (a) of this section, the municipality or membership corporation may provide written notice of the noncompliant lines, equipment, or attachments, and make demand that the communications service provider bring such lines, equipment, and attachments into compliance with the specified safety rules and regulations. Within the 60-day period following the date of the notice and demand, the communications service provider shall either contest the notice of noncompliance in writing or bring its lines, equipment, and attachments into compliance with the specified applicable safety rules and regulations. If the work required to bring the facilities into compliance is not reasonably capable of being completed within the 60-day period, the period for compliance shall be extended as may be deemed reasonable under the circumstances so long as the communications service provider promptly commences and diligently pursues within the 60-day period such actions as are reasonably necessary to cause the facilities to be brought into compliance.

(2) When the communications service provider or, if applicable, another responsible attaching party fails to bring any noncompliant lines, equipment, or attachments into compliance (i) within the 60-day period following the date of notice and demand pursuant to subdivision (1) of this subsection, or (ii) within 120 days following the date of notice and demand when the period is extended pursuant to subdivision (1) of this subsection, the municipality or membership corporation shall be entitled to take such remedial actions as are reasonably necessary to bring the lines, equipment, and attachments of the communications service provider into compliance, including removal of the lines,

equipment, or attachments should removal be required to achieve compliance with the applicable safety rules and regulations.

(3)   A municipality or membership corporation that removes or brings into compliance the noncompliant lines, equipment, or attachments of a communications service provider pursuant to subdivision (2) of this subsection shall be entitled to recover its reasonable and actual costs for such activities from the communications service provider or other attaching party whose action or inaction caused the noncompliance, and the responsible attaching party shall reimburse the municipality or membership corporation within 45 days of being billed for such costs.

(4)   All attaching parties shall work cooperatively to determine the causation of, and to effectuate any remedy for, noncompliant lines, equipment, and attachments. In the event of disputes under this subsection, the involved municipality or membership corporation or any attaching party may bring an action in the Business Court in accordance with the procedures for a mandatory business case set forth in G.S. 7A-45.4, and the Business Court shall have exclusive jurisdiction over such actions. The Business Court shall resolve such disputes consistent with the public interest and necessity. Nothing herein shall prevent a municipality or membership corporation from taking such action as may be necessary to remedy any exigent issue which is an imminent threat of death or injury to persons or damage to property.

(e)   For purposes of this section, the term "communications service provider" means a person or entity that provides or intends to provide: (i) telephone service as a public utility under Chapter 62 of the General Statutes or as a telephone membership corporation organized under Chapter 117 of the General Statutes; (ii) broadband service, but excluding broadband service over energized electrical conductors owned by a municipality or membership corporation; or (iii) cable service over a cable system as those terms are defined in Article 42 of Chapter 66 of the General Statutes.

(f)   The Business Court may adopt such rules as it deems necessary to implement its jurisdiction and authority under this section.

(g)   Nothing herein shall preclude a party from bringing civil action in the appropriate division of the General Court of Justice seeking enforcement of an agreement concerning the rates, terms, and conditions for the use of or attachment to the poles, ducts, or conduits of a municipality or membership corporation. (2009-278, s. 1.)

Chapter 62A.

Public Safety Telephone Service and Wireless Telephone Service.

Article 1.

Public Safety Telephone Service.

§ 62A-1: Repealed by Session Laws 2007-383, s. 2(a), effective January 1, 2008.

§ 62A-2: Repealed by Session Laws 2007-383, s. 2(a), effective January 1, 2008.

§ 62A-3: Repealed by Session Laws 2007-383, s. 2(a), effective January 1, 2008.

§ 62A-4: Repealed by Session Laws 2007-383, s. 2(a), effective January 1, 2008.

§ 62A-5: Repealed by Session Laws 2007-383, s. 2(a), effective January 1, 2008.

§ 62A-6: Repealed by Session Laws 2007-383, s. 2(a), effective January 1, 2008.

§ 62A-7: Repealed by Session Laws 2007-383, s. 2(a), effective January 1, 2008.

§ 62A-8: Repealed by Session Laws 2007-383, s. 2(a), effective January 1, 2008.

§ 62A-9: Repealed by Session Laws 2007-383, s. 2(a), effective January 1, 2008.

§ 62A-10: Repealed by Session Laws 2007-383, s. 2(a), effective January 1, 2008.

§ 62A-11: Repealed by Session Laws 2007-383, s. 2(a), effective January 1, 2008.

§ 62A-12: Repealed by Session Laws 2007-383, s. 2(a), effective January 1, 2008.

§§ 62A-13 through 62A-20: Reserved for future codification purposes.

Article 2.

Wireless Telephone Service.

§ 62A-21: Repealed by Session Laws 2007-383, s. 3(a), effective January 1, 2008.

§ 62A-22: Repealed by Session Laws 2007-383, s. 3(a), effective January 1, 2008.

§ 62A-22.1: Repealed by Session Laws 2007-383, s. 3(a), effective January 1, 2008.

§ 62A-23: Repealed by Session Laws 2007-383, s. 3(a), effective January 1, 2008.

§ 62A-24: Repealed by Session Laws 2007-383, s. 3(a), effective January 1, 2008.

§ 62A-25: Repealed by Session Laws 2007-383, s. 3(a), effective January 1, 2008.

§ 62A-25.1: Repealed by Session Laws 2007-383, s. 3(a), effective January 1, 2008.

§ 62A-26: Repealed by Session Laws 2007-383, s. 3(a), effective January 1, 2008.

§ 62A-27: Repealed by Session Laws 2007-383, s. 3(a), effective January 1, 2008.

§ 62A-28: Repealed by Session Laws 2007-383, s. 3(a), effective January 1, 2008.

§ 62A-29: Repealed by Session Laws 2007-383, s. 3(a), effective January 1, 2008.

§ 62A-30: Repealed by Session Laws 2007-383, s. 3(a), effective January 1, 2008.

§ 62A-31: Repealed by Session Laws 2007-383, s. 3(a), effective January 1, 2008.

§ 62A-32: Repealed by Session Laws 2007-383, s. 3(a), effective January 1, 2008.

§ 62A-33. Reserved for future codification purposes.

§ 62A-34. Reserved for future codification purposes.

§ 62A-35. Reserved for future codification purposes.

§ 62A-36. Reserved for future codification purposes.

§ 62A-37. Reserved for future codification purposes.

§ 62A-38. Reserved for future codification purposes.

§ 62A-39. Reserved for future codification purposes.

Article 3.

Emergency Telephone Service.

§ 62A-40. Definitions.

The following definitions apply in this Article.

(1)   911 Board. - The 911 Board established in G.S. 62A-41.

(2)   911 Fund. - The North Carolina 911 Fund established in G.S. 62A-43.

(3)   911 State Plan. - A document prepared, maintained, and updated by the 911 Board that provides a comprehensive plan for communicating 911 call information across networks and among PSAPs, addresses all aspects of the State's 911 system, and describes the allowable uses of revenue in the 911 Fund.

(4)   911 system. - An emergency telephone system that does all of the following:

a.   Enables the user of a voice communications service connection to reach a PSAP by dialing the digits 911.

b.   Provides enhanced 911 service.

(5)   Call taking. - The act of processing a 911 call for emergency assistance by a primary PSAP, including the use of 911 system equipment, call classification, location of a caller, determination of the appropriate response

level for emergency responders, and dispatching 911 call information to the appropriate responder.

(6)   Commercial Mobile Radio Service (CMRS). - Defined in 47 C.F.R. § 20.3.

(7)   CMRS connection. - Each mobile handset telephone number assigned to a CMRS subscriber with a place of primary use in North Carolina.

(8)   CMRS provider. - An entity, whether facilities-based or nonfacilities-based, that is licensed by the Federal Communications Commission to provide CMRS or that resells CMRS within North Carolina.

(9)   Enhanced 911 service. - Directing a 911 call to an appropriate PSAP by selective routing or other means based on the geographical location from which the call originated and providing information defining the approximate geographic location and the telephone number of a 911 caller, in accordance with the FCC Order.

(10)   Exchange access facility. - The access from a subscriber's premises to the telephone system of a service supplier. The term includes service supplier provided access lines, private branch exchange trunks, and centrex network access registers, as defined by applicable tariffs approved by the North Carolina Utilities Commission. The term does not include service supplier owned and operated telephone pay station lines, Wide Area Telecommunications Service (WATS), Foreign Exchange (FX), or incoming only lines.

(11)   FCC Order. - The Order of the Federal Communications Commission, FCC Docket No. 94-102, adopted on December 1, 1997, and any consent decrees, rules, and regulations adopted by the Federal Communications Commission pursuant to the Order.

(12)   GIS mapping. - Computerized geographical information that can be used to assist in locating a person who calls emergency assistance, including street centerlines, ortho photography, and oblique imaging.

(13)   Interconnected VoIP service. - Defined in 47 C.F.R. § 9.3.

(14)   Local exchange carrier. - An entity that is authorized to provide telephone exchange service or exchange access in North Carolina.

(15) Prepaid wireless telecommunications service. - A wireless telecommunications service that allows a caller to dial 911 to access the 911 system, which service must be paid for in advance and is sold in predetermined units or dollars of which the number declines with use in a known amount.

(16) Primary PSAP. - The first point of reception of a 911 call by a public safety answering point.

(17) Proprietary information. - Subscriber lists, technology descriptions, technical information, or trade secrets that are developed, produced, or received internally by a voice communications service provider or by a voice communications service provider's employees, directors, officers, or agents.

(18) Public safety answering point (PSAP). - The public safety agency that receives an incoming 911 call and dispatches appropriate public safety agencies to respond to the call.

(18a) Retail transaction. - The sale of prepaid wireless telecommunications service for any purpose other than resale.

(19) Service supplier. - An entity that provides exchange telephone service to a telephone subscriber.

(20) Subscriber. - A person who purchases a voice communications service and is able to receive it or use it periodically over time.

(21) Voice communications service. - Any of the following:

a. The transmission, conveyance, or routing of real-time, two-way voice communications to a point or between or among points by or through any electronic, radio, satellite, cable, optical, microwave, wireline, wireless, or other medium or method, regardless of the protocol used.

b. The ability to receive and terminate voice calls to and from the public switched telephone network.

c. Interconnected VoIP service.

(22) Voice communications service connection. - Each telephone number assigned to a residential or commercial subscriber by a voice communications service provider, without regard to technology deployed.

(23)   Voice communications service provider. - An entity that provides voice communications service to a subscriber.

(24)   VoIP provider. - An entity that provides interconnected VoIP service. (2007-383, s. 1(a); 2010-158, s. 1; 2011-122, s. 2.)

§ 62A-41. 911 Board.

(a)   Membership. - The 911 Board is established in the Office of Information Technology Services. Neither a local government unit that receives a distribution from the fund under G.S. 62A-46 nor a telecommunication service provider may have more than one representative on the 911 Board. The 911 Board consists of 17 members as follows:

(1)   Four members appointed by the Governor as follows:

a.   An individual who represents a municipality where a primary PSAP is located, appointed upon the recommendation of the North Carolina League of Municipalities.

b.   An individual who represents a county where a primary PSAP is located, appointed upon the recommendation of the North Carolina Association of County Commissioners.

c.   An individual who represents a VoIP provider.

d.   An individual who represents the North Carolina chapter of the National Emergency Number Association (NENA).

(2)   Six members appointed by the General Assembly upon the recommendation of the Speaker of the House of Representatives as follows:

a.   An individual who is a sheriff, appointed upon the recommendation of the North Carolina Sheriffs' Association, Inc.

b.   An individual who represents CMRS providers operating in North Carolina.

c. An individual who represents the North Carolina chapter of the Association of Public Safety Communications Officials (APCO).

d. Two individuals who represent local exchange carriers operating in North Carolina, one of whom represents a local exchange carrier with less than 50,000 access lines.

e. A fire chief with experience operating or supervising a PSAP, appointed upon the recommendation of the North Carolina Firemen's Association.

(3) Six members appointed by the General Assembly upon the recommendation of the President Pro Tempore of the Senate as follows:

a. An individual who is a chief of police, appointed upon the recommendation of the North Carolina Association of Chiefs of Police.

b. Two individuals who represent CMRS providers operating in North Carolina.

c. A Rescue or Emergency Medical Services Chief with experience operating or supervising a PSAP, appointed upon the recommendation of the North Carolina Association of Rescue and Emergency Medical Services.

d. Two individuals who represent local exchange carriers operating in North Carolina, one of whom represents a local exchange carrier with less than 200,000 access lines.

(4) The State Chief Information Officer or the State Chief Information Officer's designee, who serves as the chair.

(b) Term. - A member's term is four years. No member may serve more than two terms. Members remain in office until their successors are appointed and qualified. Vacancies are filled in the same manner as the original appointment. The Governor may remove any member for misfeasance, malfeasance, or nonfeasance in accordance with G.S. 143B-13(d).

(c) Meetings. - Members of the 911 Board serve without compensation. Members receive per diem, subsistence, and travel allowances at the rate established in G.S. 138-5. A quorum of the 911 Board is nine members. The 911 Board meets upon the call of the chair.

(d) Public Servants. - The members of the 911 Board are public servants under G.S. 138A-3 and are subject to the provisions of Chapter 138A of the General Statutes. (2007-383, s. 1(a); 2010-158, s. 2(a); 2013-286, s. 2.)

§ 62A-42. Powers and duties of the 911 Board.

(a) Duties. - The 911 Board has the following powers and duties:

(1) To develop the 911 State Plan. In developing and updating the plan, the 911 Board must monitor trends in voice communications service technology and in enhanced 911 service technology, investigate and incorporate GIS mapping and other resources into the plan, and formulate strategies for the efficient and effective delivery of enhanced 911 service.

(2) To administer the 911 Fund and the monthly 911 service charge authorized by G.S. 62A-43.

(3) To distribute revenue in the 911 Fund to CMRS providers and PSAPs in accordance with this Article and advise CMRS providers and PSAPs of the requirements for receiving a distribution from the 911 Fund.

(4) To establish policies and procedures to fund advisory services and training for PSAPs, to set operating standards for PSAPs, and to provide funds in accordance with these policies, procedures, and standards.

(5) To investigate the revenues and expenditures associated with the operation of a PSAP to ensure compliance with restrictions on the use of amounts distributed from the 911 Fund.

(6) To make and enter into contracts and agreements necessary or incidental to the performance of its powers and duties under this Article and to use revenue available to the 911 Board under G.S. 62A-44 for administrative expenses to pay its obligations under the contracts and agreements.

(6a) To use funds available to the 911 Board under G.S. 62-47 to pay its obligations incurred for statewide 911 projects.

(7) To accept gifts, grants, or other money for the 911 Fund.

(8) To undertake its duties in a manner that is competitively and technologically neutral as to all voice communications service providers.

(8a) To design, create, or acquire printed or Web-based public education materials regarding the proper use of 911.

(9) To adopt rules to implement this Article. This authority does not include the regulation of any enhanced 911 service, such as the establishment of technical standards for telecommunications service providers to deliver 911 voice and data.

(10) To take other necessary and proper action to implement the provisions of this Article.

(b) Prohibition. - In no event shall the 911 Board or any other State agency lease, construct, operate, or own a communications network for the purpose of providing 911 service. The 911 Board may pay private sector vendors for provisioning a network for the purpose of providing 911 service. (2007-383, s. 1(a); 2010-158, s. 3.)

§ 62A-43. Service charge for 911 service.

(a) Charge Imposed. - A monthly 911 service charge is imposed on each active voice communications service connection that is capable of accessing the 911 system. The service charge for service other than prepaid wireless telecommunications service is seventy cents (70¢) or a lower amount set by the 911 Board under subsection (d) of this section. The service charge is payable by the subscriber to the voice communications service provider. The provider may list the service charge separately from other charges on the bill. Partial payments made by a subscriber are applied first to the amount the subscriber owes the provider for the voice communications service.

(b) Prepaid Wireless. - A 911 service charge is imposed on each retail purchase of prepaid wireless telecommunications service occurring in this State of seventy cents (70¢) for each retail transaction of prepaid wireless telecommunications service or a lower amount set as provided by subsection (d) of this section. The service charge is collected and remitted as provided in G.S. 62A-54.

(c) Remittance to 911 Board. - A voice communications service provider must remit the service charges collected by it under subsection (a) of this section to the 911 Board. The provider must remit the collected service charges by the end of the calendar month following the month the provider received the charges from its subscribers. A provider may deduct and retain from the service charges it receives from its subscribers and remits to the 911 Board an administrative allowance equal to the greater of one percent (1%) of the amount of service charges remitted or fifty dollars ($50.00) a month.

(d) Adjustment of Charge. - The 911 Board must monitor the revenues generated by the service charges imposed by this section. If the 911 Board determines that the rates produce revenue that exceeds or is less than the amount needed, the 911 Board may adjust the rates. The rates must ensure full cost recovery for voice communications service providers and for primary PSAPs over a reasonable period of time. The 911 Board must set the service charge for prepaid wireless telecommunications service at the same rate as the monthly service charge for nonprepaid service. A change in the rate becomes effective only on July 1. The 911 Board must notify providers of a change in the rates at least 90 days before the change becomes effective. The 911 Board must notify the Department of Revenue of a change in the rate for prepaid wireless telecommunications service at least 90 days before the change becomes effective. The Department of Revenue must provide notice of a change in the rate for prepaid wireless telecommunications service at least 45 days before the change becomes effective only on the Department's Web site.

(e) Collection. - A voice communications service provider has no obligation to take any legal action to enforce the collection of the service charge billed to a subscriber. The 911 Board may initiate a collection action, and reasonable costs and attorneys' fees associated with that collection action may be assessed against the subscriber. At the request of the 911 Board, but no more than annually, a voice communications service provider must report to the 911 Board the amount of the provider's uncollected service charges. The 911 Board may request, to the extent permitted by federal privacy laws, the name, address, and telephone number of a subscriber who refuses to pay the 911 service charge.

(f) Restriction. - A local government may not impose a service charge or other fee on a subscriber to support the 911 system. (2007-383, s. 1(a); 2010-158, s. 4; 2011-122, ss. 1(a), 3.)

§ 62A-44. 911 Fund.

(a) Fund. - The 911 Fund is created as an interest-bearing special revenue fund within the State treasury. The 911 Board administers the Fund. The 911 Board must credit to the 911 Fund all revenues remitted to it from the service charge imposed by G.S. 62A-43 on voice communications service connections in the State. Revenue in the Fund may only be used as provided in this Article.

(b) Allocation of Revenues. - The 911 Board may deduct and retain for its administrative expenses a percentage of the total service charges remitted to it under G.S. 62A-43 for deposit in the 911 Fund. The percentage may not exceed two percent (2%). The percentage is one percent (1%) unless the 911 Board sets the percentage at a different amount. The 911 Board must monitor the amount of funds required to meet its financial commitment to provide technical assistance to primary PSAPs and set the rate at an amount that enables the 911 Board to meet this commitment. The remaining revenues remitted to the 911 Board for deposit in the 911 Fund are allocated as follows:

(1) A percentage of the funds remitted by CMRS providers, other than the funds remitted by the Department of Revenue from prepaid wireless telecommunications service, to the 911 Fund are allocated for reimbursements to CMRS providers pursuant to G.S. 62A-45.

(2) A percentage of the funds remitted by CMRS providers, all funds remitted by the Department of Revenue from prepaid wireless telecommunications service, and all funds remitted by all other voice communications service providers are allocated for monthly distributions to primary PSAPs pursuant to G.S. 62A-46 and grants to PSAPs pursuant to G.S. 62A-47.

(3) The percentage of the funds remitted by CMRS providers allocated to CMRS providers and PSAPs shall be set by the 911 Board and may be adjusted by the 911 Board as necessary to ensure full cost recovery for CMRS providers and, to the extent there are excess funds, for distributions to primary PSAPs.

(c) Report. - In February of each odd-numbered year, the 911 Board must report to the Joint Legislative Commission on Governmental Operations and the Revenue Laws Study Committee. The report must contain complete information regarding receipts and expenditures of all funds received by the 911 Board during the period covered by the report, the status of the 911 system in North Carolina at the time of the report, and the results of any investigations by the

Board of PSAPs that have been completed during the period covered by the report.

(d) Nature of Revenue. - The General Assembly finds that distributions of revenue from the 911 Fund are not State expenditures for the purpose of Section 5(3) of Article III of the North Carolina Constitution. Therefore, the Governor may not reduce or withhold revenue in the 911 Fund. (2007-383, s. 1(a); 2008-134, s. 1(a); 2010-158, s. 5; 2011-122, s. 4; 2011-291, s. 2.17.)

§ 62A-45. Fund distribution to CMRS providers.

(a) Distribution. - CMRS providers are eligible for reimbursement from the 911 Fund for the actual costs incurred by the CMRS providers in complying with the requirements of enhanced 911 service. Costs of complying include costs incurred for designing, upgrading, purchasing, leasing, programming, installing, testing, or maintaining all necessary data, hardware, and software required to provide service as well as the recurring and nonrecurring costs of providing the service. To obtain reimbursement, a CMRS provider must comply with all of the following:

(1) Invoices must be sworn.

(2) All costs and expenses must be commercially reasonable.

(3) All invoices for reimbursement must be related to compliance with the requirements of enhanced 911 service.

(4) Prior approval must be obtained from the 911 Board for all invoices for payment of costs that exceed the lesser of:

a. One hundred percent (100%) of the eligible costs allowed under this section.

b. One hundred twenty-five percent (125%) of the service charges remitted to the 911 Board by the CMRS provider.

(b) Payment Carryforward. - If the total amount of invoices submitted to the 911 Board and approved for payment in a month exceeds the amount available from the 911 Fund for reimbursements to CMRS providers, the amount payable to each CMRS provider is reduced proportionately so that the amount paid does not exceed the amount available for payment. The balance of the payment is deferred to the following month. A deferred payment accrues interest at a rate equal to the rate earned by the 911 Fund until it is paid.

(c) Grant Reallocation. - If the amount of reimbursements to CMRS providers approved by the 911 Board for a fiscal year is less than the amount of funds allocated for reimbursements to CMRS providers for that fiscal year, the 911 Board may reallocate part of the excess amount to the PSAP Grant and Statewide 911 Projects Account established under G.S. 62A-47. The 911 Board may reallocate funds under this subsection only once each calendar year and may do so only within the three-month period that follows the end of the fiscal year. If the 911 Board reallocates more than a total of three million dollars ($3,000,000) to the PSAP Grant and Statewide 911 Projects Account in a calendar year, it must consider reducing the amount of the service charge in G.S. 62A-44 to reflect more accurately the underlying costs of providing 911 system services.

The 911 Board must make the following findings before it reallocates funds to the PSAP Grant and Statewide 911 Projects Account:

(1) There is a critical need for additional funding for PSAPs in rural or high-cost areas to ensure that enhanced 911 service is deployed throughout the State.

(2) The reallocation will not impair cost recovery by CMRS providers.

(3) The reallocation will not result in the insolvency of the 911 Fund. (2007-383, s. 1(a); 2010-158, s. 6.)

§ 62A-46. Fund distribution to PSAPs.

(a) Monthly Distribution. - The 911 Board must make monthly distributions to primary PSAPs from the amount allocated to the 911 Fund for PSAPs. A PSAP is not eligible for a distribution under this section unless it provides enhanced 911 service and received distributions from the 911 Board in the 2008-2009 fiscal year. The Board must comply with all of the following:

(1) Administration. - The Board must notify PSAPs of the estimated distributions no later than December 31 of each year. The Board must determine actual distributions no later than June 1 of each year. The Board must determine a method for establishing distributions that is equitable and sustainable and that ensures distributions for eligible operating costs and anticipated increases for all funded PSAPs. The Board must establish a formula to determine each PSAP's base amount. The formula must be determined and published to PSAPs in the first quarter of the fiscal year preceding the fiscal year in which the formula is used. The Board may not change the funding formula for the base amount more than once every year.

(2) Reports. - The Board must report to the Joint Legislative Commission on Governmental Operations and the Revenue Laws Study Committee within 45 days of a change in the funding formula. The report must contain a description of the differences in the old and new formulas and the projected distributions to each PSAP from the new formula.

(3) Formula. - The funding formula established by the Board must consider all of the following:

a. The population of the area served by a PSAP.

b. PSAP reports and budgets, disbursement histories, and historical costs.

c. PSAP operations, 911 technologies used by the PSAP, compliance with operating standards of the 911 Board, level of service a PSAP delivers dispatching fire, emergency medical services, law enforcement, and Emergency Medical Dispatch.

d. The tier designation of the county in which the PSAP is located as designated in G.S. 143B-437.08.

e. Any interlocal government funding agreement between a primary PSAP and a secondary PSAP, if the secondary PSAP was in existence as of June 1, 2010, receives funding under the agreement, and is within the service area of the primary PSAP.

f. Any other information the Board considers relevant.

(4) Additional distributions. - In the first quarter of the Board's fiscal year, the Board must determine whether payments to PSAPs during the preceding

fiscal year exceeded or were less than the eligible costs incurred by each PSAP during the fiscal year. If a PSAP receives less than its eligible costs in any fiscal year, the Board may increase a PSAP's distribution in the following fiscal year above the base amount as determined by the formula to meet the estimated eligible costs of the PSAP as determined by the Board. The Board may not distribute less than the base amount to each PSAP except as provided in subsection (b1) of this section. The Board must provide a procedure for a PSAP to request a reconsideration of its distribution or eligible expenses.

(b) Percentage Designations. - The 911 Board must determine how revenue that is allocated to the 911 Fund for distribution to primary PSAPs and is not needed to make the base amount distribution required by subdivision (a)(1) of this section is to be used. The 911 Board must designate a percentage of the remaining funds to be distributed to primary PSAPs on a per capita basis and a percentage to be allocated to the PSAP Grant Account established in G.S. 62A-47. If the 911 Board does not designate an amount to be allocated to the PSAP Grant Account, the 911 Board must distribute all of the remaining funds on a per capita basis. The 911 Board may not change the percentage designation more than once each fiscal year.

(b1) Carryforward. - A PSAP may carry forward distributions for eligible expenditures for capital outlay, capital improvements, or equipment replacement. Amounts carried forward to the next fiscal year from distributions made by the 911 Board may not be used to lower the distributions in subsection (a) of this section unless the amount is greater than twenty percent (20%) of the average yearly amount distributed to the PSAP in the prior two years. The 911 Board may allow a PSAP to carry forward a greater amount without changing the PSAP's distribution.

(c) Use of Funds. - A PSAP that receives a distribution from the 911 Fund may not use the amount received to pay for the lease or purchase of real estate, cosmetic remodeling of emergency dispatch centers, hiring or compensating telecommunicators, or the purchase of mobile communications vehicles, ambulances, fire engines, or other emergency vehicles. Distributions received by a PSAP may be used only to pay for the following:

(1) The lease, purchase, or maintenance of:

a. Emergency telephone equipment, including necessary computer hardware, software, and database provisioning.

b. Addressing.

c. Telecommunicator furniture.

d. Dispatch equipment located exclusively within a building where a PSAP is located, excluding the costs of base station transmitters, towers, microwave links, and antennae used to dispatch emergency call information from the PSAP.

(1a) The nonrecurring costs of establishing a 911 system.

(2) Expenditures for in-State training of 911 personnel regarding the maintenance and operation of the 911 system. Allowable training expenses include the cost of transportation, lodging, instructors, certifications, improvement programs, quality assurance training, training associated with call taking, and emergency medical, fire, or law enforcement procedures, and training specific to managing a PSAP or supervising PSAP staff. Training outside the State is not an eligible expenditure unless the training is unavailable in the State or the PSAP documents that the training costs are less if received out-of-state. Training specific to the receipt of 911 calls is allowed only for intake and related call taking quality assurance and improvement. Instructor certification costs and course required prerequisites, including physicals, psychological exams, and drug testing, are not allowable expenditures.

(3) Charges associated with the service supplier's 911 service and other service supplier recurring charges. The PSAP providing 911 service is responsible to the voice communications service provider for all 911 installation, service, equipment, operation, and maintenance charges owed to the voice communications service provider. A PSAP may contract with a voice communications service provider on terms agreed to by the PSAP and the provider.

(d) Local Fund. - The fiscal officer of a PSAP to whom a distribution is made under this section must deposit the funds in a special revenue fund, as defined in G.S. 159-26(b)(2), designated as the Emergency Telephone System Fund. The fiscal officer may invest money in the Fund in the same manner that other money of the local government may be invested. Income earned from the invested money in the Emergency Telephone System Fund must be credited to the Fund. Revenue deposited into the Fund must be used only as permitted in this section.

(e) Compliance. - A PSAP, or the governing entity of a PSAP, must comply with all of the following in order to receive a distribution under this section:

(1) A county or municipality that has one or more PSAPs must submit in writing to the 911 Board information that identifies the PSAPs in the manner required by the FCC Order.

(2) A participating PSAP must annually submit to the 911 Board a copy of its governing agency's proposed or approved budget detailing the revenues and expenditures associated with the operation of the PSAP. The PSAP budget must identify revenues and expenditures for eligible expense reimbursements as provided in this Article and rules adopted by the 911 Board.

(3) A PSAP must be included in its governing entity's annual audit required under the Local Government Budget and Fiscal Control Act. The Local Government Commission must provide a copy of each audit of a local government entity with a participating PSAP to the 911 Board.

(4) A PSAP must comply with all requests by the 911 Board for financial information related to the operation of the PSAP.

(5) A primary PSAP must comply with the rules, policies, procedures, and operating standards for primary PSAPs adopted by the 911 Board.

(f) Application to Cherokees. - The Eastern Band of Cherokee Indians is an eligible PSAP. The Tribal Council of the Eastern Band is the local governing entity of the Eastern Band for purposes of this section. The Tribal Council must give the 911 Board information adequate to determine the Eastern Band's base amount. The 911 Board must use the most recent federal census estimate of the population living on the Qualla Boundary to determine the per capita distribution amount. (2007-383, s. 1(a); 2008-134, ss. 1(b), (c); 2010-158, ss. 7(a)-(d); 2011-291, s. 2.18.)

§ 62A-47. PSAP Grant and Statewide 911 Projects Account.

(a) Account Established. - A PSAP Grant and Statewide 911 Projects Account is established within the 911 Fund for the purpose of making grants to PSAPs in rural and other high-cost areas and funding projects that provide statewide benefits for 911 service. The Account consists of revenue allocated by the 911 Board under G.S. 62A-45(c) and G.S. 62A-46.

(b) Grant Application. - A PSAP may apply to the 911 Board for a grant from the Account. An application must be submitted in the manner prescribed by the 911 Board. The 911 Board may approve a grant application and enter into a grant agreement with a PSAP if it determines all of the following:

(1) The costs estimated in the application are reasonable and have been or will be incurred for the purpose of promoting a cost-effective and efficient 911 system.

(2) The expenses to be incurred by the applicant are consistent with the 911 State Plan.

(3) There are sufficient funds available in the fiscal year in which the grant funds will be distributed.

(4) The costs are authorized PSAP costs under G.S. 62A-46(c), or the costs are for consolidating one or more PSAPs with a primary PSAP, or the relocation costs of primary PSAPs, including costs not authorized under G.S. 62A-46(c) and construction costs.

(c) Grant Agreement. - A grant agreement between the 911 Board and a PSAP must include the purpose of the grant, the time frame for implementing the project or program funded by the grant, the amount of the grant, and a provision for repaying grant funds if the PSAP fails to comply with any of the terms of the grant. The amount of the grant may vary among grantees. If the grant is intended to promote the deployment of enhanced 911 service in a rural area of the State, the grant agreement must specify how the funds will assist with this goal. The 911 Board must publish one or more notices each fiscal year advertising the availability of grants from the PSAP Grant and Statewide 911 Projects Account and detailing the application process, including the deadline for submitting applications, any required documents specifying costs, either incurred or anticipated, and evidence demonstrating the need for the grant. Any grant funds awarded to PSAPs under this section are in addition to any funds reimbursed under G.S. 62A-46.

(d) Statewide 911 Projects. - The 911 Board may use funds from the Account for a statewide project if the Board determines the project meets all of the following requirements:

(1)   The project is consistent with the 911 plan.

(2)   The project is cost-effective and efficient when compared to the aggregated costs incurred by primary PSAPs for implementing individual projects.

(3)   The project is an eligible expense under G.S. 62A-46(c).

(4)   The project will have statewide benefit for 911 service. (2007-383, s. 1(a); 2010-158, s. 8.)

§ 62A-48. Recovery of unauthorized use of funds.

The 911 Board must give written notice of violation to any voice communications service provider or PSAP found by the 911 Board to be using monies from the 911 Fund for purposes not authorized by this Article. Upon receipt of notice, the voice communications service provider or PSAP must cease making any unauthorized expenditures. The voice communications service provider or PSAP may petition the 911 Board for a hearing on the question of whether the expenditures were unauthorized, and the 911 Board must grant the request within a reasonable period of time. If, after the hearing, the 911 Board concludes the expenditures were in fact unauthorized, the 911 Board may require the voice communications service provider or PSAP to refund the monies improperly spent within 90 days. Money received under this section must be credited to the 911 Fund. If a voice communications service provider or PSAP does not cease making unauthorized expenditures or refuses to refund improperly spent money, the 911 Board must suspend funding to the provider or PSAP until corrective action is taken. (2007-383, s. 1(a).)

§ 62A-49. Conditions for providing enhanced 911 service.

In accordance with the FCC Order, no CMRS provider is required to provide enhanced 911 service until all of the following conditions are met:

(1) The provider receives a request for the service from the administrator of a PSAP that is capable of receiving and utilizing the data elements associated with the service.

(2) Funds for reimbursement of the CMRS provider's costs are available pursuant to G.S. 62A-45.

(3) The local exchange carrier is able to support the requirements of enhanced 911 service. (2007-383, s. 1(a).)

§ 62A-50. Audit.

The State Auditor may perform audits of the 911 Board pursuant to Article 5A of Chapter 147 of the General Statutes to ensure that funds in the 911 Fund are being managed in accordance with the provisions of this Article. The State Auditor must perform an audit of the 911 Board at least every two years. The 911 Board must reimburse the State Auditor for the cost of an audit of the 911 Board. (2007-383, s. 1(a).)

§ 62A-51. Subscriber records.

Each CMRS provider must provide its 10,000 number groups to a PSAP upon request. This information remains the property of the disclosing CMRS provider and must be used only in providing emergency response services to 911 calls. CMRS voice communications service provider connection information obtained by PSAP personnel for public safety purposes is not public information under Chapter 132 of the General Statutes. No person may disclose or use, for any purpose other than the 911 system, information contained in the database of the telephone network portion of a 911 system. (2007-383, s. 1(a).)

§ 62A-52. Proprietary information.

All proprietary information submitted to the 911 Board or the State Auditor is confidential. Proprietary information submitted pursuant to this Article is not subject to disclosure under Chapter 132 of the General Statutes, and it may not be released to any person other than to the submitting CMRS voice communications service provider, the 911 Board, and the State Auditor without the express permission of the submitting CMRS voice communications service provider. Proprietary information is considered a trade secret under the Trade Secrets Protection Act, Article 24 of Chapter 66 of the General Statutes. General information collected by the 911 Board or the State Auditor may be released or published only in aggregate amounts that do not identify or allow identification of numbers of subscribers or revenues attributable to an individual CMRS voice communications service provider. (2007-383, s. 1(a).)

§ 62A-53. Limitation of liability.

Except in cases of wanton or willful misconduct, a voice communications service provider and its employees, directors, officers, and agents are not liable for any damages in a civil action resulting from death or injury to any person or from damage to property incurred by any person in connection with developing, adopting, implementing, maintaining, or operating the 911 system or in complying with emergency-related information requests from State or local government officials. This section does not apply to actions arising out of the operation or ownership of a motor vehicle. (2007-383, s. 1(a).)

§ 62A-54. Service charge for prepaid wireless telecommunications service; seller collects 911 service charge on each retail transaction occurring in this State; remittances to Department of Revenue and transfer to 911 Fund.

(a) Retail Collection. - A seller of prepaid wireless telecommunications service shall collect the 911 service charge for prepaid wireless telecommunications service from the consumer on each retail transaction occurring in this State. The 911 service charge for prepaid wireless telecommunications service is in addition to the sales tax imposed on the sale or recharge of prepaid telephone calling service under G.S. 105-164.4(a)(4d). The amount of the 911 service charge for prepaid wireless telecommunications service must be separately stated on an invoice, receipt, or other reasonable notification provided to the consumer by the seller at the time of the retail transaction. For purposes of this Article, a retail transaction is occurring in this State if the sale is sourced to this State under G.S. 105-164.4B(a).

(b) Administrative Allowance; Remittance to Department of Revenue. - A seller may deduct and retain from the 911 service charges it collects from consumers and remits to the Department of Revenue an administrative allowance of five percent (5%). A seller shall remit the 911 service charge for prepaid wireless telecommunications service collected by it under subsection (a) of this section in either of the following ways:

(1) Monthly to the Department of Revenue. The service charges collected in a month are due by the 20th day of the month following the calendar month covered by the return.

(2) Semiannually to the Department of Revenue. The service charges collected in the first six months of the calendar year are due by July 20. The service charges collected in the second six months of the calendar year are due by January 20.

(c) Administration. - Administration, auditing, requests for review, making returns, promulgation of rules and regulations by the Secretary of Revenue, additional taxes and liens, assessments, refunds, and penalty provisions of Article 9 of Chapter 105 of the General Statutes apply to the collection of the 911 service charge for prepaid wireless telecommunications service. An audit of the collection of the 911 service charge for prepaid wireless telecommunications service shall only be conducted in connection with an audit of the taxes imposed by Article 5 of Chapter 105 of the General Statutes. Underpayments shall be subject to the same interest rate as imposed for taxes under G.S. 105-241.21. Overpayments shall be subject to the same interest rate as imposed for taxes under G.S. 105-241.21(c)(2). Excessive and erroneous collections of the service charge will be subject to G.S. 105-164.11. The Department of Revenue shall establish procedures for a seller of prepaid wireless telecommunications service to document that a sale is not a retail transaction, and the procedures established shall substantially coincide with the procedures for documenting a sale for resale transaction under G.S. 105-164.28. The Secretary of Revenue may retain the costs of collection from the remittances received under subsection (b) of this section, not to exceed five hundred thousand dollars ($500,000) a year of the total 911 service charges for prepaid wireless telecommunications service remitted to the Department. Within 45 days of the end of each month in which 911 service charges for prepaid wireless telecommunications service are remitted to the Department, the Secretary of Revenue shall transfer the total 911 service charges remitted to the Department less the costs of collection to the 911 Fund established under G.S. 62A-44.

(d) Liability of Consumer. - The 911 service charge for prepaid wireless telecommunications service is the liability of the consumer and not of the seller or of any provider, except that the seller shall be liable for remitting to the Department of Revenue all 911 service charges for prepaid wireless telecommunications service that the seller collects from consumers as provided in subsection (b) of this section. (2011-122, s. 5; 2013-414, s. 30.)

§ 62A-55. Limitation of liability, prepaid wireless.

In addition to the limitation of liability provided in subsection G.S. 62A-53, each provider and seller of prepaid wireless telecommunications service is entitled to the following limitations of liability:

(1) No provider or seller of prepaid wireless telecommunications service shall be liable for damages to any person resulting from or incurred in connection with the provision of or the failure to provide 911 service, or for identifying or failing to identify the telephone number, address, location, or name associated with any person or device that is accessing or attempting to access 911 service.

(2) No provider or seller of prepaid wireless telecommunications service shall be liable for damages to any person resulting from or incurred in connection with the provision of any lawful assistance to any investigative or law enforcement officer of the United States, this State or any other state, or any political subdivision of this State or any other state in connection with any lawful investigation or other law enforcement activity by the law enforcement officer. (2011-122, s. 5.)

§ 62A-56. Exclusivity of 911 service charge for prepaid wireless telecommunications service.

The 911 service charge for prepaid wireless telecommunications service imposed by this Article is the only 911 funding obligation imposed with respect to prepaid wireless telecommunications service in this State, and no tax, fee, surcharge, or other charge shall be imposed in this State, any subdivision of this State, or any intergovernmental agency for 911 funding purposes upon any provider, seller, or consumer with respect to the sale, purchase, use, or provision of prepaid wireless telecommunications service. (2011-122, s. 5.)

§ 62A-57: Reserved for future codification purposes.

§ 62A-58: Reserved for future codification purposes.

Chapter 63.

Aeronautics.

Article 1.

Municipal Airports.

§ 63-1. Definitions; singular and plural.

(a) Definitions. - For the purpose of this Chapter the following words, terms, and phrases shall have the meanings herein given, unless otherwise specifically defined, or unless another intention clearly appears, or the context otherwise requires:

(1) "Aeronautics" means transportation by aircraft; the operation, construction, repair, or maintenance of aircraft, aircraft power plants and accessories, including the repair, packing, and maintenance of parachutes; the design, establishment, construction, extension, operation, improvement, repair, or maintenance of airports, restricted landing areas, or other air navigation facilities, and air instruction.

(2) "Aeronautics instructor" means any individual engaged in giving instruction or offering to give instruction in aeronautics, either in flying or ground subjects, or both, for hire or reward, without advertising such occupation, without calling his facilities an "air school" or anything equivalent thereto, and without employing or using other instructors. It does not include any instructor in any public school or university of this State, or any institution of higher learning

duly accredited and approved for carrying on collegiate work, while engaged in his duties as such instructor.

(3) "Aircraft" means any contrivance now known, or hereafter invented, used or designed for navigation of or flight in the air.

(4) "Air instruction" means the imparting of aeronautical information by any aeronautics instructor or in or by any air school or flying club.

(5) "Airman" means any individual who engages, as the person in command, or as pilot, mechanic, or member of the crew, in the navigation of aircraft while underway and (excepting individuals employed outside the United States, any individual employed by a manufacturer of aircraft, aircraft engines, propellers, or appliances to perform duties as inspector or mechanic in connection therewith, and any individual performing inspection or mechanical duties in connection with aircraft owned or operated by him) any individual who is directly in charge of the inspection, maintenance, overhauling, or repair of aircraft engines, propellers, or appliances; and any individual who serves in the capacity of aircraft dispatcher or air traffic control tower operator.

(6) "Air navigation" means the operation or navigation of aircraft in the air space over this State, or upon any airport or restricted landing area within this State.

(7) "Air navigation facility" means any facility other than one owned or controlled by the federal government, used in, available for use in, or designed for use in aid of air navigation, including airports, restricted landing areas, and any structures, mechanisms, lights, beacons, marks, communicating systems, or other instrumentalities or devices used or useful as an aid, or constituting an advantage or convenience to the safe taking off, navigation, and landing of aircraft, or the safe and efficient operation or maintenance of an airport or restricted landing area, and any combination of any or all of such facilities.

(8) "Airport" means any area of land or water, except a restricted landing area, which is designed for the landing and take off of aircraft, whether or not facilities are provided for the shelter, servicing, or repair of aircraft, or for receiving or discharging passengers or cargo, and all appurtenant areas used or suitable for airport buildings or other airport facilities, and all appurtenant rights-of-way, whether heretofore or hereafter established.

(9)   "Airport hazard" means any structure, object of natural growth, or use of land, which obstructs the air space required for the flight of aircraft in landing or taking off at any airport or restricted landing area or is otherwise hazardous to such landing or taking off.

(10)   "Airport protection privileges" means easements through, or other interests in, air space over land or water, interests in airport hazards outside the boundaries of airports or restricted landing areas, and other protection privileges, the acquisition or control of which is necessary to insure safe approaches to the landing areas of airports and restricted landing areas and the safe and efficient operation thereof.

(11)   "Air school" means any person engaged in giving or offering to give instruction in aeronautics, either in flying or ground subjects, or both, for or without hire or reward, and advertising, representing, or holding himself out as giving or offering to give such instruction. It does not include any public school or university of this State, or any institution of higher learning duly accredited and approved for carrying on collegiate work.

(12)   "Civil aircraft" means any aircraft other than a public aircraft.

(13)   "Flying club" means any person other than an individual which, neither for profit nor reward, owns, leases, or uses one or more aircraft for the purpose of instruction or pleasure, or both.

(14)   "Municipality" means any county, city, or town of this State, and any other political subdivision, public corporation, authority, or district in this State, which is or may be authorized by law to acquire, establish, construct, maintain, improve, and operate airports and other air navigation facilities.

(15)   "Navigable air space" means air space above the minimum altitudes of flight prescribed by the laws of this State, or by regulations of the Commission consistent therewith.

(16)   "Operation of aircraft" or "operation aircraft" means the use of aircraft for the purpose of air navigation and includes the navigation or piloting of aircraft. Any person who causes or authorizes the operation of aircraft, whether with or without the right of legal control (in the capacity of owner, lessee, or otherwise) of the aircraft, shall be deemed to be engaged in the operation of aircraft within the meaning of the statutes of this State.

(17) "Person" means any individual, firm, partnership, corporation, company, association, joint stock association, or body politic; and includes any trustee, receiver, assignee, or other similar representative thereof.

(18) "Public aircraft" means an aircraft used exclusively in the service of any government or of any political subdivision thereof, including the government of any state, territory, or possession of the United States, or the District of Columbia, but not including any government owned aircraft engaged in carrying persons or property for commercial purposes.

(19) "Restricted area" means any area of land, water, or both, which is used or is made available for the landing and take off of aircraft, the use of which shall, except in case of emergency, be only as provided from time to time by the Commission.

(20) "State" or "this State" means the State of North Carolina.

(21) "State airway" means a route in the navigable air space over and above the lands or water of this State designated by the Commission as a route suitable for air navigation.

(b) Singular and Plural. - The singular shall include the plural, and the plural the singular. (1945, c. 490, s. 1; 1949, c. 865, s. 3; 1971, c. 936, s. 2.)

§ 63-2. Cities and towns authorized to establish airports.

The governing body of any city or town in this State is hereby authorized to acquire, establish, construct, own, control, lease, equip, improve, maintain, operate, and regulate airports or landing fields for the use of airplanes and other aircraft, either within or without the limits of such cities and towns and may use for such purpose or purposes any property suitable therefor that is now or may at any time hereafter be owned or controlled by such city or town. (1929, c. 87, s. 2.)

§ 63-3. Counties authorized to establish airports.

The governing body of any county in this State is hereby authorized to acquire, establish, construct, own, control, lease, equip, improve, maintain, operate, and regulate airports or landing fields for the use of airplanes and other aircraft within or without the limits of such counties, and may use for such purpose or purposes any property suitable therefor that is now or may at any time hereafter be owned or controlled by such county. (1929, c. 87, s. 3.)

§ 63-4. Joint airports established by cities, towns and counties.

The governing bodies of any city, town and county in this State are hereby authorized to jointly acquire, establish, construct, own, control, lease, equip, improve, maintain, operate, and regulate airports or landing fields for the use of airplanes and other aircraft within or without the limits of such cities, towns and counties, and may use for such purpose or purposes any property suitable therefor that is now or may at any time hereafter be jointly owned or controlled by such city, town and county. (1929, c. 87, s. 4.)

§ 63-5. Airport declared public purpose; eminent domain.

Any lands acquired, owned, controlled, or occupied by such cities, towns, and/or counties, for the purposes enumerated in G.S. 63-2, 63-3 and 63-4, shall and are hereby declared to be acquired, owned, controlled and occupied for a public purpose, and such cities, towns and/or counties shall have the right to acquire property for such purpose or purposes under the power of eminent domain as and for a public purpose. (1929, c. 87, s. 5.)

§ 63-6. Acquisition of sites; appropriation of moneys.

Private property needed by a city, town and/or county for an airport or landing field may be acquired by gift or devise or shall be acquired by purchase if the city, town and/or county is or are able to agree with the owners on the terms thereof, and otherwise by condemnation, in the manner provided by Chapter 40A. The purchase price, or award for property acquired for an airport or landing field may be paid for by appropriation of moneys available therefor, or wholly or partly from the proceeds of the sale of bonds of the city, town and/or county, as the governing body and/or bodies of such city, town and/or county shall determine. (1929, c. 87, s. 6; 1981, c. 919, s. 7.)

§ 63-7. Airports already established declared public charge; regulations and fees for use of.

The governing body or bodies of a city, town and/or county which has or have established an airport or landing field, and acquired, leased, or set apart real property for such purpose, may construct, improve, equip, maintain, and operate the same. The expenses of such construction, improvement, maintenance, and operation shall be a city, town and/or county charge as the case may be. The governing body or bodies of a city, town and/or county may adopt regulations and establish fees or charges for the use of such airport or landing field. (1929, c. 87, s. 7.)

§ 63-8. Appropriations.

The governing body or bodies of a city, town and/or county to which this Article is applicable, having power to appropriate, individually or jointly, money therein, are hereby authorized to annually appropriate and cause to be raised by taxation in such city, town and/or county or to use from the net proceeds derived from the operation, by such city, town or county, of any public utility a sum sufficient to carry out the provisions of this Article in such proportion and upon such pro-rata basis as may be determined upon by a joint board to be appointed by and from the governing body or bodies of the city, town and/or the county or individually as the case may be. Provided, nothing herein shall be construed to permit the governing bodies of any county, city or town to issue bonds under the provisions of this Article without a vote of the people. (1929, c. 87, s. 8.)

§ 63-8.1. Repealed by Session Laws 1973, c. 803, s. 3.

§ 63-9. Partial invalidity.

If any part or parts of this Article shall be held to be unconstitutional, such unconstitutionality shall not affect the validity of the remaining parts of this Article. The General Assembly expressly declares that it would have passed the remaining parts of this Article, if it had known that such part or parts thereof would be declared unconstitutional. (1929, c. 87, s. 9.)

Article 2.

State Regulation.

§ 63-10. Repealed by Session Laws 1971, c. 936, s. 1.

§ 63-11. Sovereignty in space.

Sovereignty in space above the lands and waters of this State is declared to rest in the State, except where granted to and assumed by the United States. (1929, c. 190, s. 2.)

§ 63-12. Ownership of space.

The ownership of the space above the lands and waters of this State is declared to be vested in the several owners of the surface beneath, subject to the right of flight described in G.S. 63-13. (1929, c. 190, s. 3.)

§ 63-13. Lawfulness of flight.

Flight in aircraft over the lands and waters of this State is lawful, unless at such a low altitude as to interfere with the then existing use to which the land or water, or the space over the land or water, is put by the owner, or unless so conducted as to be injurious to the health and happiness, or imminently dangerous to persons or property lawfully on the land or water beneath. The landing of an aircraft on the lands or waters of another, without his consent, is unlawful, except in the case of a forced landing. For damages caused by a forced landing, however, the owner or lessee of the aircraft or the aeronaut shall be liable as provided in G.S. 63-14. (1929, c. 190, s. 4; 1947, c. 1001, s. 1.)

§ 63-14. Repealed by Session Laws 1947, c. 1069, s. 3.

§ 63-15. Collision of aircraft.

The liability of the owners of one aircraft to the owner of another aircraft, or to aeronauts or passengers on either aircraft, for damages caused by collision on land or in the air shall be determined by the rules of law applicable to torts on land. (1929, c. 190, s. 6.)

§ 63-16. Jurisdiction over crimes and torts.

All crimes, torts, and other wrongs committed by or against an airman or passenger while in flight over this State shall be governed by the laws of this State; and the question whether damage occasioned by or to an aircraft while in flight over this State constitutes a tort, crime or other wrong by or against the owner of such aircraft shall be determined by the laws of this State. (1929, c. 190, s. 7; 1971, c. 936, s. 3.)

§ 63-17. Jurisdiction over contracts.

All contractual and other legal relations entered into by airmen or passengers while in flight over this State shall have the same effect as if entered into on the land or water beneath. (1929, c. 190, s. 8; 1971, c. 936, s. 3.)

§ 63-18. Dangerous flying a misdemeanor.

Any airman or passenger who, while in flight over a thickly inhabited area or over a public gathering within this State, shall engage in trick or acrobatic flying, or in any acrobatic feat, or shall except while in landing or taking off, fly at such a low level as to disturb the public peace or the rights of private persons in the enjoyment of their homes, or injure the health, or endanger the persons or property on the surface beneath, or drop any object except loose water or loose sand ballast, shall be guilty of a Class 1 misdemeanor. (1929, c. 190, s. 9; 1947, c. 1001, s. 2; 1971, c. 936, s. 3; 1993, c. 539, s. 493; 1994, Ex. Sess., c. 24, s. 14(c).)

§ 63-19. Repealed by Session Laws 1943, c. 543.

§ 63-20. Qualifications of operator; federal license.

The public safety requiring, and the advantages of uniform regulation making it desirable, in the interest of aeronautical progress, that a person engaging within this State in operating aircraft, in any form of aerial navigation for which a license to operate aircraft issued by the United States government would then be required if such aerial navigation were interstate, should have the qualifications necessary for obtaining and holding such a license, it shall be unlawful for any person to engage in operating aircraft within the State, in any such form of aerial navigation, unless he have such federal license. (1929, c. 190, s. 11.)

§ 63-21. Possession and exhibition of license certificate.

The certificate of the license, herein required, shall be kept in the personal possession of the licensee when he is operating aircraft within this State and must be presented for inspection upon the demand of any passenger, any peace officer of this State, or any official, manager or person in charge of any airport or landing field in this State upon which he shall land. (1929, c. 190, s. 12.)

§ 63-22. Aircraft; construction, design and airworthiness; federal registration.

The public safety requiring, and the advantages of uniform regulation making it desirable, in the interest of aeronautical progress, that aircraft to be operated within this State should conform, with respect to design, construction and airworthiness, to standards then prescribed by the United States government with respect to aerial navigation of aircraft subject to its jurisdiction, it shall be unlawful for any person to operate an aircraft within this State unless it is registered pursuant to the lawful rules and regulations of the United States government then in force, if the circumstances of such aerial navigation are of a character that such registration would be required in the case of interstate aerial navigation. (1929, c. 190, s. 13.)

§ 63-23. Penalties.

A person who violates any provision of G.S. 63-20, 63-21 or 63-22 of this Article shall be guilty of a Class 2 misdemeanor; provided, however, that acts or omissions made unlawful by G.S. 63-20, 63-21 or 63-22 of this Article shall not be deemed to include any act or omission which violates the laws or lawful regulations of the United States. (1929, c. 190, s. 14; 1993, c. 539, s. 494; 1994, Ex. Sess., c. 24, s. 14(c).)

§ 63-24. Jurisdiction of State over crimes and torts retained.

Provided that this Article shall not be construed as a waiver of jurisdiction of the courts of the State of North Carolina over any crime or tort committed within the State of North Carolina, and provided, further, that the General Assembly of North Carolina may at any time amend, regulate or control any of the powers which may be assumed by the United States Department of Commerce under this Article. (1929, c. 190, s. 15.)

Article 3.

Stealing, Tampering with, or Operating Aircraft While Intoxicated.

§ 63-25. Taking of aircraft made crime of larceny.

Any person who, under circumstances not constituting larceny shall, without the consent of the owner, take, use or operate or cause to be taken, used or operated, an airplane or other aircraft or its equipment, for his own profit, purpose or pleasure, steals the same, is guilty of a Class H felony. (1929, c. 90, s. 1; 1993, c. 539, s. 1278; 1994, Ex. Sess., c. 24, s. 14(c).)

§ 63-26. Tampering with aircraft made crime.

Any person who shall, without the consent of the owner, go upon or enter, tamper with or in any way damage or injure any airplane or other aircraft, or any personal property under the control of or being used by any public or private airport or aircraft landing facility shall be guilty of a Class 1 misdemeanor, and the showing of willful or malicious intent shall not be necessary to sustain a conviction hereunder. (1929, c. 90, s. 2; 1987, c. 818, s. 3; 1993, c. 539, s. 495; 1994, Ex. Sess., c. 24, s. 14(c).)

§ 63-26.1. Trespass upon airport property made a crime.

(a) It shall be unlawful for any person to trespass upon airport property. For purposes of this section "airport property" means property that is under the control of or is being used by any public or private airport or aircraft landing facility.

(b) A person commits the offense of trespass upon airport property if, without authorization, he enters or remains on airport property that is so enclosed or posted or secured as to demonstrate clearly an intent to keep out intruders. Violation of this section is a Class 2 misdemeanor. (1987, c. 818, s. 4; 1993, c. 539, s. 496; 1994, Ex. Sess., c. 24, s. 14(c).)

§ 63-27. Operation of aircraft while impaired.

(a) Offense. - A person commits the offense of operation of an aircraft while impaired if he operates an aircraft, whether on the ground or in the air or on water, within this State:

(1) While under the influence of an impairing substance; or

(2) After having consumed sufficient alcohol that he has, at any relevant time after the operating of an aircraft, an alcohol concentration of 0.04 or more.

The relevant definitions contained in G.S. 20-4.01 shall apply to this section.

(b) Defense precluded. - The fact that a person charged with violating this section is or has been legally entitled to use alcohol or a drug is not a defense to a charge under this section.

(c) Pleading. - In any prosecution for operating an aircraft while impaired, the pleading is sufficient if it states the time and place of the alleged offense in the usual form and charges that the defendant operated the aircraft within this State while subject to an impairing substance.

(d) Chemical Analysis. - Any person who operates an airplane or other aircraft, whether on the ground or in the air or on the water within the territorial limits of this State gives consent to chemical analysis if he is charged with the offense of operating an aircraft while impaired. The charging officer must designate the type of chemical analysis to be administered, and it may be administered when he has reasonable grounds to believe that the person charged has committed the specified crime. The chemical analysis shall be performed pursuant to the procedures established under Chapter 20 of the General Statutes applying to motor vehicle violations with the exception that if the person charged refuses to be tested, the charging officer shall, in writing, notify the local office of the Federal Aviation Administration of the individual's refusal. The results of any chemical tests administered pursuant to this section will be admissible into evidence at trial on the offense charged and a written report of the test results shall be made available to the local office of the Federal Aviation Administration.

(e) Punishment. - A person violating this section shall be guilty of a Class 1 misdemeanor. Provided, however, for a second and all subsequent convictions of this section, a person shall be guilty of a Class I felony. (1929, c. 90, s. 3; 1953, c. 675, s. 8; 1987, c. 818, s. 1; 1993, c. 539, ss. 497, 1279; 1994, Ex. Sess., c. 24, s. 14(c).)

§ 63-28. Infliction of serious bodily injury by operation of an aircraft while impaired.

(a)   Offense. - A person commits the offense of infliction of serious bodily injury by operation of an aircraft while impaired if, while in violation of G.S. 63-27, he does serious bodily injury to another.

(b)   Defense precluded. - The fact that a person charged with violating this section is or has been legally entitled to use alcohol or a drug is not a defense to a charge under this section.

(c)   Pleading. - In any prosecution for infliction of serious bodily injury by operation of an aircraft while impaired, the pleading is sufficient if it states the time and place of the alleged offense in the usual form and charges that the defendant did serious bodily injury to another while operating an aircraft within this State while subject to an impairing substance.

(d)   Punishment. - Violation of this section is a Class F felony. (1929, c. 90, s. 4; 1953, c. 675, s. 9; 1987, c. 818, s. 2; 1993, c. 539, s. 1280; 1994, Ex. Sess., c. 24, s. 14(c).)

Article 4.

Model Airport Zoning Act.

§ 63-29: Repealed by Session Laws 1971, c. 936, s. 1.

§ 63-30. Airport hazards not in public interest.

It is hereby found and declared that an airport hazard endangers the lives and property of users of the airport and of occupants of land in its vicinity, and also, if of the obstruction type, in effect reduces the size of the area available for the landing, taking off and maneuvering of aircraft, thus tending to destroy or impair the utility of the airport and the public investment therein, and is therefore not in the interest of the public health, public safety, or general welfare. (1941, c. 250, s. 2.)

§ 63-31. Adoption of airport zoning regulations.

(a) Every political subdivision may adopt, administer, and enforce, under the police power and in the manner and upon the conditions hereinafter prescribed, airport zoning regulations, which regulations shall divide the area surrounding any airport within the jurisdiction of said political subdivision into zones, and, within such zones, specify the land uses permitted, and regulate and restrict the height to which structures and trees may be erected or allowed to grow. In adopting or revising any such zoning regulations, the political subdivision shall consider, among other things, the character of the flying operations expected to be conducted at the airport, the nature of the terrain, the height of existing structures and trees above the level of the airport, the possibility of lowering or removing existing obstructions, and the views of the agency of the federal government charged with the fostering of civil aeronautics, as to the aerial approaches necessary to safe flying operations at the airport.

(b) In the event that a political subdivision has adopted, or hereafter adopts, a general zoning ordinance regulating, among other things, the height of buildings, any airport zoning regulations adopted for the same area or portion thereof under this Article may be incorporated in and made a part of such general zoning regulations, and be administered and enforced in connection therewith, but such general zoning regulations shall not limit the effectiveness or scope of the regulations adopted under this Article.

(c) Any two or more political subdivisions may agree, by ordinance duly adopted, to create a joint board and delegate to said board the powers herein conferred to promulgate, administer and enforce airport zoning regulations to protect the aerial approaches of any airport located within the corporate limits of any one or more of said political subdivisions. Such joint board shall have as members two representatives appointed by the chief executive officer of each political subdivision participating in the creation of said board and a chairman elected by a majority of the members so appointed.

(d) The jurisdiction of each political subdivision is hereby extended to the promulgating, adopting, administering and enforcement of airport zoning regulations to protect the approaches of any airport or landing field which is owned by said political subdivision, although the area affected by the zoning regulations may be located outside the corporate limits of said political subdivision. In case of conflict with any airport zoning or other regulations promulgated by any political subdivision, the regulations adopted pursuant to this section shall prevail.

(e) All airport zoning regulations adopted under this Article shall be reasonable, and none shall require the removal, lowering, or other change or alteration of any structure or tree not conforming to the regulations when adopted or amended, or otherwise interfere with the continuance of any nonconforming use, except as provided in G.S. 63-32, subsection (a).

(f) A political subdivision may not adopt an airport zoning regulation in violation of G.S. 63A-18. (1941, c. 250, s. 3; 1945, cc. 300, 635; 1991, c. 749, s. 3.)

§ 63-32. Permits, new structures, etc., and variances.

(a) Permits. - Where advisable to facilitate the enforcement of zoning regulations adopted pursuant to this Article, a system may be established by any political subdivision for the granting of permits to establish or construct new structures and other uses and to replace existing structures and other uses or make substantial changes therein or substantial repairs thereof. In any event, before any nonconforming structure or tree may be replaced, substantially altered or repaired, rebuilt, allowed to grow higher, or replanted, a permit must be secured from the administrative agency authorized to administer and enforce the regulations, authorizing such replacement, change or repair. No such permit shall be granted that would allow the structure or tree in question to be made higher or become a greater hazard to air navigation than it was when the applicable regulation was adopted; and whenever the administrative agency determines that a nonconforming structure or tree has been abandoned or more than eighty percent (80%) torn down, destroyed, deteriorated, or decayed: (i) no permit shall be granted that would allow said structure or tree to exceed the applicable height limit or otherwise deviate from the zoning regulations; and (ii) whether application is made for a permit under this paragraph or not, the said agency may by appropriate action compel the owner of the nonconforming structure or tree, at his own expense, to lower, remove, reconstruct, or equip such object as may be necessary to conform to the regulations or, if the owner of the nonconforming structure or tree shall neglect or refuse to comply with such order for 10 days after notice thereof, the said agency may proceed to have the object so lowered, removed, reconstructed, or equipped. Except as indicated, all applications for permits for replacement, change or repair of nonconforming uses shall be granted.

(b)   Variances. - Any person desiring to erect any structures, or increase the height of any structure, or permit the growth of any tree, or otherwise use his property, in violation of airport zoning regulations adopted under this Article, may apply to the board of appeals, as provided in G.S. 63-33, subsection (c), for a variance from the zoning regulations in question. Such variances shall be allowed where a literal application or enforcement of the regulations would result in practical difficulty or unnecessary hardship and the relief granted would not be contrary to the public interest but do substantial justice and be in accordance with the spirit of the regulations and this Article.

(c)   Obstruction Marking and Lighting. - In granting any permit or variance under this section, the administrative agency or board of appeals may, if it deems such action advisable to effectuate the purposes of this Article and reasonable in the circumstances, so condition such permit or variance as to require the owner of the structure or tree in question to permit the political subdivision, at its own expense, to install, operate, and maintain suitable obstruction markers and obstruction lights thereon. (1941, c. 250, s. 4.)

§ 63-33. Procedure.

(a)   Adoption of Zoning Regulations. - No airport zoning regulations shall be adopted, amended, or changed under this Article except by action of the legislative body of the political subdivision in question, or the joint board provided for in G.S. 63-31, subsection (c), after a public hearing in relation thereto, at which parties in interest and citizens shall have an opportunity to be heard. At least 10 days' notice of the hearing shall be published in an official paper, or a paper of general circulation, in the political subdivision or subdivisions in which the airport is located.

(b)   Administration of Zoning Regulations - Administrative Agency. - The legislative body of any political subdivision adopting airport zoning regulations under this Article may delegate the duty of administering and enforcing such regulations to any administrative agency under its jurisdiction, or may create a new administrative agency to perform such duty, but such administrative agency shall not be or include any member of the board of appeals. The duties of such administrative agency shall include that of hearing and deciding all permits under G.S. 63-32, subsection (a), but such agency shall not have or exercise any of the powers delegated to the board of appeals.

(c) Administration of Airport Zoning Regulations - Board of Appeals. - Airport zoning regulations adopted under this Article shall provide for a board of appeals to have and exercise the following powers:

(1) To hear and decide appeals from any order, requirement, decision, or determination made by the administrative agency in the enforcement of this Article or of any ordinance adopted pursuant thereto;

(2) To hear and decide special exceptions to the terms of the ordinance upon which such board may be required to pass under such ordinance;

(3) To hear and decide specific variances under G.S. 63-32, subsection (b).

Where a zoning board of appeals or adjustment already exists, it may be appointed as the board of appeals. Otherwise, the board of appeals shall consist of five members, each to be appointed for a term of three years and to be removable for cause by the appointing authority upon written charges and after public hearing.

The board shall adopt rules in accordance with the provisions of any ordinance adopted under this Article. Meetings of the board shall be held at the call of the chairman and at such other times as the board may determine. The chairman, or in his absence the acting chairman, may administer oaths and compel the attendance of witnesses. All meetings of the board shall be public. The board shall keep minutes of its proceedings, showing the vote of each member upon each question, or, if absent or failing to vote, indicating such fact, and shall keep records of its examinations and other official actions, all of which shall immediately be filed in the office of the board and shall be a public record.

Appeals to the board may be taken by any person aggrieved, or by any officer, department, board, or bureau of the political subdivision affected, by any decision of the administrative agency. An appeal must be taken within a reasonable time, as provided by the rules of the board, by filing with the agency from which the appeal is taken and with the board, a notice of appeal specifying the grounds thereof. The agency from which the appeal is taken shall forthwith transmit to the board all the papers constituting the record upon which the action appealed from was taken.

An appeal shall stay all proceedings in furtherance of the action appealed from, unless the agency from which the appeal is taken certifies to the board, after the notice of appeal has been filed with it, that by reason of the facts stated in the certificate a stay would, in its opinion, cause imminent peril to life or property. In such case proceedings shall not be stayed otherwise than by a restraining order which may be granted by the board or by a court of record on application on notice to the agency from which the appeal is taken and on due cause shown.

The board shall fix a reasonable time for the hearing of the appeal, give public notice and due notice to the parties in interest, and decide the same within a reasonable time. Upon the hearing any party may appear in person or by agent or by attorney.

The board may, in conformity with the provisions of this Article, reverse or affirm, wholly or partly, or modify, the order, requirement, decision or determination appealed from and may make such order, requirement, decision or determination as ought to be made, and to that end shall have all the powers of the administrative agency from which the appeal is taken.

The concurring vote of a majority of the members of the board shall be sufficient to reverse any order, requirement, decision, or determination of the administrative agency, or to decide in favor of the applicant on any matter upon which it is required to pass under any such ordinance, or to effect any variation in such ordinance. (1941, c. 250, s. 5; 1981, c. 891, s. 11.)

§ 63-34. Judicial review.

(a) Any person aggrieved by any decision of the board of appeals, or any taxpayer, or any officer, department, board, or bureau of the political subdivision, may present to the superior court a verified petition setting forth that the decision is illegal, in whole or in part, and specifying the grounds of the illegality. Such petition shall be presented to the court within 30 days after the decision is filed in the office of the board. Such petition shall comply with the provisions of G.S. 160A-393.

(b) The allowance of the writ shall not stay proceedings upon the decision appealed from, but the court may, on application, on notice to the board and on due cause shown, grant a restraining order.

(c)   The board of appeals shall not be required to return the original papers acted upon by it, but it shall be sufficient to return certified or sworn copies thereof or of such portions thereof as may be called for by the writ. The return shall concisely set forth such other facts as may be pertinent and material to show the grounds of the decision appealed from and shall be verified.

(d)   Repealed by Session Laws 2009-421, s. 3, effective January 1, 2010.

(e)   Costs shall not be allowed against the board of appeals unless it appears to the court that it acted with gross negligence, in bad faith, or with malice, in making the decision appealed from. (1941, c. 250, s. 6; 2009-421, s. 3.)

§ 63-35. Enforcement and remedies.

Each violation of this Article or of any regulations, order, or ruling promulgated or made pursuant to this Article, shall constitute a Class 3 misdemeanor, and each day a violation continues to exist shall constitute a separate offense. In addition, the political subdivision within which the property is located may institute in any court of competent jurisdiction, an action to prevent, restrain, correct or abate any violation of this Article, or of airport zoning regulations adopted under this Article, or of any order or ruling made in connection with their administration or enforcement, and the court shall adjudge to the plaintiff such relief, by way of injunction (which may be mandatory) or otherwise, as may be proper under all the facts and circumstances of the case, in order fully to effectuate the purposes of this Article and of the regulations adopted and orders and rulings made pursuant thereto. (1941, c. 250, s. 7; 1993, c. 539, s. 498; 1994, Ex. Sess., c. 24, s. 14(c).)

§ 63-36. Acquisition of air rights.

In any case in which:

(1)   It is desired to remove, lower, or otherwise terminate a nonconforming use; or

(2) The approach protection necessary cannot, because of constitutional limitations, be provided by airport zoning regulations under this Article; or

(3) It appears advisable that the necessary approach protection be provided by acquisition of property rights rather than by airport zoning regulations,

the political subdivision within which the property or nonconforming use is located or the political subdivision owning the airport or served by it may acquire, in the manner provided by the law under which municipalities are authorized to acquire real property for public purposes, such an air right, easement, or other estate or interest in the property or nonconforming use in question as may be necessary to effectuate the purposes of this Article.

If any political subdivision, or if any board or administrative agency appointed or selected by a political subdivision, shall adopt, administer or enforce any airport zoning regulations which results in the taking of, or in any other injury or damage to any existing structure, such political subdivision shall be liable therefor in damages to the owner or owners of any such property and the liability of the political subdivision shall include any expense which the owners of such property are required to incur in complying with any such zoning regulations. (1941, c. 250, s. 8.)

§ 63-37. Short title.

This Article shall be known and may be cited as the "Model Airport Zoning Act." (1941, c. 250, s. 10.)

§ 63-37.1. Airport obstructions illegal.

Any person, other than the owner or operator of an airport, who intentionally obstructs the lawful takeoff and landing operations and patterns of aircraft at an existing public or private airport shall be guilty of a Class 1 misdemeanor. (1995, c. 507, s. 19.5(m).)

Article 5.

Aeronautics Commission; Federal Regulations.

§§ 63-38 through 63-44: Repealed by Session Laws 1949, c. 865, s. 1.

§ 63-45. Enforcement of Article.

It shall be the duty of every State, county and municipal officer charged with the enforcement of State and municipal laws to enforce and assist in the enforcement of this Article. (1945, c. 198, s. 8.)

§ 63-46. Repealed by Session Laws 1949, c. 865, s. 2.

§ 63-47. Enforcement of regulations of Civil Aeronautics Administration.

In the general public interest and safety, the safety of persons receiving instructions concerning or operating, using or traveling in aircraft, and of persons and property on the ground, and in the interest of aeronautical progress, the public officers of the State, counties and cities shall enforce the rules and regulations of the Civil Aeronautics Administration. (1945, c. 198, s. 10.)

Article 6.

Public Airports and Related Facilities.

§ 63-48. Transferred to § 63-1 by Session Laws 1971, c. 936, s. 2.

§ 63-49. Municipalities may acquire airports.

(a) Every municipality is hereby authorized, through its governing body, to acquire property, real or personal, for the purpose of establishing, constructing, and enlarging airports and other air navigation facilities and to acquire, establish, construct, enlarge, improve, maintain, equip, operate, and regulate such airports and other air navigation facilities and structures and other property incidental to their operation, either within and without the territorial limits of such municipality and within or without this State; to make, prior to any such acquisition, investigations, surveys, and plans; to construct, install, and maintain airport facilities for the servicing of aircraft and for the comfort and accommodation of air travelers; and to purchase and sell equipment and supplies as an incident to the operation of its airport properties. It may not, however, acquire or take over any airport or other air navigation facility owned or controlled by any other municipality of the State without the consent of such municipality. It may use for airport purposes any available property that is now or may at any time hereafter be owned or controlled by it. Such air navigation facilities as are established on airports shall be supplementary to and coordinated in design and operation with those established and operated by the federal government.

(b) All property needed by a municipality for an airport or restricted landing area, or for the enlargement of either, or for other airport purposes, may be acquired by purchase, gift, devise, lease or other means if such municipality is able to agree with the owners of said property on the terms of such acquisition, and otherwise by condemnation in the manner provided by the Chapter entitled Eminent Domain, full power to exercise the right of eminent domain for such purposes being hereby granted every municipality both within and without its territorial limits. If but one municipality is involved and the charter of such municipality prescribes a method of acquiring property by condemnation, proceedings shall be had pursuant to the provisions of such charter and may be followed as to property within or without its territorial limits. The fact that the property needed has been acquired by any agency or corporation authorized to institute condemnation proceedings under power of eminent domain shall not prevent its acquisition by the municipality by the exercise of the right of eminent domain herein conferred when such right is exercised on the approach zone or on the airport site. For the purpose of making surveys and examinations relative to any condemnation proceedings, it shall be lawful to enter upon any land, doing no unnecessary damage. Provided that municipalities building airports after the ratification of this Article shall not acquire by condemnation any property of any corporation engaged in the operation of a railroad or railroad bridge in this State if such property is used in the business of such corporation.

(c) Where necessary, in order to provide unobstructed air space for the landing and taking off of aircraft utilizing airports or restricted landing areas acquired or operated under the provisions of this Article, every municipality is authorized to acquire, in the same manner as is provided for the acquisition of property for airport purposes, easements through or other interests in air space over land or water, interests in airport hazards, or airport hazards outside the boundaries of the airports or restricted landing areas and such other airport protection privileges as are necessary to insure safe approaches to the landing areas of said airports or restricted landing areas and the safe and efficient operation thereof. It is also hereby authorized to acquire, in the same manner, land for the removal of airport hazards and the right of easement for a term of years or perpetually, to place or maintain suitable marks for the daytime marking and suitable lights for the nighttime marking of airport hazards, including the right of ingress or egress to or from such airport hazards for the purpose of maintaining and repairing such lights and marks. This authority shall not be so construed as to limit any right, power or authority to zone property adjacent to airports and restricted landing areas under the provisions of any law of this State.

(d) It shall be unlawful for anyone to build, rebuild, create, or cause to be built, rebuilt, or created any object, or plant, cause to be planted, or permit to grow higher any tree or trees or other vegetation which shall encroach upon any airport protection privileges acquired pursuant to the provisions of this section. Any such encroachment is declared to be a public nuisance and may be abated in the manner prescribed by law for the abatement of public nuisances, or the municipality in charge of the airport or restricted landing area for which airport protection privileges have been acquired as in this section provided, may go upon the land of others and remove any such encroachment without being liable for damages in so doing. (1945, c. 490, s. 2; c. 810; 1981, c. 919, s. 8.)

§ 63-50. Airports a public purpose.

The acquisition of any lands for the purpose of establishing airports or other air navigation facilities; the acquisition of airport protection privileges; the acquisition, establishment, construction, enlargement, improvement, maintenance, equipment and operation of airports and other air navigation facilities, and the exercise of any other powers herein granted to municipalities, are hereby declared to be public, governmental and municipal functions exercised for a public purpose and matters of public necessity, and such lands and other property, easements and privileges acquired and used by such municipalities in the manner and for the purposes enumerated in this Article, shall and are hereby declared to be acquired and used for public, governmental and municipal purposes and as a matter of public necessity. (1945, c. 490, s. 3.)

§ 63-51. Prior acquisition of airport property validated.

Any acquisition of property within or without the limits of any municipality for airports and other air navigation facilities or of airport protection privileges heretofore made by any such municipality in any manner, together with the conveyance and acceptance thereof, is hereby legalized and made valid and effective. (1945, c. 490, s. 4.)

§§ 63-51.1 through 63-52. Repealed by Session Laws 1973, c. 695, s. 10.

§ 63-53. Specific powers of municipalities operating airports.

In addition to the general powers in this Article conferred, and without limitation thereof, a municipality which has established or may hereafter establish airports, restricted landing areas or other air navigation facilities, or which has acquired or set apart or may hereafter acquire or set apart real property for such purpose or purposes is hereby authorized:

(1)   To vest authority for the construction, enlargement, improvement, maintenance, equipment, operation and regulation thereof in an officer, a board or body of such municipality by ordinance or resolution which shall prescribe the powers and duties of such officer, board or body. The expense of such construction, enlargement, improvement, maintenance, equipment, operation and regulation shall be a responsibility of the municipality.

(2)   To adopt and amend all needful rules, regulations and ordinances for the management, government and use of any properties under its control whether within or without the territorial limits of the municipality; to appoint airport guards or police with full police powers; to fix by ordinance, penalties for the violation of said ordinances and enforce said penalties in the same manner

in which penalties prescribed by other ordinances of the municipality are enforced. It may also adopt ordinances designed to safeguard the public upon or beyond the limits of private airports or landing strips within such municipality or its police jurisdiction against the perils and hazards of instrumentalities used in aerial navigation. Such ordinances shall be published as provided by general law or the charter of the municipality for the publication of similar ordinances. They must conform to and be consistent with the laws of this State and shall be kept in conformity, as nearly as may be, with the then current federal legislation governing aeronautics and the regulations duly promulgated thereunder and rules and standards issued from time to time pursuant thereto.

(3)   To lease such airports or other air navigation facilities, or real property acquired or set apart for airport purposes, to private parties, to any municipal or State government or to the national government, or to any department of either thereof, for operation; to lease to private parties, to any municipal or State government or to the national government, or any department of either thereof, for operation or use consistent with the purpose of this Article, space, area, improvements, or equipment on such airports; to sell any part of such airports, other air navigation facilities or real property to any municipal government, or to the United States or to any department or instrumentality thereof, for aeronautical purposes or purposes incidental thereto, and to confer the privileges of concessions of supplying upon its airports goods, commodities, things, services and facilities; provided that in each case in so doing the public is not deprived of its rightful, equal, and uniform use thereof.

(4)   To sell or lease any property, real or personal, acquired for airport purposes and belonging to the municipality, which, in the judgment of its governing body, may not be required for aeronautic purposes in accordance with the laws of this State or the provisions of the charter of the municipality governing the sale or leasing of similar municipally owned property.

(5)   To determine the charge or rental for the use of any properties under its control and the charges for any services or accommodations and the terms and conditions under which such properties may be used, provided that in all cases the public is not deprived of its rightful, equal, and uniform use of such property. Charges shall be reasonable and uniform for the same class of service and established with due regard to the property and improvements used and the expense of operation to the municipality. The municipality shall have and may enforce liens as provided by law for liens and enforcement thereof, for repairs to or improvement or storage or care of any personal property, to enforce the payment of any such charges.

(6) To engage, on an airport, in commercial and industrial land development projects which relate to, develop, or further airborne commerce and cargo and passenger traffic, and, in connection with any project, to improve real estate on an airport and lease that improved real estate to public or private commercial and industrial enterprises, or contract with others to do so.

(7) To exercise all powers necessarily incidental to the exercise of the general and special powers herein created. (1945, c. 490, s. 6; 1991, c. 501, s. 1.)

§ 63-54. Federal aid.

(a) A municipality is authorized to accept, receive, and receipt for federal moneys and other moneys, either public or private, for the acquisition, construction, enlargement, improvement, maintenance, equipment, or operation of airports and other air navigation facilities and sites therefor, and to comply with the provisions of the laws of the United States and any rules and regulations made thereunder for the expenditures of federal moneys upon such airports and other air navigation facilities.

(b) The governing body of any municipality is authorized, if necessary, to comply with any federal law or regulation of any agency thereof to designate the North Carolina Aeronautics Commission as its agents to accept, receive, and receipt for federal moneys in its behalf for airport purposes. Such moneys as are paid over by the United States government shall be paid over to said municipality under such terms and conditions as may be imposed by the United States government in making such grant.

(c) All contracts for the acquisition, construction, enlargement, improvement, maintenance, equipment, or operation of airports or other air navigation facilities made by the municipality shall be made pursuant to the laws of this State governing the making of like contracts, provided, however, that where such acquisition, construction, improvement, enlargement, maintenance, equipment or operation is financed wholly or partly with federal moneys the municipality may let contracts in the manner prescribed by the federal authorities, acting under the laws of the United States and any rules or regulations made thereunder notwithstanding any other State law to the contrary. (1945, c. 490, s. 7.)

§ 63-55. Airports on public waters and reclaimed land.

(a) The powers herein granted to a municipality to establish and maintain airports shall include the power to establish and maintain such airports in, over, and upon any public waters of this State within the limits or jurisdiction of or bordering on the municipality, any submerged land under such public water, and any artificial or reclaimed land which before the artificial making or reclamation thereof constituted a portion of the submerged land under such public waters, and as well the power to construct and maintain terminal buildings, landing floats, causeways, roadways and bridges for approaches to or connecting with the airport, and landing floats and breakwaters for the protection of any such airport.

(b) All the other powers herein granted municipalities with reference to airports on land or granted to them with reference to such airports in, over, and upon public waters, submerged land under public waters, and artificial or reclaimed land. (1945, c. 490, s. 8.)

§ 63-56. Joint operation of airports.

(a) All powers, rights and authority granted to any municipality in this Article may be exercised and enjoyed by two or more municipalities either within or without the territorial limits of either or any of said municipalities and within or without this State, or by any municipality acting jointly with any other municipality therein either within or without this State, provided the laws of such other state permit such joint action.

(b) Any two or more municipalities may enter into agreements with each other, duly authorized by ordinance or resolution, as may be appropriate, for joint action pursuant to the provisions of this section. Concurrent action by the governing bodies of the municipalities involved shall constitute joint action.

(c) Each such agreement shall specify its terms; the proportionate interest which each municipality shall have in the property, facilities and privileges involved, and the proportion of preliminary costs, costs of acquisition, establishment, construction, enlargement, improvement and equipment, and of expenses of maintenance, operation and regulation to be borne by each, and make such other provisions as may be necessary to carry out the provisions of this section. It shall provide for amendments thereof and for conditions and methods of termination; for the disposition of all or any part of the property, facilities and privileges jointly owned if said property, facilities and privileges, or any part thereof, shall cease to be used for the purposes herein provided or if the agreement shall be terminated, and for the distribution of the proceeds received upon any such disposition, and of any funds or other property jointly owned and undisposed of, and the assumption or payment of any indebtedness arising from the joint venture which remains unpaid, upon any such disposition or upon a termination of the agreement.

(d)   Municipalities acting jointly as herein authorized may create a board from the inhabitants of such municipalities for the purpose of acquiring property for establishing, constructing, enlarging, improving, maintaining, equipping, operating and regulating the airports and other air navigation facilities and airport protection privileges to be jointly acquired, controlled, and operated. Such board shall consist of members to be appointed by the governing body of each municipality involved, the number to be appointed by each to be provided for by the agreement for the joint venture. Each member shall serve for such time and upon such terms and as to compensation, if any, as may be provided for in the agreement.

(e)   Each such board shall organize, select officers for terms to be fixed by the agreement, and adopt and from time to time amend rules of procedure.

(f)   Such board may exercise, on behalf of the municipalities acting jointly by which it is appointed, all the powers of each of such municipalities granted by this Article, except as herein provided, subject, however, to such limitations as may be contained in the agreement between such municipalities. Real property, airports, restricted landing areas, air protection privileges, or personal property costing in excess of a sum to be fixed by the joint agreement, may be acquired, and condemnation proceedings may be instituted, only by authority of the governing bodies of each of the municipalities involved. The total amount of expenditures to be made by the board for any purpose in any calendar year shall be determined by the municipalities involved by the approval by each. No real property and no airport, other air navigation facility, or air protection privilege, owned jointly, shall be disposed of by the board, by sale, or otherwise, except by authority of the appointed governing bodies, but the board may lease space, area or improvements and grant concessions on airports for aeronautical purposes or purposes incidental thereto.

(g) Each municipality is authorized and empowered to enact such ordinances as are provided for by this Article, and to fix by such ordinances penalties for the violation thereof, which ordinances shall have the same force and effect within the municipality which enacted them, and on any property controlled by it, either separately or jointly with another municipality, or adjacent thereto, whether within or without the territorial limits of it, or either or any of them, as ordinances of the municipality involved, and may be enforced in such municipality in like manner as are its other ordinances.

(h) Condemnation proceedings may be instituted in the names of two or more municipalities jointly, and the property acquired by such joint condemnation proceedings shall be held by the municipalities as tenants in common, each municipality being entitled to a pro rata interest in said property as the value of its contribution to the acquisition of said property bears to the total cost of acquiring said property, and in the event one municipality desires to acquire property for expansion of or addition to the facilities, and the other or others do not elect to join in the acquisition of such property, such municipality may institute condemnation proceedings in its name individually, and all property now owned or hereafter acquired by a municipal corporation for additions to or expansions of aeronautical facilities operated jointly shall be and remain the sole property of the municipal corporation acquiring same.

(i) For the purpose of providing funds for necessary expenditures in carrying out the provisions of this section, a joint fund shall be created and maintained, into which each of the municipalities involved shall deposit its proportionate share as provided by the joint agreement, and into which shall be paid the revenues obtained from the ownership, control and operation of the airports and other air navigation facilities jointly controlled.

(j) All disbursements from such fund shall be made by order of the board, subject, however, to such limitations as shall be contained in the agreement between such municipalities.

(k) Specific performance of the provisions of any joint agreement entered into as provided for in this section may be enforced as against any party thereto by the other party or parties thereto.

(l) In the event any property is now held or may hereafter be acquired by two or more municipalities for aeronautical purposes, and such municipalities do not agree upon the terms of an agreement, as heretofore provided, and shall not agree to create a board as heretofore provided, then and in that event a board of not less than five nor more than seven members shall be created from the inhabitants of such municipalities, each municipality being entitled to appoint as nearly as possible the proportionate number of representatives on said board as the value of its contribution shall bear to the entire amount of money or property so held by such municipalities for aeronautical purposes. In determining the value of the contribution of any municipality, the value of any funds or property used for the development of said property or the building of facilities on said property shall be taken into consideration.

(m)   The said board shall have all powers given by this Article to boards created by agreements between municipalities, provided, however, that any funds appropriated by a municipality and turned over to the board for aeronautical purposes shall only be used for these purposes designated by the municipality furnishing such funds.

(n)   The actions of such board shall be determined by a majority vote of the members thereof, and a majority of the members shall constitute a quorum for any meeting of the board, and such boards so created shall have full control of all revenues received by reason of the airport or other aeronautical facilities, and shall have power to expend all sums so received for such aeronautical purposes as the board deems proper, and pay over any surplus to municipalities in proportion to their respective interests.

(o)   In the event the aeronautical facilities or any part thereof shall cease to be used for aeronautical purposes, such of the facilities as are jointly owned by two or more municipalities shall be sold, and each municipality shall receive its pro rata proportion of the sums realized from the sale of facilities jointly owned.

(p)   In the event aeronautical facilities are now owned or hereafter acquired by two or more municipalities, and are operated under a board as hereinabove provided, and one or more of such municipalities deem it advisable to expand or enlarge the facilities or invest more money in such facilities, all of the municipalities then having representation on the board shall be entitled, if they so desire, to contribute their pro rata part of such additional investment and maintain their pro rata representation on said board, provided, however, that if one or more of the municipalities involved shall fail to contribute its or their proportionate part of such additional investment, the representation of such municipality on such board shall be readjusted, to the end that the representation of each municipality on said board shall represent as nearly as possible its pro rata contribution to the entire investment.

Provided further that where one municipality at the time of the passage of this Article shall have invested more than one half of the total investment in a jointly owned airport, then, and in that event the minority owner or owners shall be allowed five years from the date of the passage of this Article in which to pay over to the majority owner a sum sufficient to equalize the amount of ownership of the present minority owner or owners with the total ownership of the majority owner. Provided further that this Article shall not be construed to amend or impair in any respect contracts or agreements in effect at the time of the adoption of this Article.

(q)   In the case of an airport board or commission authorized by agreement between two cities, as defined in G.S. 160A-1(2), pursuant to this section, one of which is located partially but not wholly in the county in which the jointly owned airport is located, and where the board or commission provided water and wastewater services off the airport premises before January 1, 1995, the board or commission shall have the authority to acquire, construct, establish, enlarge, improve, maintain, own, operate and contract for the operation of water supply and distribution systems and wastewater collection, treatment and disposal systems of all types, on and off the airport premises. In no event, however, shall such a board or commission be held liable for damages to those off the airport premises for failure to provide such water or wastewater services. (1945, c. 490, s. 9; 1995 (Reg. Sess., 1996), c. 644, s. 1.)

§ 63-57. Powers specifically granted to counties.

(a)   The purposes of this Article are specifically declared to be county purposes as well as generally public, governmental and municipal.

(b)   The powers herein granted to all municipalities are specifically declared to be granted to counties in this State, any other statute to the contrary notwithstanding. (1945, c. 490, s. 10.)

§ 63-58. Municipal jurisdiction exclusive.

Every airport and other air navigation facility controlled and operated by any municipality, or jointly controlled and operated pursuant to the provisions of this

Article, shall, subject to federal and State laws, rules, and regulations, be under the exclusive jurisdiction and control of the municipality or municipalities controlling and operating it, and no other municipality in which such airport or air navigation facility is located shall have any police jurisdiction of the same. (1945, c. 490, s. 11.)

§§ 63-59 through 63-64. Reserved for future codification purposes.

Article 7.

State and Federal Aid; Authority of Department of Transportation.

§ 63-65. Authority of Department of Transportation generally; "airport" defined.

(a)   The Department of Transportation is hereby authorized, subject to the limitations and conditions of this Article, to provide State aid in form of loans and grants to cities, counties, and public airport authorities of North Carolina for the purpose of planning, acquiring, constructing, or improving municipal, county, and other publicly owned or controlled airport facilities, and to authorize related programs of aviation safety, education, promotions, and long-range planning.

(b)   Repealed by Session Laws 1979, c. 148, s. 1. (1967, c. 1006, s. 1; 1975, c. 716, s. 3; 1977, 2nd Sess., c. 1219, s. 39; 1979, c. 148, ss. 1, 5.)

§ 63-66. Administration of Article; powers of Department of Transportation.

The Department of Transportation shall carry out the provisions of this Article. In exercising such power, the Department shall:

(1)   Promote the further development and improvement of air routes, airport facilities, seaplane bases, heliports, protect their approaches and stimulate the development of aviation, commerce and air facilities. In exercising this power, the Department shall prepare and develop goals, objectives, standards and policies for the most efficient and economical expenditure of State funds as may be appropriated for the purposes of this Article.

(2) Publish and make available to aviation interests, the Federal Aviation Administration, and the people of the State generally, current information regarding such criteria, standards, and policies.

(3) Prepare and keep current a State airport plan and submit annual revisions of that plan to the Federal Aviation Administration.

(4) Make a detailed and thorough study of all applications for State assistance authorized herein and make specific recommendations regarding applications to the Federal Aviation Administration for federal grants.

(5) Develop a plan of priorities and allocations of State funds to be revised annually.

(6) Represent the State before all federal agencies and elsewhere where the aviation interests of the State may be affected.

(7) Subject to the availability of funds for the purpose, promote aviation safety throughout the State and conduct such promotional, educational and other programs as may be necessary to keep the people of the State properly informed with respect to aviation and to further aeronautics generally throughout the State. (1967, c. 1006, s. 1; 1973, c. 507, s. 5; c. 1262, ss. 28, 86; c. 1443, s. 1; 1975, c. 716, s. 3; 1979, c. 148, ss. 2, 5; 2011-266, s. 1.21(c).)

§ 63-67. Activities eligible for State aid.

Loans and grants of State funds may be made for the planning, acquisition, construction, or improvement of any airport, seaplane base, or heliport owned or controlled, or which will be owned or controlled by any city, county or public airport authority acting by itself or jointly with any other city or county. An airport, seaplane base, or heliport development project or activity eligible for State aid under this Article shall also be deemed to include projects such as air navigation facilities, aviation easements, and the acquisition of land, lighting, marking, security items, terminal improvements, and the elimination of aviation safety hazards, and the preservation or enhancement of essential air service as defined by the Federal Aviation Act of 1958, as amended. (1967, c. 1006, s. 1; 1973, c. 1443, s. 2; 1977, 2nd Sess., c. 1219, s. 39.1; 1979, c. 148, s. 5; 1987 (Reg. Sess., 1988), c. 1086, s. 164.)

§ 63-68. Limitations on State financial aid.

Grants and loans of funds authorized by this Article shall be subject to the following conditions and limitations:

(1) Loans and grants may be for such projects, activities, or facilities as would in general be eligible for approval by the Federal Aviation Administration or its successor agency or agencies with the exception that the requirement that the airport be publicly owned shall not be applicable. Further, airport terminal and security areas, seaplane bases, and heliports are also eligible for State financial aid.

(2) Loans and grants of State funds shall be limited to a maximum of fifty percent (50%) of the nonfederal share of the total cost of any project for which aid is requested, and shall be made only for the purpose of supplementing such other funds, public or private, as may be available from federal or local sources provided, however, using one hundred percent (100%) State funding in its discretion the Department of Transportation may purchase, install and maintain navigational aids necessary for the safe, efficient use of airspace and may conduct other projects or programs to improve the safety and planning of the air transportation system, including but not limited to, marking serviceable runways and taxiways. Further, the Department of Transportation may contract out the maintenance and installation of state-owned navigational aids when necessary and may give or transfer such aids to the Federal Aviation Administration.

(3) Loans and grants of State funds shall be made from General Assembly appropriations specifically designated for aviation improvement, and from no other source. The Department of Transportation may utilize the State Aviation Grant Funds to cover the direct and indirect costs of administering airport grant projects, other services authorized by this Article including planning, and the costs of services provided by nonadministrative Department of Transportation divisions or other State agencies in connection with these projects.

(4) Notwithstanding the provisions of this section or G.S. 63-67, the Department of Transportation may allow up to ten percent (10%) of State aviation grant funds to be used for maintenance on General Aviation and Air Carrier Airports having a Department of Transportation approved maintenance

plan on a seventy-five percent (75%) local - twenty-five percent (25%) State basis.

(5) Notwithstanding the provisions of this section, the Department of Transportation may allow loans and grants of State funds up to eighty percent (80%) of the nonfederal share of the total cost of the development of new or unpaved publicly owned airports identified in the North Carolina Airport System Plan, provided that such funding shall be limited to land acquisition, site preparation, basic runway, taxiway, and apron system construction, together with associated lighting and navigational aids, and construction of the primary airport access road. Electronic navigational aids, terminal buildings, access taxiways, and other items eligible for State airport aid at the rate of fifty percent (50%) of the nonfederal share of project cost shall not be eligible for the foregoing eighty percent (80%) State funding, even though constructed as part of the initial airport development.

(6) Notwithstanding the provisions of this section, the Department of Transportation may allow loans and grants of State funds up to ninety percent (90%) of the total cost of the development of new or unpaved publicly owned rural airports identified in the North Carolina Airport System Plan and receiving no federal funding. Such State funding shall be limited to land acquisition, site preparation, basic runway, taxiway, and apron system construction, together with associated lighting and navigational aids, and construction of the primary airport access road.

The Department of Transportation shall develop rules and regulations to define rural airports. (1967, c. 1006, s. 1; 1969, c. 293; 1973, c. 1262, s. 28; c. 1443, s. 3; 1975, c. 716, s. 3; 1977, 2nd Sess., c. 1219, s. 39.2; 1979, c. 148, ss. 3, 5; c. 149; 1981, c. 1117, ss. 1, 2; 1983, c. 319; 1983 (Reg. Sess., 1984), c. 1094; 1985, c. 782; 1989, c. 636; 1991, c. 430, s. 1.)

§ 63-69. Sources of State funds.

State financial assistance under this Article shall be limited to appropriations of funds made for the purpose by the General Assembly to the Department of Transportation, or to private funds which may become available to the Department for such purpose. (1967, c. 1006, s. 1; 1973, c. 1262, s. 86; 1975, c. 716, s. 3; 1979, c. 148, s. 5.)

§ 63-70. Acceptance, receipt, accounting, and expenditure of State and federal funds.

All North Carolina municipalities, counties and public airport authorities are hereby authorized to accept, receive, receipt for, disburse and expend State funds, and other funds, public and private, which may be made available to them to accomplish any purpose of this Article. All federal funds accepted and expended by any municipality or county shall be accepted, accounted for, and expended according to such terms and conditions as may be prescribed by the United States and not inconsistent with State law. All State funds accepted by any municipality, county or public airport authority shall be accepted, accounted for, and expended according to such terms and conditions as may be prescribed by the Department of Transportation. Unless otherwise prescribed by the federal or State agency from which funds were made available, the chief financial officer of the municipality, county or public airport authority shall deposit all funds received and keep the same in separate funds according to the purpose for which they were received. The accounting of all such funds shall be subject to the municipal and county fiscal control acts. (1967, c. 1006, s. 1; 1973, c. 1262, s. 86; 1975, c. 716, s. 3; 1979, c. 148, s. 5.)

§ 63-71. Receipt of federal grants.

(a) The Department of Transportation is hereby designated the State agency to accept grants for public airport development and improvements made by the United States pursuant to federal law. The Department shall have authority to comply with federal-aid provisions, to obtain and to disburse said grants in accordance with applicable federal laws and regulations, and to enter into contracts with the federal government, municipalities, counties, or airport authorities in connection with said grants. The Department shall also have the authority to enter into contracts with the Federal Aviation Administration or its successor agency for aeronautics related purposes, including joint acquisition and installation of aviation related equipment in accordance with the procurement procedures of the Federal Aviation Administration where such method of acquisition would result in a cost savings to the Department.

(b) The Department of Transportation shall have authority to act as an agent of any public agency which, either individually or jointly with one or more other public agencies, submits to the Secretary of Transportation of the United States an application for federal aid in connection with airport development, improvement, or planning. (1969, c. 1109, ss. 1, 2; 1973, c. 1262, s. 86; 1975, c. 716, s. 3; 1979, c. 148, ss. 4, 5; 1983 (Reg. Sess., 1984), c. 1093.)

§ 63-72. Authority of Department of Transportation to operate airports and expend funds therefor.

The Department is authorized to operate state-owned or leased airports or any airport for which the State has obtained a special use permit to operate. The Department may expend funds appropriated for grants to airports for the purpose of operating, maintaining, and improving state-owned or leased airports, or any airport for which the State has obtained a special use permit to operate and maintain. (1969, c. 1109, s. 3; 1973, c. 1262, s. 86; 1975, c. 716, s. 3; 1979, c. 148, s. 5.)

§ 63-73. Letting of contracts.

All contracts that the Department of Transportation may let for construction, repair, maintenance or those services listed in 49 U.S.C. App. § 2210(a)(16) in furtherance of this Article shall be let in accordance with the provisions of G.S. 136-28.1. (1983 (Reg. Sess., 1984), c. 1033, s. 1; 1991, c. 430, s. 2.)

§§ 63-74 through 63-77. Reserved for future codification purposes.

Article 8.

North Carolina Special Airport Districts Act.

§ 63-78. Short title.

This Article shall be known and may be cited as the "North Carolina Special Airport Districts Act." (1979, c. 689, s. 1.)

§ 63-79. Definitions.

As used in this Article, the following words and terms shall have the following meanings, unless the context shall indicate another or different meaning or intent:

(1) "Aeronautical facilities" means airports, runways, terminals, hangars and other facilities related thereto;

(2) "District" means a special airport district created under the provisions of this Article;

(3) "District board" or "board" means a special airport district board established under the provisions of this Article as the governing body of a district;

(4) "Governing body" means the board, commission, council or other body, by whatever name it may be known, of a unit of local government in which the general legislative powers thereof are vested;

(5) "Unit" or "unit of local government" means counties, cities, towns and incorporated villages. (1979, c. 689, s. 2.)

§ 63-80. Procedure for creation of districts; concurrent resolutions; notice and public hearing; submission of question to voters; publication of notice; actions to set aside proceedings.

(a) Any unit of local government in this State and any one or more other units of local government in this State may, by concurrent resolutions adopted by the governing body of each such unit, create special airport districts under the provisions of this Article which shall be public bodies corporate and politic and political subdivisions of the State. The district shall comprise the territory of the participating units. The district shall be designated "Special Airport District of __" and shall be of such duration as the participating units shall determine.

(b)   Prior to the adoption of any resolutions creating a special airport district, there shall be held a joint public hearing convened by the governing bodies of each of the participating units of government concerning the creation of the proposed special airport district. The presiding officers of the governing body of the units proposing to create such district shall name a time and place within the proposed district at which the public hearing shall be held. The presiding officers shall give prior notice of such hearing at the courthouse of the county or counties within which the district lies and also by publication at least once a week for two successive weeks in a newspaper having general circulation in the proposed district, the first publication to be at least 30 days prior to such hearing. In the event all matters pertaining to the creation of such special airport district cannot be concluded at such hearing, such hearing may be continued to a time and place within the proposed district determined by the governing body of each of the respective units of local government.

(c)   Following the joint public hearing but prior to the adoption by a unit of local government of any resolution creating a special airport district, the governing body of such unit may submit the question of the unit's participation in a special airport district to the qualified voters of such unit. The form of the question as stated on the ballot shall be in substantially the following words:

"Shall the governing body of _____ approve _____'s participation in the proposed _____ special airport district?

[ ] YES   [ ] NO"

If a majority of the qualified voters of the unit who vote thereon approve such participation, the governing body of such unit may adopt a resolution creating the particular special airport district. The election shall be conducted in accordance with G.S. 163-287 and the results thereof certified, declared and published in the same manner as bond elections within the unit.

(d)   Following the adoption of the resolutions creating the district by the governing body of each participating unit, the presiding officer of each such governing body shall cause to be published a single time in a newspaper circulating within the unit a notice in substantially the following form:

The governing body of _____ and the governing body of ___ passed resolutions on ____, __, and on ____, __, respectively, creating the Special Airport District of _____. Notice of the creation of such special airport district is hereby given on the date hereof. Any action or proceeding questioning the validity of the resolutions or the creation of the special airport district must be commenced within 30 days after the publication of this notice.

_____

Presiding Officer

(e) Any action or proceeding in any court to set aside the resolutions or the creation of a special airport district, or to obtain any other relief upon the ground that such resolutions or any proceeding or action taken with respect to the creation of such district is invalid, must be commenced within 60 days after the publication of the foregoing notice. After the expiration of such period of limitation, no right of action or defense founded upon the invalidity of the resolutions or the creation of the special airport district shall be asserted nor shall the validity of the resolutions or the creation of such airport district be open to question in any court upon any ground whatever, except in an action or proceeding commenced within such period. (1979, c. 689, s. 3; 1999-456, s. 59; 2013-381, s. 10.4.)

§ 63-81. District board; composition, appointment, terms and oaths; organization; meetings; quorum.

(a) Appointment of Board for District. - The board of the special airport district shall be composed of two representatives from each of the participating units of local government appointed annually by the governing body of each of said units of local government, respectively, from among their members at the first regular meeting thereof in January. Each member of the district board must be a member of the governing body of the unit of local government by which he was appointed. Membership on the district board may be held in addition to the offices authorized by G.S. 128-1 or 128-1.1. Said representatives shall hold office from their appointment until their successors are appointed and qualified, except that when any member of the district board ceases for any reason to be a member of the governing body of the unit of local government by which he was appointed, he shall simultaneously cease to be a member of said district board. Upon the occurrence of any vacancy on said district board, the vacancy shall be filled within 30 days after notice thereof by the governing body of the participating unit of local government having a vacancy in its representation. Within 30 days after the expiration of the period set forth in G.S. 63-80 hereof, the governing body of each participating unit of local government shall appoint its representatives to hold office until successors shall be appointed in the manner hereinbefore provided. Each member of the district board, before entering upon his duties, shall take and subscribe an oath or affirmation to support the Constitution and laws of the United States and of this State and to discharge faithfully the duties of his office; and a record of each such oath shall be filed in the minutes of the respective participating units of local government.

(b) District Board Procedures. - The district board shall meet regularly at such places and on such dates as are determined by the board. Special meetings may be called by the chairman on his own initiative and shall be called by him upon request of two or more members of the board. All members shall be notified in writing at least 24 hours in advance of such meeting. A majority of the members of the district board shall constitute a quorum. No vacancy in the membership of the district board shall impair the right of a quorum to exercise all the rights and perform all the duties of the district board. No action, other than an action to recess or adjourn, shall be taken except upon a majority vote of the entire authorized membership of said district board. Each member, including the chairman, shall be entitled to vote on any question.

(c) District Board Officers. - The district board shall elect annually in January from among its members a chairman, vice-chairman, secretary and treasurer. (1979, c. 689, s. 4.)

§ 63-82. Procedure for inclusion of additional units of local government; notice and hearing; actions to set aside proceedings.

(a) If, at any time subsequent to the creation of a special airport district, there shall be filed with the district board a resolution of the governing body of a unit of local government requesting inclusion in the district of such unit of local government, and if the district board shall favor the inclusion in the district of such unit of local government, the district board shall notify the governing body of each of the participating units of local government within which the district lies and shall propose to such governing bodies an appropriate amendment of the concurrent resolutions creating the special airport district.

(b) The procedures set forth in G.S. 63-79 regarding the creation of a special airport district shall apply to the inclusion in such special airport district of additional units of local government.

(c) If all of the participating units of local government agree to the amendment of the concurrent resolutions creating the special airport district to include such unit of local government in the special airport district, the presiding officer of the governing body of each of such participating units of local government, including the unit proposed to be included, shall cause to be published in the manner provided in G.S. 63-79, a notice of the inclusion of such unit of local government.

(d) Any action or proceeding in any court to set aside such amendatory resolutions providing for the inclusion of a unit of local government within a special airport district or to obtain any other relief upon the ground that such amendatory resolutions or any proceeding or action taken with respect to the inclusion of the unit of local government within the district is invalid, must be commenced within 30 days after publication of the notice. After the expiration of such period of limitation, no right of action or defense founded upon the invalidity of the amendatory resolutions or the inclusion of the unit of local government in the district shall be asserted, nor shall the validity of the amendatory resolutions or the inclusion of the unit of local government in the district be open to question in any court upon any ground whatever, except in an action or proceeding commenced within such period. Provided that no such action or proceeding to set aside such amendatory resolutions shall impair or otherwise affect the conclusivity of the concurrent resolutions as provided in G.S. 63-80.

(e) Immediately following the inclusion of any additional unit of local government within an existing district, members representing such additional unit of local government shall be appointed to the district board in the manner provided in G.S. 63-81 hereof.

(f) The annexation by a participating unit of local government of an area lying outside the district shall not be construed as the inclusion within the district of an additional unit of local government within the meaning of the provisions of this section; but any such area so annexed shall become a part of the district and shall be subject to all debts and supplemental tax obligations thereof. (1979, c. 689, s. 5.)

§ 63-83. Powers of districts generally.

Each district shall be deemed to be a public body and body politic and corporate exercising public and essential governmental functions to aid counties, cities, towns, incorporated villages and airport authorities in constructing and financing aeronautical facilities and enhancing the security of airport revenue bonds issued by counties, cities, towns, incorporated villages and airport authorities, and each district is hereby authorized and empowered:

(1)   To adopt bylaws for the regulation of its affairs and the conduct of its business not in conflict with this or other laws;

(2)   To adopt an official seal and alter the same at pleasure;

(3)   To maintain an office at such place or places in the district as it may designate;

(4)   To sue and be sued in its own name, plead and be impleaded;

(5)   To acquire in the name of the district by gift, purchase or exercise of the power of eminent domain any improved or unimproved lands or rights-in-land and make a conveyance thereof to a county, city, town, incorporated village or airport authority for use as or in connection with aeronautical facilities;

(6)   To enter into contracts with any person, firm or corporation, public or private, or any airport authority or other public authority or governmental entity, upon such terms as the district board may determine with respect to aeronautical facilities owned or operated by counties, cities, towns, incorporated villages or airport authorities;

(7)   To lend to any airport authority heretofore or hereafter created by statute such sum or sums of money and at such rate of interest and upon such other terms as the district and the airport authority shall contract and agree upon, for the purpose of establishing, enlarging, improving, or maintaining any airport under the control of such airport authority;

(8)   To issue bonds or other obligations of the district as hereinafter provided and apply the proceeds thereof to the financing of aeronautical facilities owned or operated by counties, cities, towns, incorporated villages or airport authorities or to the retirement of bonds theretofore issued by such units for such purposes or by the district and to refund, whether or not in advance of maturity or the earliest redemption date, any such bonds or other obligations;

(9) To levy for the life of airport revenue bonds issued by counties, cities, towns, incorporated villages or airport authorities an annual property tax for operating supplements or debt service reserved supplements as hereinafter provided;

(10) To cause taxes to be levied and collected upon all taxable property within the district sufficient to meet the obligations of the district; and

(11) To do all acts and things necessary or convenient to carry out the powers granted by this Article. (1979, c. 689, s. 6.)

§ 63-84. Bonds and notes authorized.

In addition to the powers hereinbefore granted, a district shall have power to issue bonds and notes pursuant to the provisions of the Local Government Bond Act and the Local Government Revenue Bond Act for the purpose of financing aeronautical facilities and to refund such bonds and notes, whether or not in advance of their maturity or earliest redemption date, and such bond or note issues may include bonds or notes, the proceeds of which are to be applied to the retirement of outstanding bonds or notes of counties, cities, towns, incorporated villages or airport authorities theretofore issued for the purpose of financing aeronautical facilities. (1979, c. 689, s. 7.)

§ 63-85. Taxes for supplementing airport revenue bond projects.

A district shall have power from time to time to levy taxes or cause the levy thereof for operating supplements and debt service reserve supplements with respect to aeronautical facilities under and subject to the Local Government Revenue Bond Act. (1979, c. 689, s. 8.)

§ 63-86. Determination of tax rate by district board; levy and collection of tax; remittance and deposit of funds.

After each assessment for taxes following the creation of the district, the board or boards of commissioners of the county or counties within which the district is located shall file with the district board the valuation of assessable property within the district. The district board shall then determine the amount of funds to be raised by taxation for the ensuing year in excess of available funds to provide for the payment of interest on and principal of all outstanding general obligation bonds as the same shall become due and payable and to pay all obligations incurred by the district in the performance of its lawful undertakings and functions.

The district board shall determine the number of cents per hundred dollars necessary to raise said amount and certify such rate to the appropriate board or boards of commissioners of the appropriate county or counties. The board or boards of commissioners of such county or counties shall include the number of cents per hundred dollars certified by the district board in its next annual levy against all taxable property within the district, which tax shall be collected as other county taxes are collected, and every month the amount of tax so collected shall be remitted to the district board and deposited by the district board in a separate account in a bank in the State. Such levy may include an amount for reimbursing the particular county for the cost to the county of levying and collecting any such taxes. The officer or officers having charge or custody of the funds of the district shall require security for protection of deposits as provided in the Local Government Budget and Fiscal Control Act. (1979, c. 689, s. 9.)

§ 63-87. Bond elections.

Elections for the purpose of authorizing the levy of taxes for the issuance of bonds shall be called by the district board and shall be conducted in accordance with G.S. 163-287 and the results canvassed by the boards of elections having jurisdiction within the participating units. Such results shall be certified to the district board and such board shall certify and declare the result of the election and publish a statement of the result once as provided in the Local Government Bond Act. (1979, c. 689, s. 10; 2013-381, s. 10.5.)

§ 63-88. Advances.

Any participating unit of local government is hereby authorized to make advances, from any moneys that may be available for such purpose, in connection with the creation of the special airport district and to provide for the preliminary expenses of such district. Any such advances may be repaid to such participating units of local government from the proceeds of the bonds issued by such district or from other available funds of the district. (1979, c. 689, s. 11.)

§ 63-89. Inconsistent laws declared inapplicable.

All general, special or local laws, or parts thereof, inconsistent herewith, are hereby declared to be inapplicable, unless otherwise specified in the provisions of this Article. (1979, c. 689, s. 12.)

Article 9.

Changes in Special Use Airspaces.

§ 63-90. Public purpose declared.

It is the intent of the General Assembly that the legislative branch review and comment on all applications and actions of the Federal Aviation Administration concerning the creation of or changes in special use airspaces for aircraft operation over North Carolina. (1987, c. 494, s. 1.)

§ 63-91. General Assembly review and approval.

The Division of Aviation of the Department of Transportation shall bring before the General Assembly or the Joint Legislative Commission on Governmental Operations all applications to the Federal Aviation Administration and all proposed rule changes by the Federal Aviation Administration for the creation of or changes in special use airspaces, including military operation areas and restricted areas for aircraft operation over North Carolina during the period for public comment. If the General Assembly is in session during that period, information on the pending application or rule change shall be presented to the standing Transportation Committees of the House of Representatives and the

Senate. If the comment period occurs when the General Assembly is not in session then the Division of Aviation of the Department of Transportation shall bring the relevant information before the Joint Legislative Commission on Governmental Operations. The General Assembly or the Joint Legislative Commission on Governmental Operations will then review and comment on those applications. (1987, c. 494, s. 1.)

§ 63-92. Effect of General Assembly review.

(a) If the General Assembly or the Joint Legislative Commission on Governmental Operations determines that the proposed change is in the best interests of the citizens of this State, then the Division of Aviation of the Department of Transportation shall notify the Federal Aviation Administration of the General Assembly's official position on the pending application or rule change when it submits the State's official position on the pending application or rule change.

(b) If the General Assembly or the Joint Legislative Commission on Governmental Operations determines that the proposed change is not in the best interests of the citizens of this State, then the Division of Aviation of the Department of Transportation shall notify the Federal Aviation Administration of the General Assembly's official position opposing the pending application or rule change when it submits the State's official position on the pending application or rule change. (1987, c. 494, s. 1.)

Chapter 63A.

North Carolina Global TransPark Authority.

§ 63A-1. Short title and intent.

This Chapter is the "North Carolina Global TransPark Authority Act." It is enacted in part pursuant to Article V, Section 13, of the North Carolina Constitution with the intent that the body politic and corporate created by this Chapter shall have all power and authority as may be provided to it under that section of the Constitution. (1991, c. 749, s. 1; 1993 (Reg. Sess., 1994), c. 777, s. 4(b).)

§ 63A-2. Definitions.

The following definitions apply in this Chapter:

(1) Aircraft. - A contrivance that is used or designed for flight.

(2) Airport project. - Any of the following that is part of or is used in connection with a cargo airport or a facility at a cargo airport complex site and is not a special user project:

a. Land, equipment, or buildings or other structures, whether located on one or more sites.

b. The addition to or the rehabilitation, improvement, renovation, or enlargement of any property described in subpart a.

The term includes infrastructure improvements, such as improvements to railroad facilities, roads, bridges, and water, sewer, or electric utilities even if not located on a cargo airport complex site. An airport project may include a facility leased to one or more entities under a true lease.

(3) Authority. - The North Carolina Global TransPark Authority.

(4) Board. - The Board of Directors of the Authority.

(5) Bonds. - The revenue bonds or other interest bearing obligations authorized to be issued by the Authority under this Chapter.

(6) Cargo airport. - Any area of land or water that is designed for the landing and takeoff of aircraft, any appurtenant area used or suitable for airport buildings or other airport facilities, and any appurtenant right-of-way. In addition to facilities for the transportation of cargo by aircraft, a cargo airport may contain facilities to shelter, service, or repair aircraft and facilities to discharge and receive passengers.

(7) Cargo airport complex. - A cargo airport and all other facilities, including private facilities, related to the cargo airport that are located within the cargo airport complex site.

(8) Cargo airport complex site. - The area designated by the Authority as the location of a cargo airport complex. An area may not be so designated by

the Authority unless all or a substantial portion of the land on which the cargo airport is located or is to be located is or shall be owned by the Authority or is or shall be controlled by the Authority pursuant to lease, joint operating agreement, or other contractual arrangements.

(9) Costs. - The capital cost of a project, including:

a. The costs of doing any or all of the following:

1. Acquiring, constructing, erecting, providing, developing, installing, furnishing, and equipping.

2. Reconstructing, remodeling, altering, renovating, replacing, refurnishing, and reequipping.

3. Enlarging, expanding, and extending.

4. Demolishing, relocating, improving, grading, draining, landscaping, paving, widening, and resurfacing.

b. The costs of all property, both real and personal and both improved and unimproved, and of plants, works, appurtenances, structures, facilities, furnishings, machinery, equipment, vehicles, easements, water rights, air rights, franchises, and licenses used or useful in connection with the project.

c. The costs of demolishing or moving structures from land acquired and acquiring land to which the structures are to be moved.

d. Financing charges, including estimated interest during the acquisition or construction of a project and for one year thereafter.

e. The costs of services to provide plans, specifications, studies, reports, surveys, and estimates of costs and revenues.

f. The costs of paying any interim financing, including principal, interest and premium, related to the acquisition or construction of the project.

g. Administrative and legal expenses and administrative charges.

h. The costs of obtaining bond and reserve fund insurance and investment contracts, of credit-enhancement facilities, liquidity facilities, and interest-rate agreements, and of establishing and maintaining debt service and other reserves.

i. Any other services, costs, and expenses necessary or incidental to the project.

(10) Credit facility. - An agreement with a banking institution, an insurance institution, an investment institution, or other financial institution located inside or outside the United States of America that provides for prompt payment, whether at maturity, presentment, or tender for purchase, redemption, or acceleration, of part or all of the principal or purchase price, redemption premium, if any, and interest on a bond or note issued by the Authority and for repayment of the institution.

(11) Financing agreement. - A written instrument establishing the rights and responsibilities of the Authority and the operator concerning a special user project financed by the issuance of bonds. A financing agreement may be a lease, a lease and lease-back, a sale and lease-back, a lease purchase, an installment sale and purchase agreement, a conditional sales agreement, a secured or unsecured loan agreement, or other similar contract, and may involve property in addition to the property financed with the bonds.

(12) Local Government Commission. - The Local Government Commission of the Department of State Treasurer, established by Article 2 of Chapter 159 of the General Statutes.

(13) Notes. - Revenue notes or revenue bond anticipation notes issued by the Authority under this Chapter.

(14) Obligor. - A person, including an operator, who has entered into a financing or other agreement obligating the person to make payments to the Authority or to holders of bonds issued to finance a special user project.

(15) Operator. - The person entitled to the use or occupancy of a special user project.

(16) Par formula. - A provision or formula to make periodic adjustments in the interest rate of a bond or note, including:

a. A provision for an adjustment to keep the purchase price of the bond or note in the open market as close to par as possible.

b. A provision for an adjustment based on one or more percentages of a prime rate or base rate that may vary or apply for specified periods of time.

c. Any other provision that does not materially and adversely affect the financial position of the Authority and the marketing of the bonds or notes at a reasonable interest cost to the Authority.

(17) Person. - Any person, corporation, partnership, association, trust, or other legal entity.

(18) Project. - An airport project or a special user project.

(19) Revenues. - For a special user project, the term means rents, fees, charges, payments, proceeds, or other income or profit derived from the special user project or from the financing agreement or security document for the special user project. For an airport project, the term means rents, fees, charges, payments, proceeds, or other income or profit derived from the airport project or from any pledge of nontax revenues, appropriation, or payment made by the State or a county in which the cargo airport is located.

(20) Security document. - One or more written instruments establishing the rights and responsibilities of the Authority and the holders of bonds issued to finance a special user project. A security document may provide for, or be in the form of an agreement with, a trustee for the benefit of the bondholders. A security document may contain an assignment, pledge, mortgage, or other encumbrance of part or all of the Authority's interest in, or right to receive revenues from, a special user project or any other property provided by the operator or other obligor under a financing agreement. A financing agreement and a security document may be combined as one instrument.

(21) Special user project. - Any land, equipment, or buildings or other structures located on one or more sites within a cargo airport complex site and the addition to or the rehabilitation, improvement, renovation, or enlargement of a structure located within a cargo airport complex site when the property is to be used as or in connection with any of the following:

a. An undertaking for industry, including an industrial or a manufacturing factory, mill, assembly plant, or fabricating plant, a freight terminal, an industrial research, development, or laboratory facility, or an industrial processing or distribution facility for industrial or manufactured products.

b. A commercial, processing, mining, transportation, distribution, storage, marine, aviation, or environmental facility or improvement.

c. Any combination of items mentioned in subparts a. and b.

A special user project, during its economic life, is to be principally used by one or more for-profit entities other than as lessee under a true lease. A special user project may include all appurtenances and incidental facilities such as land, a headquarters or office facility, warehouses, distribution centers, access roads, sidewalks, utilities, railway sidings, trucking and similar facilities, parking facilities, waterways, docks, wharves, and other improvements necessary or convenient for the construction, maintenance, and operation of any structure.

(22) True lease. - A lease that has a fair market value rental and is not treated as a financing lease or installment sale for federal tax law purposes. (1991, c. 749, s. 1; 1991 (Reg. Sess., 1992), c. 900, s. 108(a); 1993 (Reg. Sess., 1994), c. 777, s. 4(c).)

§ 63A-3. Creation of Authority and Board.

(a) Creation. - The North Carolina Global TransPark Authority is created as a body corporate and politic having the powers and jurisdiction as provided under this Chapter or any other law. The Authority is a State agency created to perform essential governmental and public functions. The Authority shall be located within the Department of Transportation and shall be subject to the direction and supervision of the Secretary.

(b) Board of Directors. - The Authority shall be governed by a Board of Directors. The Board shall consist of at least the following 20 members:

(1) Six members appointed by the Governor. One member shall be representative of the economic development industry, two members shall be representative of the commercial real estate development industry, two members shall be representative of the banking and finance industry, and one member shall be representative of environmental interests. Of the Governor's six appointments, at least one member shall come from each of the State's three regions: Western, Piedmont, and Eastern.

(2) Three members appointed by the General Assembly upon the recommendation of the Speaker of the House of Representatives in accordance with G.S. 120-121. One member shall be representative of the aerospace and aviation industry, one member shall be representative of advanced manufacturing industries, and one member shall be representative of the logistics and supply chain management industry.

(3) Three members appointed by the General Assembly upon the recommendation of the President Pro Tempore of the Senate in accordance with G.S. 120-121. One member shall be representative of the aerospace and aviation industry, one member shall be representative of the emergency response and disaster relief industries, and one member shall be representative of the defense and security industry.

(4) The State Treasurer, who shall serve as an ex officio nonvoting member.

(5) The President of the North Carolina System of Community Colleges, provided that the President of the North Carolina Community Colleges may instead appoint to the Board of Directors one member of the board of trustees of a community college or one president of a community college. If such an appointment is made, the appointee shall serve at the pleasure of the President.

(6) The President of The University of North Carolina, provided that the President of the University of North Carolina may instead appoint to the Board of Directors one member of the board of trustees of a constituent institution of The University of North Carolina, or one chancellor of a constituent institution of The University of North Carolina. If such an appointment is made, the appointee shall serve at the pleasure of the President.

(7) The Chairman of the State Ports Authority.

(8) One member appointed by the board of county commissioners of any county in which the cargo airport complex site is located.

(9) One member appointed by the city council of the city which is a county seat of any county in which the cargo airport complex site is located.

(10) The Commissioner of Agriculture.

(11) The Secretary of the Department of Commerce.

Within 90 days after the Authority acquires land, either by purchase or condemnation, for development as part of a cargo airport complex site, the board of county commissioners in any county in which a portion of the land is located and the city council of the city which is the county seat of the county shall, by resolution, each appoint a person to serve as a member of the Board. If the board of commissioners or the city council appoints one of its own members to the Board, the county commissioner or the member of the city council who is appointed is considered to be serving on the Board as an ex officio voting member as part of the duties of the office of county commissioner or the office of city council member, in accordance with G.S. 128-1.2, and is not considered to be serving in a separate office. Notwithstanding G.S. 116-31(h), a member of the board of trustees of a constituent institution of The University of North Carolina appointed to the Board of Directors under subdivision (6) of this subsection may concurrently serve on the board of trustees and the Board of Directors. Notwithstanding any other provision of law, the Governor may serve on the Board of Directors by his own appointment on or after July 16, 1991, under subdivision (1) of this subsection.

As the holder of an office, each member of the Board shall take the oath required by Article VI, § 7 of the North Carolina Constitution before assuming the duties of a Board member.

(c) Repealed by Session Laws 2011-340, s. 1(c), effective July 1, 2011.

(d) Terms. - The terms of the initial members appointed by the Governor or the General Assembly end June 30, 1993. The initial term of a member appointed by a board of county commissioners or by a city council ends on the second June 30 after the appointment. Subsequent appointments by a board of county commissioners or by a city council shall be for terms of four years. The seven members appointed by the Governor for subsequent terms shall be appointed for terms of two years ending on June 30 of each odd-numbered year. The six members appointed by the General Assembly for subsequent terms shall be divided into two classes. The first class shall consist of three persons, two of whom shall be appointed upon recommendation of the Speaker of the House of Representatives and one of whom shall be appointed upon recommendation of the President Pro Tempore of the Senate, to serve an initial term expiring June 30, 1995, with subsequent terms expiring each fourth June 30th thereafter. The second class shall consist of three persons, two of whom shall be appointed upon recommendation of the President Pro Tempore of the Senate and one of whom shall be appointed upon recommendation of the

Speaker of the House of Representatives, to serve an initial term expiring June 30, 1997, with subsequent terms expiring each fourth June 30th thereafter.

(d1)   Notwithstanding the terms of board members appointed by the General Assembly as specified in subsection (d) of this section, terms of board members appointed by the General Assembly shall end June 30, 2011. After June 30, 2011, the six members appointed by the General Assembly shall be divided into two classes. The first class shall consist of three persons, two of whom shall be appointed upon recommendation of the Speaker of the House of Representatives and one of whom shall be appointed upon recommendation of the President Pro Tempore of the Senate, to serve an initial term expiring June 30, 2013, with subsequent terms expiring each fourth June 30th thereafter. The second class shall consist of three persons, two of whom shall be appointed upon recommendation of the President Pro Tempore of the Senate and one of whom shall be appointed upon recommendation of the Speaker of the House of Representatives, to serve an initial term expiring June 30, 2015, with subsequent terms expiring each fourth June 30th thereafter.

(e)   Chair and Vice-chair of the Board. - The Governor shall designate one of the members appointed by the Governor as the Chair of the Board. The Governor shall convene the first meeting of the Board, at which time the members of the Board shall elect from their membership a Vice-chair of the Board.

(f)   Vacancies. - All members of the Board shall remain in office until their successors are appointed and qualify. A vacancy in an appointment made by the Governor or a board of county commissioners shall be filled by the Governor or the board of county commissioners for the remainder of the unexpired term. A vacancy in an appointment made by the General Assembly shall be filled in accordance with G.S. 120-122. A person appointed to fill a vacancy shall qualify in the same manner as a person appointed for a full term.

(g)   Removal of Board Members. - The Governor may remove any member of the Board for misfeasance, malfeasance, or nonfeasance in accordance with G.S. 143B-13(d). The person who appointed a member of the Board may remove the member for using improper influence in accordance with G.S. 143B-13(c).

(h)   Organization of the Board. - The Board shall adopt bylaws with respect to the calling of meetings, quorums, voting procedures, the keeping of records, and other organizational and administrative matters as the Board may determine. A quorum shall consist of a majority of the members of the Board. No vacancy in the membership of the Board shall impair the right of a quorum to exercise all rights and to perform all the duties of the Board and the Authority.

(i)   Compensation of the Board. - No part of the revenues or assets of the Authority shall inure to the benefit of or be distributable to the members of the Board or officers or other private persons. The members of the Board shall receive no salary for their services but shall be entitled to receive per diem and allowances in accordance with the provisions of G.S. 138-5.

(j)   Treasurer. - The Board shall select the Authority's treasurer. The Board shall require a surety bond of the appointee in the amount as the Board may fix, and the premium shall be paid by the Authority as a necessary expense of the Authority.

(k)   Executive Director and other Employees. - The Board shall appoint an executive director, whose salary shall be fixed by the Board, to serve at its pleasure. The executive director or a person designated by the executive director shall appoint, employ, dismiss, and, within the limits of available funding, fix the compensation of other employees as considered necessary.

(l)   Office. - The Board shall establish an office for the transaction of the Authority's business at the place the Board finds advisable or necessary to implement the provisions of this Chapter. (1991, c. 749, s. 1; 1991 (Reg. Sess., 1992), c. 900, s. 108(b)-(e); 1993 (Reg. Sess., 1994), c. 777, s. 4(d), (d1); 2011-340, ss. 1(a)-(d); 2012-194, s. 17.)

§ 63A-4. Powers of the Authority.

(a)   The Authority shall have all of the powers necessary to execute the provisions of this Chapter, which shall include at least the following powers:

(1)   The powers of a corporate body, including the power to sue and be sued, to make contracts, to adopt and use a common seal, and to alter the adopted seal as needed.

(2)   To establish, finance, purchase, construct, operate, and regulate cargo airport complexes and to own, finance, lease, sell, or manage real or personal property.

(3) To charge and collect fees and rents for the use of the cargo airport complexes or for services rendered in the operation of the complexes.

(4) To contract and enter into agreements with the State, local governments, other authorities of North Carolina, and other states for the interchange of business and to facilitate the business of cargo airport complexes.

(5) To rent, lease, purchase, acquire, own, encumber, dispose of, or mortgage real or personal property, including the power to acquire property by eminent domain pursuant to G.S. 63A-6.

(6) To establish, construct, purchase, maintain, equip, and operate any structure or facilities to aid commerce associated with a cargo airport complex, including the construction of highways, bridges, shipping facilities, electronic cargo transfer systems, mass transit systems, and other transportation facilities. Before constructing a highway or a bridge, the Authority shall consult with the Department of Transportation.

(7) To create and operate agencies and departments needed to implement this Chapter.

(8) To pay all necessary costs and expenses in the formation, organization, administration, and operation of the Authority.

(9) To apply for, accept, and administer loans and grants of money from any federal agency, from the State or its political subdivisions, or from any other public or private sources available, to expend the money in accordance with the requirements imposed by the lender or donor, and to give any evidences of indebtedness that are required. No indebtedness of any kind incurred or created by the Authority shall constitute an indebtedness of the State or its political subdivisions, and no indebtedness of the Authority shall involve or be secured by the faith, credit, or taxing power of the State or its political subdivisions.

(10) To adopt, alter, or repeal its own bylaws or rules implementing the provisions of this Chapter.

(11) To execute financing agreements, security documents, and other instruments necessary in exercising its power under this Chapter.

(12) To fix, charge, collect, pledge, or assign revenues of the Authority.

(13) To employ consulting engineers, architects, attorneys, real estate counselors, appraisers, and other consultants and employees as may be required in the judgment of the Board and to fix and pay their compensation from funds available to the Authority, and, when approved by the Local Government Commission under G.S. 159-123(e) and (f) as if the Authority were an issuing unit, to select and retain financial consultants, underwriters, and bond attorneys in connection with the issuance of any bonds and to pay for their services out of the proceeds of any bond issue for which their services were performed.

(14) To issue bonds or notes of the Authority as provided under this Chapter to pay the costs of a project.

(15) To issue revenue refunding bonds of the Authority as provided under this Chapter.

(16) To procure and maintain adequate insurance or otherwise provide for adequate protection to indemnify the Authority and its officers, directors, agents, employees, adjoining property owners, or the general public against loss or liability resulting from any act or omission by or on behalf of the Authority.

(17) To purchase or finance real or personal property in the manner provided for cities and counties under G.S. 160A-20.

(18) To enter into agreements with counties pursuant to G.S. 63A-15.

(19) To exercise the powers granted political subdivisions under Article 4, Chapter 63 of the General Statutes, and to exercise the powers granted to municipalities and counties under Article 6, Chapter 63 of the General Statutes, governing public airports and related facilities.

(20) To act as agent for the United States of America or any agency of the United States in any matter within the purpose of this Chapter. When acting as agent for the United States or one of its agencies, the Authority shall keep the interest of the State paramount.

(21) With the approval of any unit of local government, to use officers, employees, agents, and facilities of the unit of local government for the purposes and upon the terms as may be mutually agreeable.

(22) Repealed by Session Laws 2013-360, s. 6.3(b), effective July 1, 2013.

(23) To receive and use appropriations from the State, including an appropriation from the proceeds of State general obligation bonds or notes.

(b) To execute the powers provided in subsection (a) of this section, the Board shall determine the policies of the Authority by majority vote of the members of the Board present and voting, a quorum having been established. Once a policy is determined, the Board shall communicate it to the executive director, who shall have the sole and exclusive authority to execute the policy of the Authority. No member of the Board shall have the responsibility or authority to give operational directives to any employee of the Authority other than the executive director. (1991, c. 749, s. 1; 2000-67, s. 25.3; 2013-360, s. 6.3(b).)

§ 63A-5. Taxation of property of Authority.

Property owned by the Authority is exempt from taxation in accordance with Article V, § 2 of the North Carolina Constitution. Property that is part of or is located on a cargo airport complex site and is not owned by the Authority, including property that is part of a special user project, is not exempt from tax due to its location. (1991, c. 749, s. 1.)

§ 63A-6. Acquisition, disposition, or exchange of real property.

(a) General. The Authority may acquire real property by purchase, negotiation, gift, devise, or eminent domain. Any acquisition by eminent domain by the Authority of real property or an estate or interest in real property must be reviewed and approved by the Council of State before it can become effective. When the Authority acquires real property owned by the State, the Secretary of the Department of Administration shall execute and deliver to the Authority a deed transferring fee simple title to the property to the Authority.

(b) Eminent Domain. To exercise the power of eminent domain, the Authority shall commence a proceeding in its name and may follow any procedure set by law by which a State agency or a political subdivision of the State may exercise the power of eminent domain. The Authority's exercise of the power of eminent domain is subject to review and approval by the Council of State.

The Authority's power of eminent domain applies to all property, including property that is owned by a State agency or a political subdivision of the State and is already devoted to a specific use other than as an airport established under Chapter 63 of the General Statutes. The Authority may acquire by eminent domain property that is owned by a political subdivision and is used as an airport established under Chapter 63 of the General Statutes only after obtaining the approval of the governing body of each political subdivision that established the airport. The Authority may not begin an eminent domain proceeding before it obtains the Council of State's approval for the acquisition of the property to be condemned.

(c) Exchange. The Authority may exchange any property it acquires for other property usable in carrying out the powers conferred on the Authority and also, upon the payment of just compensation, may remove a building, a terminal, or another structure from land needed for its purposes and reconstruct the structure on another location. The Authority may not use the power of eminent domain to acquire property for exchange.

(d) Site Selection. In selecting a site for a cargo airport complex, the Authority shall consider comprehensive plans and land-use regulations adopted by local governments and the capability of local governments to provide services as specified in subdivisions (1) through (3) of this subsection. This subsection shall not be construed to require the Authority to comply with any local ordinance, regulation, or plan except as may be otherwise specifically provided by federal or State law, regulation, or rule. Plans, regulations, and capabilities to be considered are:

(1) Local comprehensive plans, including education, emergency response, law enforcement, water supply, stormwater management, solid waste management, and wastewater treatment.

(2) Local land use regulations, including appearance, floodplain zoning, subdivision zoning, and watershed protection elements.

(3) The capability of local governments to provide services and manage growth and development related to establishment of a cargo airport complex. (1991, c. 749, s. 1; 1991 (Reg. Sess., 1992), c. 900, s. 108(f), (g).)

§ 63A-7. Police power.

(a) The Authority has jurisdiction within a cargo airport complex site. The Board may adopt ordinances regulating traffic and parking within the cargo airport complex site and for the safety and welfare of those using the cargo airport complex. An ordinance adopted under this subsection shall be recorded in the minutes of the Board. A copy of the ordinance shall be filed in the office of the Attorney General of North Carolina and shall be posted at appropriate places in the cargo airport complex site. Any person who violates an ordinance of the Authority is guilty of a Class 3 misdemeanor.

(b) The executive director of the Authority may designate employees of the Authority as special police officers. A person designated as a special police officer has jurisdiction within the cargo airport complex site to arrest a person who violates any federal or State law or any ordinance of the Authority and has other powers to the same extent as police officers of incorporated municipalities. An employee designated as a special police officer shall take the oath of a law enforcement officer set out in G.S. 11-11. (1991, c. 749, s. 1; 1993, c. 539, s. 499; 1994, Ex. Sess., c. 24, s. 14(c).)

§ 63A-8. Authority funds.

All Authority funds shall be deposited in one or more banks to be designated by the Board. Funds of the Authority shall be paid out only upon warrants signed by the treasurer or assistant treasurer of the Authority and countersigned by the chair, the acting chair, or the executive director. No warrants shall be drawn or issued disbursing any of the funds of the Authority except for a purpose authorized by this Chapter and only when the account or expenditure has been audited and approved by the Authority or its executive director. (1991, c. 749, s. 1.)

§ 63A-9. Bonds and notes.

(a) The Authority may provide for the issuance, at one time or from time to time, of bonds and notes, including bond anticipation notes and renewal notes, of the Authority to carry out its corporate purposes including financing the costs of projects. The principal of and interest on the bonds or notes shall be payable from funds provided under this Chapter for their payment. A bond anticipation note may be made payable from the proceeds of bonds or renewal notes or, in the event bond or renewal note proceeds are not available, from any available Authority revenues or other funds provided for this purpose. Bonds and notes may also be paid from the proceeds of any credit facility.

All bonds, notes, or refunding bonds or notes of the Authority are subject to this section and G.S. 63A-10. All bonds, notes, or refunding bonds or notes to finance or refinance a special user project are also subject to G.S. 63A-11.

The bonds and notes of each issue shall be dated and may be made redeemable prior to maturity at the option of the Authority or otherwise, at one or more prices, on one or more dates, and upon the terms and conditions set by the Authority. The bonds or notes may also be made payable from time to time on demand or tender for purchase by the owner upon terms and conditions set by the Authority.

A bond or note shall bear interest at a rate or rates, including variable rates, as determined by the Local Government Commission with the approval of the Authority. A bond or note may be secured by a reserve fund created for that purpose and funded from proceeds of the bond or note, revenues, or any other source of funds available to the Authority.

(b) In fixing the details of bonds or notes, the Authority may provide that the bonds or notes may:

(1) Be payable from time to time on demand or tender for purchase by the owner of the bond or note if a credit facility supports the bond or note, unless the Local Government Commission specifically determines that a credit facility is not required because the absence of a credit facility will not materially and adversely affect the financial position of the Authority and the marketing of the bonds or notes at a reasonable interest cost to the Authority.

(2) Be additionally supported by a credit facility.

(3) Be made subject to redemption or a mandatory tender for purchase prior to maturity.

(4) Be capital appreciation bonds.

(5) Bear interest at a rate or rates that may vary, including variations permitted pursuant to a par formula.

(6) Be made the subject of a remarketing agreement whereby an attempt is made to remarket the bonds or notes to new purchasers prior to their presentment for payment to the provider of the credit facility or to the Authority.

(c) Notes and bonds shall mature at the times determined by the Authority, not to exceed 40 years from the date of issue. The Authority shall determine the form and manner of execution of a bond or note, including any interest coupons to be attached to the bond or note. The Authority shall fix the denominations and places of payment of principal and interest of the bond or note. The principal of and interest on a bond or note may be paid at any bank or trust company, whether located inside or outside the United States of America.

(d) The validity of a bond, note, or coupon that has the signature or facsimile signature of a person who was an officer when the bond, note, or coupon was signed or the facsimile signature attached but who is not that officer when the bond, note, or coupon is delivered is not affected by the change in officers. A bond, note, or coupon may bear the signature or facsimile signature of a person who will be the proper officer to sign the bond, note, or coupon when it is executed but who is not the officer on the date of the bond, note, or coupon.

(e) The Authority may provide for any of the following:

(1) Authentication of a bond or note by a trustee or other authenticating agent.

(2) Issuance of a bond or note as a certificated obligation, an uncertificated obligation, or both.

(3) Issuance of a bond or note in coupon form, in registered form, or both.

(4) Registration of a coupon bond or note as to principal alone or as to both principal and interest.

(5) The reconversion of a bond or note registered as to both principal and interest into a coupon bond or note.

(6) The interchange of registered and coupon bonds or notes.

(7) A system for registration in accordance with Chapter 159E of the General Statutes.

(8) Replacement of a bond or note that has been mutilated, lost, or destroyed.

(f) The Authority may not issue a bond or note under this Chapter, other than an obligation permitted under G.S. 63A-4(a)(22), unless its issuance is approved by the Local Government Commission, and it is sold by the Local Government Commission. To obtain approval of a bond or note, the Authority shall file an application for approval with the Local Government Commission. The application shall contain the information required by the Local Government Commission.

In determining whether to approve a proposed bond or note issue of the Authority, the Local Government Commission shall consider the following:

(1) For bonds or notes to finance airport projects, the criteria for its approval of revenue bonds under G.S. 159-86.

(2) For bonds or notes to finance special user projects, the criteria used for its approval of industrial bonds under G.S. 159C-8.

(3) The effect of the proposed financing upon any proposed or scheduled sale of obligations by the State, another State agency, or a unit of local government.

The Local Government Commission shall approve the proposed bond or note issue if it determines that the proposed financing for the issue meets the criteria and will effect the purposes of this Chapter.

When the Local Government Commission approves a bond or note issue of the Authority, the Authority may submit a written request to the Local Government Commission to sell the approved bonds or notes. Upon receiving a written request, the Local Government Commission shall consult with the Authority on the manner in which the bonds or notes will be sold and the price or prices at which the bonds or notes will be sold. With the approval of the Authority, the Local Government Commission shall sell the bonds or notes either at public or private sale in the manner and at the prices determined to be in the best interest of the Authority and to effect the purposes of this Chapter.

Bonds or notes may be issued under this Chapter without obtaining, except as otherwise expressly provided in this Chapter, the consent of any department, division, commission, board, body, bureau, or other agency of the State or without any other proceedings or conditions except as specifically authorized by this Chapter or by the provisions of the resolution authorizing the issuance of, or any trust agreement securing, the bonds or notes.

(g) Each bond or note that is represented by an instrument shall contain a statement signed by the Secretary of the Local Government Commission, or an assistant designated by the Secretary, certifying that the issuance of the bond or note has been approved under this Chapter. The signature may be a manual signature or a facsimile signature, as determined by the Local Government Commission. Each bond or note that is not represented by an instrument shall be evidenced by a writing relating to the obligation that identifies the obligation or the issue of which it is a part, contains the signed statement certifying approval of the Local Government Commission that is required on an instrument, and is filed with the Local Government Commission. A certification of approval by the Local Government Commission is conclusive evidence that a bond or note complies with this Chapter.

(h) The proceeds of a bond or note shall be used solely for the purposes for which the bond or note was issued and shall be disbursed in accordance with the resolution authorizing the issuance of the bond or note and with any trust agreement securing the bond or note.

(i) Prior to the preparation of definitive bonds, the Authority may issue interim receipts or temporary bonds, with or without coupons, exchangeable for definitive bonds when the bonds have been executed and are available for delivery.

(j) The Authority may secure a bond or note issued under this Chapter by a trust agreement between the Authority and a corporate trustee. The corporate trustee may be any trust company or bank having the powers of a trust company inside or outside the State. The Authority may secure a bond or note issued under this Chapter by a deed of trust. The trustee of the deed of trust may be an individual who is a resident of the State. A bank or trust company that is incorporated in this State and is a depository of the proceeds of obligations, revenues, or other money of an Authority may furnish indemnifying bonds or pledge securities required by the Authority.

The pledge of any assets, income, or revenues of the Authority to the payment of the principal of or the interest on any obligations of the Authority is binding from the time the pledge is made, and any assets, income, or revenues of the Authority are immediately subject to the lien of the pledge without any physical delivery or other act. The lien created by a pledge is binding against all persons who have claims of any kind against the Authority, regardless of whether they have notice of the lien.

(k) A resolution authorizing the issuance of a bond or note and a trust agreement securing a bond or note may provide that any moneys held under the resolution or trust agreement may be temporarily invested pending disbursement. Any officer with whom, or any bank or trust company with which, the moneys are deposited is considered a trustee of the moneys and must hold and apply the moneys for their stated purpose in accordance with this Chapter and the resolution or trust agreement. The Authority may invest any moneys, other than the proceeds of bonds issued to finance special user projects, as allowed in G.S. 147-69.1 for investments of the State Treasurer or in this subsection. The proceeds of bonds issued to finance special user projects may be invested as provided in the security document for the bonds.

In connection with or incidental to the acquisition or carrying of any investment relating to bonds, program of investment relating to bonds, or carrying of bonds, the Authority may, with the approval of the Local Government Commission, enter into a contract to place the investment or obligation of the Authority, as represented by the bonds, investment, or program of investment and the contract or contracts, in whole or in part, on an interest rate, currency, cash-flow, or other basis, including the following:

(1) Interest rate swap agreements, currency swap agreements, insurance agreements, forward payment conversion agreements, and futures.

(2) Contracts providing for payments based on levels of, or changes in, interest rates, currency exchange rates, or stock or other indices.

(3) Contracts to exchange cash flows or a series of payments.

(4) Contracts to hedge payment, currency, rate, spread, or similar exposure, including interest rate floors or caps, options, puts, and calls.

The Authority may enter a contract of this type in connection with, or incidental to, entering into or maintaining any agreement that secures bonds. A contract shall contain the payment, security, term, default, remedy, and other terms and conditions the Board considers appropriate. The Authority may enter a contract of this type with any person after giving due consideration, where applicable, of the person's credit-worthiness as determined by a rating by a nationally recognized rating agency or any other criteria the Board considers appropriate. In connection with, or incidental to, the issuance or carrying of bonds, or the entering of any contract described in this subsection, the Authority may enter into credit enhancement or liquidity agreements, with payment, interest rate, termination date, currency, security, default, remedy, and other terms and conditions as the Authority determines. Proceeds of bonds and any moneys set aside and pledged to secure payment of bonds or any of the contracts entered into under this subsection may be pledged to and used to service any of the contracts entered into under this section.

(l) Bonds and notes are exempt from all State, county, and municipal taxation or assessment, direct or indirect, general or special, whether imposed for the purpose of general revenue or otherwise, excluding inheritance and gift taxes, income taxes on the gain from the transfer of bonds and notes, and franchise taxes. The interest on bonds and notes is not subject to taxation as income.

(m) Bonds or notes issued under this Chapter shall not constitute a debt secured by a pledge of the faith and credit of the State or a political subdivision of the State and shall be payable solely from the revenues, income, or assets of the Authority that are pledged for their payment. The face of each bond or note issued shall contain a statement that the Authority is obligated to pay the bond or note or the interest on the bond or note only from the revenues, income, or assets pledged in payment of the bond or note and that neither the faith and credit nor the taxing power of the State or any political subdivision of the State is pledged in payment of the principal of or the interest on the bond or note.

(n) The State pledges to the holder of a bond or note issued under this Chapter that, as long as the bond or note is outstanding and unpaid, the State will not limit or alter the power the Authority had when the bond or note was issued in a way that impairs the ability of the Authority to produce revenues sufficient with other available funds to do all of the following:

(1) Maintain and operate the project for which the bond or note was issued.

(2) Pay the principal of, interest on, and redemption premium, if any, of the bond or note.

(3) Fulfill the terms of an agreement with the holder.

The State further pledges to the holder of a bond or note issued under this Chapter that the State will not impair the rights and remedies of the holder concerning the bond or note.

(o) Obligations issued under this Chapter are made securities in which all public officers and public bodies of the State and its political subdivisions, and all insurance companies, trust companies, banking associations, investment companies, executors, administrators, trustees, and other fiduciaries may properly and legally invest funds, including capital in their control or belonging to them. The obligations are made securities that may properly and legally be deposited with and received by any State or municipal officer or any agency or political subdivision of the State for any purpose for which the deposit of bonds, notes, or obligations of the State is now or may be authorized by law. (1991, c. 749, s. 1; 1991 (Reg. Sess., 1992), c. 1030, s. 16; 1995, c. 46, s. 2.)

§ 63A-10. Refunding bonds or notes.

(a) Issuance. - The Authority may issue refunding bonds or notes for the purpose of refunding any outstanding bonds or notes issued under this Chapter, including any redemption premium on the bonds or notes and any interest accrued or to accrue to the date of redemption. Refunding bonds or notes shall be issued in accordance with the same procedures and requirements as bonds or notes. Refunding bonds or notes may be sold or exchanged for outstanding bonds and notes issued under this Chapter.

Refunding bonds or notes may have different interest rates and maturities than the bonds or notes being refunded. The proceeds of refunding bonds or notes may be applied to any of the following:

(1) The payment, purchase, and retirement of the bonds or notes being refunded by direct application to the payment, purchase, and retirement.

(2) The payment, purchase, and retirement of the bonds or notes being refunded by the deposit in trust of the proceeds.

(3) The payment of any expenses incurred in connection with the refunding.

(4) For any other uses not inconsistent with the refunding.

(b) Proceeds. - The proceedings providing for the issuance of refunding bonds or notes may limit the investments in which the proceeds of a particular refunding issue may be invested. Unless prohibited by the proceedings, the proceeds of refunding bonds or notes that are deposited in trust for the payment, purchase, and retirement of outstanding bonds or notes may be invested in any of the following:

(1) Direct obligations of the United States of America.

(2) Obligations whose principal and interest are guaranteed by the United States of America.

(3) Evidences of ownership of a proportionate interest in an obligation that is described in subdivisions (1) or (2) of this subsection and is held in a custodial capacity by a bank or trust company organized under the laws of the United States of America or a state.

(4) Obligations of the State or a unit of local government of the State when payment of the principal of and interest on the obligations has been provided for by depositing with a trustee or other escrow agent obligations that meet all of the following:

a. Are described in subdivisions (1), (2), or (3) of this subsection.

b. When due and payable, will provide enough money when added to any other money held in trust for this purpose to pay the principal of, premium, if any, and interest on the State or local obligations.

c. Are rated in the highest category by Standard & Poor's Corporation and Moody's Investors Service, Inc.

(5) Obligations of the State or a unit of local government when payment of the principal and interest on the obligations is insured by a bond insurance company rated in the highest category by Standard & Poor's Corporation and Moody's Investors Service, Inc.

(6) Full faith and credit obligations of the State or a unit of local government of the State that are rated in the highest category by Standard & Poor's Corporation and Moody's Investors Service, Inc.

(7) Any obligations or investments in which the State Treasurer is then authorized to invest funds of the State.

(c) Scope. - This section does not limit any of the following:

(1) The period for which the proceeds of refunding bonds or notes may be held in trust to retire the bonds or notes that are being refunded and have not matured, are not redeemable or, if redeemable, have not been called for redemption.

(2) The power to issue bonds or notes for the combined purpose of refunding outstanding bonds or notes and of providing funds for any other corporate purpose. (1991, c. 749, s. 1.)

§ 63A-11. Special user project bonds or notes.

(a) The Authority may, subject to the provisions of this section, G.S. 63A-9, and, if applicable, G.S. 63A-10, issue, at one time or from time to time, bonds and notes to finance or refinance special user projects. Bonds and notes to finance or refinance special user projects may be sold irrespective of the interest limitations in G.S. 24-1.1.

(b) Bonds or notes issued by the Authority under this section are special, limited obligations of the Authority payable solely from the following:

(1) The Authority's revenues, income, or assets that it specifically assigns or pledges for payment.

(2) The funds, collateral, and undertakings of a private party that are assigned or pledged by that party.

(c) Bonds and notes issued under this section may be secured by one or more agreements, including foreclosable deeds of trust and other trust instruments. An agreement may pledge and assign to the trustee or the holders of its obligations the assets, revenues, and income provided for the security of the bonds or notes, including proceeds from the sale of any special user project or part thereof, insurance proceeds, condemnation awards, and third-party agreements, and may convey or mortgage the project and other property and collateral to secure a bond issue.

The Authority may subordinate the bonds or notes or its rights, assets, revenues, and income derived from any special user project to any prior, contemporaneous, or future securities or obligations or lien, mortgage, or other security interest.

(d) Notwithstanding any other provision of law, the Authority may agree that all contracts relating to the acquisition, construction, installation, and equipping of the special user project shall be solicited, negotiated, awarded, and executed by the private parties for which the Authority is financing the special user project or any agents of the private parties subject only to approval by the Authority as the Authority may require. The Authority may, out of the proceeds of bonds or notes, make advances to or reimburse the private parties or their agents for all or a portion of the costs incurred in connection with the contracts.

(e) Repealed by Session Laws 2001-218, s. 5. (1991, c. 749, s. 1; 1993, c. 553, s. 23; 2000-169, s. 37; 2001-218, s. 5.)

§ 63A-12. Public hearing requirements.

To the extent federal tax law requires public hearings to be held with respect to the issuance of bonds to finance projects, the hearings may be called for by the executive director and held before one or more members of the Board of the Authority. The hearings may be held at any place within the State pursuant to public notice given in accordance with current federal tax regulations. To the extent federal tax law requires approval following the hearing of the issuance of bonds to finance a project, the approval shall be sought from the Governor following a report to the Governor of the results of the public hearing accompanied by information relating to the purposes for the proposed bond issue. (1991, c. 749, s. 1.)

§ 63A-13. Financing agreements.

(a) Every financing agreement shall contain provisions ensuring all of the following:

(1) That the amounts payable under the financing agreement are sufficient to pay, when due, the principal of, redemption premium, if any, and interest on the bonds issued to pay the costs of the special user project.

(2) That the operator pays all costs incurred by the Authority in connection with the financing and administration of the special user project, except costs paid out of the proceeds of bonds or otherwise, including, but without limitation, insurance costs, the cost of administering the financing agreement and the security document, and the fees and expenses of the fiscal agent or trustee, paying agents, attorneys, consultants, and others.

(3) That the operator pays all the costs and expenses of operation, maintenance, and upkeep of the special user project.

(4) That the operator's obligation to provide for the payment of the bonds in full is not subject to cancellation, termination, or abatement until the payment of the bonds or provision for their payment is made.

(b) The financing agreement, if in the nature of a lease agreement, shall either provide that the obligor shall have an option to purchase, or require that the obligor purchase, the special user project upon the expiration or termination of the financing agreement subject to the condition that payment in full of the principal of, and the interest and any redemption premium on, the bonds, or provision therefor, shall have been made.

(c) The financing agreement may provide the Authority with rights and remedies in the event of a default by the obligor including, without limitation, any one or more of the following:

(1) Acceleration of all amounts payable under the financing agreement.

(2) Reentry and repossession of the special user project.

(3) Termination of the financing agreement.

(4) Leasing or sale of foreclosure of the special user project to others.

(5) Taking whatever actions at law or in equity may appear necessary or desirable to collect the amounts payable under, and to enforce covenants made in, the financing agreement.

(d) The Authority's interest in a special user project under a financing agreement may be that of owner, lessor, lessee, conditional or installment vendor, mortgagor, mortgagee, secured party, or otherwise, but the Authority need not have any ownership or possessory interest in the special user project.

(e) The Authority may assign all or any of its rights and remedies under the financing agreement to the trustee or the bondholders under a security document.

(f) The financing agreement may contain additional provisions as in the determination of the Board are necessary or convenient to effectuate the purposes of this Chapter. When, as provided in G.S. 63A-9 and G.S. 63A-11, the Local Government Commission approves the issuance of bonds by the Authority, the Commission shall also approve all financing agreements and security documents. (1991, c. 749, s. 1; 1997-456, s. 27.)

§ 63A-14. Security documents.

Bonds issued under the provisions of this Chapter may be secured by a security document which may be a trust instrument between the Authority and a bank or trust company or individual within the State, or a bank or a trust company outside the State, as trustee. The security document may pledge and assign the revenues provided for the security of the bonds, including proceeds from the sale of any project, or part thereof, insurance proceeds and condemnation awards, and may convey or mortgage the project and other property to secure a bond issue.

The revenues and other funds derived from the project, except for any part as may be necessary to provide reserves therefor, if any, may be set aside at regular intervals as may be provided in the security document in a sinking fund which may be pledged to, and charged with, the payment of the principal of and the interest on the bonds as the same shall become due and the redemption price or the purchase price of bonds retired by call or purchase as provided. The pledge shall be valid and binding from the time when the pledge is made. The revenues pledged and received by the Authority shall immediately be subject to the lien of the pledge without any physical delivery or further act, and the lien of any pledge shall be valid and binding as against all parties having claims of any kind in tort, contract or otherwise against the Authority, irrespective of whether the parties have notice. The use and disposition of money to the credit of the sinking fund shall be subject to the provisions of the security document. The security document may contain provisions for protecting and enforcing the rights and remedies of the bondholders as may be reasonable and proper and not in violation of law, including, without limitation, any one or more of the following:

(1) Acceleration of all amounts payable under the security document.

(2) Appointment of a receiver to manage the project and any other property mortgaged or assigned as security for the bonds.

(3) Foreclosure and sale of the project and any other property mortgaged or assigned as security for the bonds.

(4) Rights to bring and maintain such other actions at law or in equity as may appear necessary or desirable to collect the amounts payable under, or to enforce the covenants made in, the security document.

It shall be lawful for any bank or trust company incorporated under the laws of this State which may act as depository of the proceeds of bonds, revenues, or other funds provided under this Chapter to furnish indemnifying bonds or to pledge securities as may be required by the Authority. All expenses incurred in carrying out the provisions of the security document may be treated as a part of the cost of the project in connection with which bonds are issued or as an expense of administration of the project.

The Authority may subordinate the bonds or its rights under the security document or otherwise to any prior, contemporaneous, or future securities or obligations or lien, mortgage, or other security interest. (1991, c. 749, s. 1.)

§ 63A-15. County agreements.

Any county in which all or part of a cargo airport complex site is located may enter into an agreement with the Authority providing for payments to be made by the county to the Authority. A county may not enter into an agreement to make payments to the Authority until after the Authority designates the cargo airport complex site. The county's obligations under the agreement shall not constitute a pledge of its faith and credit. (1991, c. 749, s. 1.)

§ 63A-16. Remedies.

Any owner of bonds or notes issued under the provisions of this Chapter or any coupons appertaining thereto, and the trustee under any trust agreement securing or resolution authorizing the issuance of such bonds or notes, except to the extent the rights given may be restricted by the trust agreement or resolution, may either at law or in equity, by suit, action, mandamus, or other proceeding, protect and enforce any and all rights under the laws of the State or granted hereunder or under the trust agreement or resolution, or under any other contract executed by the Authority pursuant to this Chapter; and may enforce and compel the performance of all duties required by this Chapter or by the trust agreement or resolution by the Authority or by any officer of the Authority. (1991, c. 749, s. 1.)

§ 63A-17. Status of bonds and notes under Uniform Commercial Code.

All bonds and notes and interest coupons, if any, issued under this Chapter are made investment securities within the meaning of and for all the purposes of Article 8 of the Uniform Commercial Code, as enacted in Chapter 25 of the General Statutes. (1991, c. 749, s. 1.)

§ 63A-18. Zoning power of Authority.

(a)   The Authority has exclusive zoning jurisdiction within a cargo airport complex site. The Authority has zoning jurisdiction within six miles of the boundaries of a cargo airport complex site.

(b)   No State agency and, in accordance with G.S. 63-31, no political subdivision may adopt, without obtaining the approval of the Authority, an airport zoning provision or other land use regulation that affects real property within six miles of any cargo airport complex site if it conflicts with a zoning provision or land use restriction adopted by the Authority.

A zoning provision or land use restriction adopted in violation of this subsection is not effective. (1991, c. 749, s. 1; 1991 (Reg. Sess., 1992), c. 900, s. 108(h).)

§ 63A-19. Goals for participation by minorities, women, and the disabled.

(a) The Authority shall verify its efforts to achieve the goals established in this section for participation by minority business enterprises, women's business enterprises, and disabled business enterprises in the total value of contracts awarded by the Authority in each of the following categories:

(1) Contracts for capital construction or repair projects.

(2) Contracts for goods.

(3) Contracts for professional and other services.

(b) The goals for the Authority are as follows:

(1) Ten percent (10%) participation by minority business enterprises.

(2) Five percent (5%) participation by women's business enterprises.

(3) Two percent (2%) participation by disabled business enterprises.

In determining participation in contract awards, a contract shall be counted as participation by a minority business enterprise without regard to the gender of the owner, but only if the business does not qualify as a disabled business enterprise. A contract shall be counted as participation by a women's business enterprise only if the business does not also qualify as a disabled business enterprise. A contract shall be counted as participation by a disabled business enterprise without regard to the race or gender of the owner. The goals in this section, instead of any goals in Article 8 of Chapter 143 of the General Statutes, apply to the Authority. With respect to projects for which the Authority would not receive federal funds if it adhered to the goals in this section because the goals are contrary to or are inconsistent with 14 C.F.R. Part 152, Subpart E, Nondiscrimination in Airport Aid Program, the federal law and regulations supersede this section to the extent it is contrary to or inconsistent with the federal law and regulations.

(c) The following definitions apply in this section:

(1) Disabled business enterprise. - A legal entity, other than a joint venture, that is organized to engage in commercial transactions and is at least fifty-one percent (51%) owned and controlled by one or more disabled persons.

(2) Disabled person. - A handicapped person as defined in G.S. 168A-3.

(3) Minority business enterprise. - A legal entity, other than a joint venture, that is organized to engage in commercial transactions and is at least fifty-one percent (51%) owned and controlled by one or more minority persons.

(4) Minority person. - A member of one of the following groups: African-Americans, Hispanic-Americans, American Indians, or Asian-Americans.

(5) Women's business enterprise means a legal entity, other than a joint venture, that is organized to engage in commercial transactions and is at least fifty-one percent owned and controlled by one or more women. (1991, c. 749, s. 1.)

§ 63A-20. Officers not liable.

No member or officer of the Authority shall be subject to any personal liability or accountability by reason of his execution of any bonds or notes or the issuance of any bonds or notes. (1991, c. 749, s. 1.)

§ 63A-21. Conflicts of interest.

If any member, officer, or employee of the Authority shall be interested either directly or indirectly, or shall be an officer or employee of or have an ownership interest in any firm or corporation, not including units of local government, interested directly or indirectly, in any contract with the Authority, the interest shall be disclosed to the Board and shall be set forth in the minutes of the Board. The member, officer, or employee having an interest shall not participate on behalf of the Authority in the authorization of any contract. Other provisions of law notwithstanding, failure to take any or all actions necessary to carry out the purposes of this section may not affect the validity of any bonds or notes issued under this Chapter. (1991, c. 749, s. 1.)

§ 63A-22. Cooperation by other State agencies.

All State officers and agencies shall render the services to the Authority within their respective functions as may be requested by the Authority. (1991, c. 749, s. 1.)

§ 63A-23. Annual reports.

The Authority shall, promptly following the close of each fiscal year, submit an annual written report of its activities for the preceding year to the Governor, the General Assembly, and the Local Government Commission. Each report shall be accompanied by an audit of its books and accounts, as well as quarterly and annual financial statements. The audit shall be conducted by the State Auditor. The costs of all audits shall be paid from funds of the Authority.

As part of the report, the Authority shall include the following performance measures of the private sector jobs within the Global TransPark:

(1)   The number, type, and wage level of jobs created or retained.

(2)   The actual full-time equivalent jobs employed, as well as the median and average salaries for those jobs.

The Authority shall submit its annual report to the General Assembly to both the Joint Legislative Commission on Governmental Operations and the Program Evaluation Division. The Authority shall also submit any information about the Authority's activities that is requested by the Commission.

The Authority shall also provide a copy of its annual report on its public Web site. (1991, c. 749, s. 1; 1996, 2nd Ex. Sess., c. 18, s. 26; 2011-340, s. 1(e).)

§ 63A-24. General laws apply to Authority; exceptions.

(a) Except as provided in this section, the general laws that apply to State agencies apply to the Authority. The following general laws, to the extent provided below, do not apply to the Authority:

(1) Article 3 of Chapter 143 of the General Statutes does not apply to contracts for services listed in 49 U.S.C. § 2210(a)(16) or contracts for special user projects. That Article also does not apply to other contracts for projects, but, with respect to these other contracts, the powers and duties established in that Article shall be exercised by the Authority and the Secretary of Administration, and other State officers, employees, or agencies shall have no duties or responsibilities concerning the contracts. However, the Authority shall: (i) submit all proposed contracts for supplies, materials, printing, equipment, and contractual services that exceed one million dollars ($1,000,000) authorized by this subdivision to the Attorney General or the Attorney General's designee for review as provided in G.S. 114-8.3; and (ii) include in all contracts to be awarded by the Authority under this subdivision a standard clause which provides that the State Auditor and internal auditors of the Authority may audit the records of the contractor during and after the term of the contract to verify accounts and data affecting fees and performance. The Authority shall not award a cost plus percentage of cost agreement or contract for any purpose.

(2) Article 8 of Chapter 143 of the General Statutes does not apply to public building contracts of the Authority, but, with respect to these contracts, the powers and duties established in that Article shall be exercised by the Authority and the Secretary of Administration, and other State officers, employees, or agencies shall have no duties or responsibilities concerning the contracts.

(3) Except for G.S. 146-29.1, 146-79, and 146-80, Chapter 146 of the General Statutes does not apply to the Authority.

(b) Notwithstanding G.S. 126-5(c1)(15), the Secretary of Transportation may designate employees of the Authority as subject to Chapter 126 of the General Statutes. (1991, c. 749, s. 1; 2010-194, s. 11; 2011-326, s. 15(k); 2011-340, s. 1(f); 2012-194, s. 18.)

§ 63A-25. Dissolution.

Whenever the Board shall by resolution determine that the purposes for which the Authority was formed have been substantially fulfilled and that all bonds issued and all other obligations incurred by the Authority have been fully paid or satisfied, the Board may declare the Authority to be dissolved. On the effective date of the resolution, the title to all funds and other property owned by the Authority at the time of the dissolution shall vest in the State and possession of the funds and other property shall be delivered to the State. (1991, c. 749, s. 1.)

Chapter 64.

Aliens.

Article 1.

Various Provisions Related to Aliens.

§ 64-1. Rights as to real property.

It is lawful for aliens to take both by purchase and descent, or other operation of law, any lands, tenements or hereditaments, and to hold and convey the same as fully as citizens of this State can or may do, any law or usage to the contrary notwithstanding. (1870-1, c. 255; Code, s. 7; Rev., s. 182; C.S., s. 192; 1935, c. 243; 1939, c. 19.)

§ 64-1.1. Secretary of State to collect information as to foreign ownership of real property.

The Secretary of State is authorized and directed to collect all information obtainable from reports by aliens made to agencies of the federal government on ownership of real property interests in North Carolina, to be updated every three months, and to maintain a file on such information which shall be available to the members of the General Assembly and the public. (1979, c. 610.)

§ 64-2. Contracts validated.

All contracts to purchase or sell real estate by or with aliens, heretofore made, shall be deemed and taken as valid to all intents and purposes. (1870-1, c. 255, s. 2; Code, s. 8; Rev., s. 183; C.S., s. 193.)

§ 64-3. Nonresident aliens' rights of inheritance.

No alien residing outside the United States or its territories shall be entitled to take personal property located in this State by succession or testamentary disposition if the laws of the nation of which such alien is a resident prohibit residents of the United States from inheriting personal property located within that nation. Except as hereinabove provided, no alien shall, by reason of his citizenship or place of residence, be disqualified from inheriting property in this State. (1959, c. 1208; 1985 (Reg. Sess., 1986), c. 797, s. 1.)

§ 64-4. Escheats.

If a decedent owning personal property located within North Carolina shall leave no heirs, heirs at law or devisees other than persons disqualified from inheritance under G.S. 64-3, then such personal property shall escheat. (1959, c. 1208; 1985 (Reg. Sess., 1986), c. 797, s. 2; 2011-284, s. 60.)

§ 64-5. Burden of proof.

The burden of proof in any action or proceeding to disqualify a nonresident alien from taking personal property located within this State by succession or testamentary disposition by reason of the provisions of G.S. 64-3, shall be upon the person asserting the disqualification. (1959, c. 1208; 1985 (Reg. Sess., 1986), c. 797, s. 3.)

§ 64-6: Reserved for future codification purposes.

§ 64-7: Reserved for future codification purposes.

§ 64-8: Reserved for future codification purposes.

§ 64-9: Reserved for future codification purposes.

§ 64-10: Reserved for future codification purposes.

§ 64-11: Reserved for future codification purposes.

§ 64-12: Reserved for future codification purposes.

§ 64-13: Reserved for future codification purposes.

§ 64-14: Reserved for future codification purposes.

§ 64-15: Reserved for future codification purposes.

§ 64-16: Reserved for future codification purposes.

§ 64-17: Reserved for future codification purposes.

§ 64-18: Reserved for future codification purposes.

§ 64-19: Reserved for future codification purposes.

§ 64-20: Reserved for future codification purposes.

§ 64-21: Reserved for future codification purposes.

§ 64-22: Reserved for future codification purposes.

§ 64-23: Reserved for future codification purposes.

§ 64-24: Reserved for future codification purposes.

Article 2.

Verification of Work Authorization.

§ 64-25. (For effective date, see Editor's note.) Definitions.

The following definitions apply in this Article:

(1) Commissioner. - The North Carolina Commissioner of Labor.

(2) Employ. - Hire an employee.

(3) Employee. - Any individual who provides services or labor for an employer in this State for wages or other remuneration. The term does not include an individual whose term of employment is less than nine months in a calendar year.

(4) Employer. - Any person, business entity, or other organization that transacts business in this State and that employs 25 or more employees in this State. This term does not include State agencies, counties, municipalities, or other governmental bodies.

(5) E-Verify. - The federal E-Verify program operated by the United States Department of Homeland Security and other federal agencies, or any successor or equivalent program used to verify the work authorization of newly hired employees pursuant to federal law.

(6) Unauthorized alien. - As defined in 8 U.S.C. § 1324a(h)(3). (2011-263, s. 3; 2013-418, s. 2(f).)

§ 64-26. (For effective date, see Editor's note) Verification of employee work authorization.

(a) Employers Must Use E-Verify. - Each employer, after hiring an employee to work in the United States, shall verify the work authorization of the employee through E-Verify.

(b) Employer Preservation of E-Verify Forms. - Each employer shall retain the record of the verification of work authorization required by this section while the employee is employed and for one year thereafter.

(c) Repealed by Session Laws 2013-418, s. 2(g), effective September 4, 2013. (2011-263, s. 3; 2013-418, s. 2(g).)

§ 64-27. (For effective date, see Editor's note) Commissioner of Labor to prepare complaint form.

(a) Preparation of Form. - The Commissioner shall prescribe a complaint form for a person to allege a violation of G.S. 64-26. The form shall clearly state that completed forms may be sent to the Commissioner.

(b) Certain Information Not Required. - The complainant shall not be required to list the complainant's social security number on the complaint form or to have the complaint notarized. (2011-263, s. 3.)

§ 64-28. (For effective date, see Editor's note) Reporting of complaints.

(a) Filing of Complaint. - Any person with a good faith belief that an employer is violating or has violated G.S. 64-26 may file a complaint with the Commissioner setting forth the basis for that belief. The complaint may be on a form prescribed by the Commissioner pursuant to G.S. 64-27 or may be made in any other form that gives the Commissioner information that is sufficient to proceed with an investigation pursuant to G.S. 64-29. Nothing in this section shall be construed to prohibit the filing of anonymous complaints that are not submitted on a prescribed complaint form.

(b) False Statements a Misdemeanor. - A person who knowingly files a false and frivolous complaint under this section is guilty of a Class 2 misdemeanor. (2011-263, s. 3.)

§ 64-29. (For effective date, see Editor's note) Investigation of complaints.

(a) Investigation. - Upon receipt of a complaint pursuant to G.S. 64-28 that an employer is allegedly violating or has allegedly violated G.S. 64-26, the Commissioner shall investigate whether the employer has in fact violated G.S. 64-26.

(b) Certain Complaints Shall Not Be Investigated. - The Commissioner shall not investigate complaints that are based solely on race, religion, gender, ethnicity, or national origin.

(c) Assistance by Law Enforcement. - The Commissioner may request that the State Bureau of Investigation assist in investigating a complaint under this section.

(d) Subpoena for Production of Documents. - The Commissioner may issue a subpoena for production of employment records that relate to the recruitment, hiring, employment, or termination policies, practices, or acts of employment as part of the investigation of a valid complaint under this section. (2011-263, s. 3.)

§ 64-30. (For effective date, see Editor's note) Actions to be taken; hearing.

If, after an investigation, the Commissioner determines that the complaint is not false and frivolous:

(1) The Commissioner shall hold a hearing to determine if a violation of G.S. 64-26 has occurred and, if appropriate, impose civil penalties in accordance with the provisions of this Article.

(2) If, during the course of the hearing required by subdivision (1) of this section, the Commissioner concludes that there is a reasonable likelihood that an employee is an unauthorized alien, the Commissioner shall notify the following entities of the possible presence of an unauthorized alien:

a. United States Immigration and Customs Enforcement.

b. Local law enforcement agencies. (2011-263, s. 3.)

§ 64-31. (For effective date, see Editor's note) Consequences of first violation.

(a) Affidavit Must Be Filed. - For a first violation of G.S. 64-26, the Commissioner shall order the employer to file a signed sworn affidavit with the Commissioner within three business days after the order issued pursuant to this subsection is issued. The affidavit shall state with specificity that the employer has, after consultation with the employee, requested a verification of work authorization through E-Verify.

(b) Effect of Failure to File Affidavit. - If an employer fails to timely file an affidavit required by subsection (a) of this section or by G.S. 64-32 or G.S. 64-33, the Commissioner shall order the employer to pay a civil penalty of ten thousand dollars ($10,000). (2011-263, s. 3.)

§ 64-32. (For effective date, see Editor's note) Consequences of second violation.

For a violation of G.S. 64-26 that occurs after an order has been issued pursuant to G.S. 64-31, the Commissioner shall order the measures required by G.S. 64-31(a) and shall also order the employer to pay a civil penalty of one thousand dollars ($1,000), regardless of the number of required employee verifications the employer failed to make. (2011-263, s. 3.)

§ 64-33. (For effective date, see Editor's note) Consequences of third or subsequent violation.

For a violation of G.S. 64-26 that occurs after an order has been issued pursuant to G.S. 64-32, the Commissioner shall order the measures required by G.S. 64-31(a), and shall also order the employer to pay a civil penalty of two thousand dollars ($2,000) for each required employee verification the employer failed to make. (2011-263, s. 3.)

§ 64-34. (For effective date, see Editor's note) Commissioner to maintain copies of orders.

The Commissioner shall maintain copies of orders issued pursuant to G.S. 64-31, 64-32, and 64-33, and shall maintain a database of the employers and business locations that have a violation of G.S. 64-26 and make the orders available on the Commissioner's Web site. (2011-263, s. 3.)

§ 64-35. (For effective date, see Editor's note) Work authorization shall be verified through the federal government.

When investigating a complaint under this Article, the Commissioner shall verify the work authorization of the alleged unauthorized alien with the federal government pursuant to 8 U.S.C. § 1373(c). The Commissioner shall not attempt to independently make a final determination of whether an alien is authorized to work in the United States. (2011-263, s. 3.)

§ 64-36. (For effective date, see Editor's note) Appeal of Commissioner's order.

A determination by the Commissioner pursuant to this Article shall be final, unless within 15 days after receipt of notice thereof by certified mail with return receipt, by signature confirmation as provided by the U.S. Postal Service, by a designated delivery service authorized pursuant to 26 U.S.C. § 7502(f)(2) with delivery receipt, or via hand delivery, the employer charged with the violation takes exception to the determination, in which event final determination shall be made in an administrative proceeding pursuant to Article 3 of Chapter 150B of the General Statutes and in a judicial proceeding pursuant to Article 4 of Chapter 150B of the General Statutes. (2011-263, s. 3.)

§ 64-37. (For effective date, see Editor's note) Rules.

The Commissioner may adopt rules needed to implement this Article. (2011-263, s. 3.)

§ 64-38. (For effective date, see Editor's note) Article does not require action that is contrary to federal or State law.

This Article shall not be construed to require an employer to take any action that the employer believes in good faith would violate federal or State law. (2011-263, s. 3.)

Chapter 65.

Cemeteries.

Article 1.

Care of Rural Cemeteries.

§ 65-1: Repealed by Session Laws 2007-118, s. 2, effective July 1, 2007.

§ 65-2: Repealed by Session Laws 2007-118, s. 2, effective July 1, 2007.

§ 65-3: Repealed by Session Laws 2007-118, s. 2, effective July 1, 2007.

Article 2.

Care of Confederate Cemetery.

§ 65-4. State Division of Adult Correction of the Department of Public Safety to furnish labor.

The Division of Adult Correction of the Department of Public Safety is hereby authorized and directed to furnish at such time, or times, as may be convenient, such prisoner's labor as may be available, to properly care for the Confederate Cemetery situated in the City of Raleigh, such services to be rendered by the State's prisoners without compensation. (1927, c. 224, s. 1; 1933, c. 172; 1957, c. 349, s. 10; 1967, c. 996, s. 13; 2011-145, s. 19.1(h); 2012-83, s. 32.)

Article 3.

Cemeteries for Inmates of County Homes.

§ 65-5. County commissioners may establish new cemeteries.

The boards of county commissioners of the various counties in the State are authorized and empowered to locate and establish new graveyards or cemeteries upon the lands of their respective counties for the burial of the inmates of the county homes. (1917, c. 151, s. 1; C.S., s. 5022.)

§ 65-6. Removal and reinterment of bodies.

Whenever the county commissioners have established new graveyards or cemeteries, they are authorized and empowered to remove to such graveyards or cemeteries all bodies of deceased inmates of the county homes. (1917, c. 151, s. 2; C.S., s. 5023.)

Article 4.

Trust Funds for the Care of Cemeteries.

§ 65-7: Repealed by Session Laws 2007-118, s. 3, effective July 1, 2007.

§ 65-8: Repealed by Session Laws 2007-118, s. 3, effective July 1, 2007.

§ 65-9: Repealed by Session Laws 2007-118, s. 3, effective July 1, 2007.

§ 65-10: Repealed by Session Laws 2007-118, s. 3, effective July 1, 2007.

§ 65-11: Repealed by Session Laws 2007-118, s. 3, effective July 1, 2007.

§ 65-12: Repealed by Session Laws 2007-118, s. 3, effective July 1, 2007.

Article 5.

Removal of Graves.

§ 65-13: Repealed by Session Laws 2007-118, s. 4, effective July 1, 2007, and applicable to all trusts created on or after that date.

§§ 65-14 through 65-15. Repealed by Session Laws 1971, c. 797, s. 2.

Article 6.

Cemetery Associations.

§ 65-16. Land holdings.

All cemetery associations or corporations created by any local, private or special act or resolution before January 10, 1917, are authorized and fully empowered to hold amounts of land in excess of the limitation provided in the local, private or special act or resolution incorporating or chartering such cemetery association or corporation. (1923, c. 76, s. 1; C.S., s. 5030(b).)

§ 65-17. Change of name of association or corporation.

Any corporation or association chartered or incorporated by any special act of the legislature, as set forth in G.S. 65-16, is authorized and fully empowered to change the name of such association or corporation by a majority vote of its directors, and upon such change in name it shall be the duty of the officers of the board of directors of such corporation or association to file with the clerk of the superior court a copy of resolution changing the name, which resolution must show the act of the legislature creating or incorporating the same and the reasons for the change thereof. (1923, c. 76, s. 2; C.S., s. 5030(c).)

§ 65-17.1. Quorum at stockholders' meeting of certain nonprofit cemetery corporations; calling meeting; amendment of charter.

Notwithstanding any conflicting provision of law or of the charter or bylaws of any corporation affected by this section, in the case of any nonprofit cemetery corporation chartered prior to the year 1900 whose charter has expired prior to May 18, 1955, a quorum at any meeting of stockholders called for the purpose of electing directors, or of amending the charter of such corporation, or both, shall consist of the holders of ten percent (10%) or more of the outstanding shares of the capital stock of such corporation having voting powers, present in person or represented by proxy; and a meeting of the stockholders of such corporation for such purpose or purposes may be called by any two stockholders after 10 days' notice by registered mail to all stockholders of record at their last known addresses as shown by the stock book of such corporation. The concurrence of a majority of the shares represented at such meeting shall be sufficient to authorize an amendment or amendments to the charter of such corporation in accordance with the provisions of G.S. 55-31. (1955, c. 1084.)

Article 7.

Cemeteries Operated for Private Gain.

§§ 65-18 through 65-36: Recodified as §§ 65-46 through 65-72.

Article 7A.

Funeral and Burial Trust Funds.

§§ 65-36.1 through 65-36.8: Recodified as §§ 90-210.30 through 90-210.37, by Session Laws 1985, c. 12, s. 1.

Article 8.

Municipal Cemeteries.

§ 65-37: Repealed by Session Laws 2007-118, s. 5, effective July 1, 2007, and applicable to all trusts created on or after that date.

§ 65-38. Repealed by Session Laws 1969, c. 1279.

§ 65-39: Repealed by Session Laws 2007-118, s. 5, effective July 1, 2007, and applicable to all trusts created on or after that date.

§ 65-40: Repealed by Session Laws 2007-118, s. 5, effective July 1, 2007, and applicable to all trusts created on or after that date.

Article 8A.

Veterans Cemeteries.

§ 65-41. Land acquisition.

The State may accept land for the establishment of not more than four veterans cemeteries. (1987, c. 183, s. 1; 2013-360, s. 36.2(e).)

§ 65-42. Location of cemeteries.

These veterans cemeteries may be located in those regions of the State with a high concentration of veterans including the 3rd, 7th and 11th United States Congressional Districts. (1987, c. 183, s. 1.)

§ 65-43. Definitions.

For purposes of this Article, the following definitions shall apply, unless the context requires otherwise:

(1) "Honorable military service" means:

a. Service on active duty, other than for training, as a member of the Armed Forces of the United States, when the service was terminated under honorable conditions;

b. Service on active duty as a member of the Armed Forces of the United States at the time of death under honorable conditions;

c. Service on active duty for training or full-time service as a member of a reserve component of the Armed Forces of the United States, the Army National Guard, the Air National Guard, or the Reserve Officer Training Corps of the Army, Navy, or Air Force, at the time of death under honorable conditions.

(2) A "legal resident" of a state means a person whose principal residence or abode is in that state, who uses that state to establish his or her right to vote and other rights in a state, and who intends to live in that state, to the exclusion of maintaining a legal residence in any other state.

(3) A "qualified veteran" means a veteran who meets the requirements of sub-subdivisions a. and b. of this subdivision:

a. A veteran who served an honorable military service or who served a period of honorable nonregular service and is any of the following:

1. A veteran who is entitled to retired pay for nonregular service under 10 U.S.C. §§ 12731-12741, as amended.

2. A veteran who would have been entitled to retired pay for nonregular service under 10 U.S.C. §§ 12731-12741, as amended, but for the fact that the person was under 60 years of age.

3. A veteran who is eligible for interment in a national cemetery under 38 U.S.C. § 2402, as amended.

b. Who is a legal resident of North Carolina:

1. At the time of death, or

2. For a period of at least 10 years, or

3. At the time he or she entered the Armed Forces of the United States. (1987 (Reg. Sess., 1988), c. 1051, s. 1; 1993, c. 553, s. 24; 2001-143, s. 1; 2011-183, s. 49.)

§ 65-43.1. Eligibility for interment in a State veterans cemetery.

(a) The following persons are eligible for interment at a State veterans cemetery:

(1) A qualified veteran.

(2) The spouse, widow, or widower of a qualified veteran, or a minor child who is unmarried and dependent on the qualified veteran at the time of death. For purposes of this subdivision, "minor child" includes a child under 21 years of age or under 23 years of age if pursuing a course of instruction at an educational institution approved by the United States Department of Veterans Affairs.

(3) An unmarried adult child of a qualified veteran when the child became permanently incapable of self-support because of a physical or mental disability before attaining the age of 18 years.

(b) Only one grave site is authorized for a qualified veteran and his eligible family members. A grave site may not be reserved until the death of a person who is eligible for interment. When a death occurs and the deceased is determined to be eligible for interment in a State veteran cemetery pursuant to subsection (b) of this section, a grave site shall be assigned in the name of the veteran.

(c) When an eligible family member dies before the qualified veteran dies, the veteran shall sign an agreement to be interred in the same plot with the family member before the deceased family member is interred in the veterans cemetery. (1987 (Reg. Sess, 1988), c. 1051, s. 1; 2001-143, s. 2.)

§ 65-43.2. Proof of eligibility.

(a) The veteran, his survivors, or his legal representative shall furnish any evidence necessary to establish the eligibility of the veteran or the family member before the veteran or eligible family member may be interred in a State veterans cemetery.

(b) The survivors or legal representative of the deceased shall notify the funeral director that the deceased is to be interred in a veterans cemetery. The survivor or legal representative shall furnish the funeral director with documentary evidence of the veteran's honorable military service and evidence to establish that the veteran is a legal resident of North Carolina. The funeral director shall notify the superintendent of the nearest State veterans cemetery to arrange for the interment and convey to the superintendent all evidence to establish the veteran's eligibility. (1987 (Reg. Sess., 1988), c. 1051, s. 1.)

§ 65-43.3. Bars to eligibility.

A veteran may not be interred in a State veterans cemetery under any of the following circumstances:

(1) He was discharged or dismissed on the grounds that:

a. He was a conscientious objector who refused to perform military duty;

b. He was a deserter; or

c. He was an officer who accepted his resignation for the good of the service;

(2) He was convicted of subversive activities against the United States after separation from active military service; or

(3) He was separated from the Armed Forces of the United States for the good of the service due to a willful and persistent unauthorized absence and issued a Clemency Discharge (DD Form 1953) pursuant to Presidential Proclamation No. 4313. (1987 (Reg. Sess., 1988), c. 1051, s. 1.)

§ 65-43.4. Disinterment.

(a) When a veteran fails to abide by his agreement to be interred in the same grave site as his previously interred eligible family member, the veteran, his legal representative, or his heirs shall have the remains of the family member removed from the cemetery at no cost to the State.

(b) A disinterment may be permitted, at no cost to the State, when the following conditions are satisfied:

(1) The disinterment is requested in writing and filed with the Program Director of the veterans cemeteries, the Assistant Secretary for Veterans Affairs, or the Division of Veterans Affairs;

(2) The request for disinterment contains the notarized signature of the nearest of kin, such as surviving spouse. If the spouse is deceased, the signatures of a majority of the surviving children of legal age will be required;

(3) The funeral director has obtained all necessary permits for disinterment. (1987 (Reg. Sess., 1988), c. 1051, s. 1.)

§ 65-43.5. Reinterment.

(a) The remains of a qualified veteran or the remains of an eligible family member may be moved to a State veterans cemetery for reinterment, at no cost to the State, when the following conditions are satisfied:

(1) The superintendent of the State veterans cemetery has been presented with proof of eligibility in accordance with G.S. 65-43.2;

(2) The reinterment is requested in writing and filed with the Program Manager of veterans cemeteries, the Assistant Secretary for Veterans Affairs, or the Division of Veterans Affairs; and

(3) The request for reinterment contains the notarized signatures of the veteran or his legal representative, all living immediate family members, and any other interested living family member;

(4) The request for reinterment contains a statement of the circumstances and reasons for reinterment; and

(5) The funeral director has obtained all necessary permits for reinterment.

(b) If permission for reinterment is granted, an agreement shall be entered into between the veteran or his living representative, all living immediate family members, and any interested living family members, and the Assistant Secretary of Veterans Affairs. (1987 (Reg. Sess., 1988), c. 1051, s. 1.)

§ 65-43.6. State veterans cemeteries cost.

(a) There may be no charge for the grave site or the interment service of a qualified veteran. There may be a minimal charge, to be set by the Division of Veteran Affairs, for only the opening and closing of the grave of an eligible family member.

(b) All other costs, including funeral expenses and costs of the headstone, transportation of the remains, or grave liner or burial vault shall be paid out of allowances by the Veterans Administration or private funds.

(c) All costs resulting from damage to, or destruction or theft of a grave site, headstone, or any other grave monument may not be borne by the State. (1987 (Reg. Sess., 1988), c. 1051, s. 1.)

§ 65-44. Days for burial.

Notwithstanding any other provision of law, burial services shall be conducted at the Coastal Carolina State Veterans Cemetery and the Sandhills State Veterans Cemetery from Monday through Sunday, except when the day for services falls on a State holiday. (2004-124, s. 19.2(a).)

§ 65-45. Reserved for future codification purposes.

Article 9.

North Carolina Cemetery Act.

§ 65-46. Short title.

This Article 9 may be cited as "North Carolina Cemetery Act." (1975, c. 768, s. 1.)

§ 65-47. Scope.

(a)   The provisions of this Article shall apply to all persons engaged in the business of operating a cemetery as defined herein, except cemeteries owned and operated by governmental agencies or churches.

(b)   Any cemetery beneficially owned and operated by a fraternal organization or its corporate agent for at least 50 years prior to September 1, 1975, shall be exempt from the provisions of Article 9 of this Chapter.

(c)   The provisions of this Article shall not apply to persons licensed under Article 13D of Chapter 90 of the General Statutes when engaging in activities for which a license is required under the Article.

(d)   (Expires January 23, 2015) A columbarium that is built on the grounds of a private, self-contained retirement community in a county where no commercially available columbarium exists, funded solely by the residents of that community, and reserved exclusively for the residents' use shall be exempt from the provisions of Article 9 of this Chapter. (1975, c. 768, s. 1; 1977, c. 686, s. 1; 1995, c. 509, s. 135.1(i); 2013-335, s. 1.)

§ 65-48. Definitions.

As used in this Article, unless otherwise stated or unless the context or subject matter clearly indicates otherwise:

(1) "Bank of belowground crypts" means any construction unit of belowground crypts acceptable to the Commission which a cemetery uses to initiate its belowground crypt program or to add to existing belowground crypt structures.

(2) "Belowground crypts" consists of an interment space in preplaced chambers, either side by side or multiple depth, covered by earth and sod and are also known as lawn crypts, westminsters or turf top crypts.

(3) "Cemetery" means any one or a combination of more than one of the following in a place used or to be used and dedicated or designated for cemetery purposes:

a. A burial park, for earth interment.

b. A mausoleum.

c. A columbarium.

(4) "Cemetery broker" means a legal entity engaged in the business of arranging sales of cemetery products between legal entities and which sale does not involve a cemetery company, but does not mean funeral establishments or funeral directors operating under G.S. 90-210.25, when dealing between legal entities wherein one such entity shall be members of the family of a deceased person or other persons authorized by law to arrange for the burial and funeral of such deceased human being. The North Carolina Cemetery Act shall not apply to any cemetery broker selling less than five grave spaces per year.

(5) "Cemetery company" means any legal entity that owns or controls cemetery lands or property and conducts the business of a cemetery, including all cemeteries owned and operated by governmental agencies, churches and fraternal organizations or their corporate agents for the duration of any sales and management contracts entered into with cemetery sales organizations or cemetery management organizations for cemetery purposes, or with any other legal entity other than direct employees of said governmental agency, church or fraternal organization.

(6) "Cemetery management organization" means any legal entity contracting as an independent contractor with a cemetery company to manage

a cemetery but does not mean individual managers employed by and contracting directly with cemetery companies operating under this Article.

(7) "Cemetery sales organization" means any legal entity contracting with a cemetery which is exempt or not exempt under this Article to conduct sales of cemetery products, but does not mean individual salesmen or sales managers employed by and contracting directly with cemetery companies operating under this Article, nor does it mean funeral establishments or funeral directors operating under licenses authorized by G.S. 90-210.25 when dealing directly with a cemetery company and with members of the family of a deceased person or other persons authorized by law to arrange for the burial and funeral of such deceased human being.

(8) "Columbarium" means a structure or building substantially exposed aboveground intended to be used for the interment of the cremated remains of a deceased person.

(9) "Commission" means the North Carolina Cemetery Commission.

(10) "Grave space" means a space of ground in a cemetery intended to be used for the interment in the ground of the remains of a deceased person.

(11) "Human remains" or "remains" means the bodies of deceased persons, and includes the bodies in any stage of decomposition, and cremated remains.

(12) "Mausoleum" means a structure or building substantially exposed aboveground intended to be used for the entombment of remains of a deceased person.

(13) "Mausoleum section" means any construction unit of a mausoleum acceptable to the Commission which a cemetery uses to initiate its mausoleum program or to add to its existing mausoleum structures.

(14) "Person" means an individual, corporation, partnership, joint venture, or association.

(15) "Vault" means a crypt or underground receptacle which is used for interment in the ground and which is designed to encase and protect caskets or similar burial devices. For the purposes of this Article, a vault is a preneed item until delivery to the purchaser. (1943, c. 644, s. 2; 1967, c. 1009, s. 2; 1971, c. 1149, s. 1; 1975, c. 768, s. 1; 1977, c. 686, ss. 2, 3.)

§ 65-49. The North Carolina Cemetery Commission.

The North Carolina Cemetery Commission is established with the power and duty to adopt rules and regulations to be followed in the enforcement of this Article. (1975, c. 768, s. 1; 1989, c. 751, s. 7(5); 1991 (Reg. Sess., 1992), c. 959, s. 19; 2012-120, s. 3(a).)

§ 65-50. Cemetery Commission; members, selection, quorum.

(a) Membership. - The Cemetery Commission shall consist of nine members. The General Assembly shall appoint two members who own or manage or who have retired from owning or managing a cemetery in North Carolina, one of whom shall be recommended by the President Pro Tempore of the Senate and one of whom shall be recommended by the Speaker of the House of Representatives. The Governor shall appoint seven members as follows:

(1) Two members who own or manage cemeteries in North Carolina.

(2) Three members who are selected from six nominees submitted by the North Carolina Cemetery Association.

(3) Two public members who have no financial interest in, and are not involved in management of, any cemetery or funeral related business.

(b) Terms. - Four members of the initial Commission shall be appointed for a term to expire June 30, 1977, and three members shall be appointed for a term to expire June 30, 1976. At the end of the respective terms of office of the initial members of the Commission, their successors shall be nominated in the same manner, selected from the same categories and appointed for terms of four years and until their successors are appointed and qualified.

(b1) Any vacancy shall be filled by the authority originally filling that position, except that any vacancy in appointments by the General Assembly shall be filled in accordance with G.S. 120-122.

(c) Removal. - The appointing authority shall have the power to remove any member of the Commission appointed by that authority from office for misfeasance, malfeasance and nonfeasance according to applicable provisions of law.

(d) Quorum. - A majority of the Commission shall constitute a quorum for the transaction of business.

(e) Officers. - At the first meeting of the Commission held after September 1, 1975, the Commission shall elect one of its members as its chair and another as its vice-chair, both to serve through June 30 of the next following year. Thereafter, at its first meeting held on or after July 1 of each year, the Commission shall elect from its members a president, vice president, and secretary-treasurer with no two offices to be held by the same person. All officers shall serve a term of one year and shall serve until their successors are elected and qualified. (1975, c. 768, s. 1; 2001-486, s. 2.1; 2012-120, s. 3(b).)

§ 65-51. Principal office.

The principal office of the Commission shall be in the City of Raleigh, North Carolina. Notice of all regular and special meetings of the Commission shall be advertised 10 or more days in advance in at least three newspapers in North Carolina having inter-county circulation in the State. Each member of the Commission shall receive per diem and allowances in accordance with G.S. 93B-5. Members of the Commission and other employees required to attend and legal counsel to the Commission shall be entitled to actual expenses while attending regular or special meetings of the Commission held other than in Raleigh, North Carolina. All salaries, compensation, and expenses of the Commission shall be paid from funds coming to the Commission pursuant to this Article. In no case shall any salary, compensation, or other expense of the Commission be charged against the General Fund. (1975, c. 768, s. 1; 2012-120, s. 3(c).)

§ 65-52. Regular and special meetings.

The Cemetery Commission shall meet at least once in each quarter and may hold special meetings at any time and place within the State at the call of the chairman or upon the written request of at least four members. (1975, c. 768, s. 1.)

§ 65-53. Powers.

In addition to other powers conferred by this Article, the Cemetery Commission shall have the following powers and duties:

(1) To employ staff, including legal counsel, as may be necessary to perform its duties and determine the compensation of its employees.

(2) To examine a cemetery company's records when a person applies for a change of control of the company.

(3) Investigate, upon its own initiative or upon a verified complaint in writing, the actions of any person engaged in the business or acting in the capacity of a licensee under this Article. The license of a licensee may be revoked or suspended for a period not exceeding two years, or until compliance with a lawful order imposed in the final order of suspension, or both, where the licensee in performing or attempting to perform any of the acts specified in this Article has been guilty of:

a. Failing to pay the fees required herein;

b. Failing to make any reports required by this Article;

c. Failing to remit to the care and maintenance trust fund, merchandise trust fund, or preconstruction trust fund the required amounts;

d. Making any substantial misrepresentation;

e. Making any false statement of a character likely to influence or persuade;

f. A continued and flagrant course of misrepresentation or making of false promises through cemetery agents or salesmen;

g. Violating any provision of this Article or rule promulgated by the Commission; or

h. Any other conduct, whether of the same or a different character than specified in this section, which constitutes fraud or dishonest dealing.

(4) To hold hearings in accordance with the provisions of this Article and Article 3A of Chapter 150B of the General Statutes to subpoena witnesses and to administer oaths to or receive the affirmation of witnesses before the Commission.

In any show cause hearing before the Commission held under the authority of Article 3A of Chapter 150B of the General Statutes where the Commission imposes discipline against a licensee, the Commission may recover the costs, other than attorneys' fees, of holding the hearing against all respondents jointly, not to exceed two thousand five hundred dollars ($2,500).

(5) To apply to the courts, in its own name, for injunctive relief to prevent violations of this Article or violations of any rules adopted pursuant to this Article. Any court may grant injunctive relief regardless of whether criminal prosecution or any other action is instituted as a result of the violation. A single violation is sufficient to invoke the injunctive relief under this subdivision. In any such action, an order or judgment may be entered awarding such temporary or permanent injunction as may be deemed proper; provided, that before any such action is brought the Commission shall give the cemetery at least 20 days' notice in writing, stating the alleged violation and giving the cemetery an opportunity within the 20-day period to cure the violation. In addition to all other means provided by law for the enforcement of a temporary restraining order, temporary injunction, or permanent injunction, the court shall have the power and jurisdiction to impound and to appoint a receiver for the property and business of the defendant, including books, papers, documents, and records appertaining thereto or so much thereof as the court may deem reasonably necessary to prevent further violation of this Article through or by means of the use of said property and business. The Commission may institute proceedings against the cemetery or its officers, whereafter an examination, pursuant to this Article, a shortage in the care and maintenance trust fund, merchandise trust fund or mausoleum and belowground crypts preconstruction trust fund is discovered, to recover said shortage.

(6) Whenever any special additional audit or examination of a licensee's premises, facilities, books or records is necessary because of the failure of the licensee to comply with the requirements imposed in this Article or by the rules and regulations of the Commission, to charge a fee based on the cost of the

special examination or audit, taking into consideration the salary of any employees involved in the special audit or examination and any expenses incurred.

(7) To promulgate rules and regulations requiring licensees to file with the Commission plans and specifications for the minimum quality of any product sold. The sale of any product for which plans and specifications required by the rules and regulations have not been filed or sale of any product of a lesser quality than the plans and specifications filed with the Commission is a violation of this Article.

(8) When the Commission finds that failure by a licensee to maintain a cemetery properly has caused that cemetery to be a public nuisance or a health or safety hazard, the Commission may bring an action for injunctive relief, against the responsible licensee, in the superior court of the county in which the cemetery or any part thereof is located.

(9) To acquire, hold, rent, encumber, alienate, and otherwise deal with real property in the same manner as a private person or corporation, subject only to approval of the Governor and Council of State. Collateral pledged by the Commission for an encumbrance is limited to the assets, incomes, and resources of the Commission.

(10) To purchase, rent, or lease equipment and supplies and purchase liability insurance to cover the activities of the Commission, its operations, or its employees. (1943, c. 644, s. 17; 1971, c. 1149, s. 8; 1973, c. 732, s. 2; 1975, c. 768, s. 1; 1977, c. 686, ss. 4-6; 1979, c. 888, ss. 1-3; 1981 (Reg. Sess., 1982), c. 1153; 1987, c. 488, s. 8; c. 827, s. 1; 1991, c. 653, s. 3; 2012-120, s. 3(d).)

§ 65-53.1. Inspectors.

(a) The Commission may appoint one or more agents who shall serve at the pleasure of the Commission and who shall have the title "Inspector of the North Carolina Cemetery Commission."

(b) To determine compliance with the provisions of this Article and regulations promulgated under this Article, inspectors may do the following:

(1) Enter the office, establishment, or place of business in North Carolina of any cemetery broker, cemetery company, cemetery management organization, cemetery sales organization, or preneed sales licensee to inspect the records, office, establishment, or facility or to inspect the practice conducted or license of any licensee.

(2) Inspect criminal and probation records of licensees and applicants for licenses under this Article to obtain evidence of their character.

(c) Inspectors may serve papers and subpoenas issued by the Commission or any office or member thereof under authority of this Article and shall perform other duties prescribed or ordered by the Commission.

(d) The Commission may prescribe an inspection form to be used by the inspectors in performing their duties.

(e) Upon request by the Commission, the Attorney General of North Carolina shall provide the inspectors with appropriate identification cards signed by the Attorney General or his or her designated agent. In lieu of identification cards, the Commission may design and issue badges to inspectors. (2012-120, s. 3(e).)

§ 65-54. Annual budget of Commission; collection of funds.

The Commission shall prepare an annual budget and shall collect the sums of money required for this budget from yearly fees and from any other sources provided in this Article. On or before July 1 of each year, each licensed cemetery shall pay a license fee to be set by the Commission in an amount not to exceed six hundred dollars ($600.00). In addition, each licensed cemetery shall pay to the Commission an inspection fee for each grave space, niche, or mausoleum crypt when the certificate of interment right is issued and shall pay a fee for each vault, belowground crypt, memorial, or opening and closing of a grave space that is included in a preneed cemetery contract. The inspection fee for each grave space, niche, or mausoleum crypt is payable when the certificate of interment right is issued and may not exceed four dollars ($4.00). The fee for each of the listed items that are included in a preneed cemetery contract is payable when the contract is made and may not exceed ten dollars ($10.00). (1975, c. 768, s. 1; 1977, c. 686, s. 7; 1987, c. 488, s. 1; 1991, c. 653, s. 1; 2004-202, s. 1.)

§ 65-54.1. Commission records are confidential.

Records, papers, and other documents containing information collected or compiled by the Commission, its members, or employees as a result of a complaint, investigation, inquiry, or interview in connection with an application for license, or in connection with a license holder's professional ethics and conduct, shall not be considered public records within the meaning of Chapter 132 of the General Statutes. Any notice or statement of charges against a license holder or applicant, or any notice to a license holder or applicant of a hearing to be held by the Commission, is a public record even though it may contain information collected and compiled as a result of a complaint, investigation, inquiry, or interview conducted by the Commission. If any record, paper, or other document containing information collected and compiled by the Commission is admitted into evidence in a hearing held by the Commission, it shall then be a public record within the meaning of Chapter 132 of the General Statutes. (2012-120, s. 3(f).)

§ 65-55. License; cemetery company.

(a) No legal entity shall engage in the business of operating a cemetery company except as authorized by this Article and without first obtaining a license from the Commission.

(b) Any legal entity wishing to establish a cemetery shall file a written application for authority with the Commission on forms provided by the Commission.

(c) Upon receipt of the application and filing fee to be set by the Commission in an amount not to exceed one thousand six hundred dollars ($1,600), the Commission shall cause an investigation to be made to establish the following criteria for approval of the application:

(1) The creation of a legal entity to conduct cemetery business, and its proposed financial structure.

(2) A perpetual care trust fund agreement, with an initial deposit of not less than fifty thousand dollars ($50,000) and with a bank cashier's check or certified check attached for the amount made payable to the trustee. The trust fund agreement must be executed by the applicant, accepted by the trustee, and conditional only upon approval of the application.

(3) A plat of the land to be used for the cemetery, showing the location of the cemetery and the access roads to the cemetery.

(4) Designation by the legal entity wishing to establish a cemetery of a general manager. The general manager must be a person of good moral character and have at least one year's experience in cemeteries.

(5) Development plans sufficient to ensure the community that the cemetery will provide adequate cemetery services and that the property is suitable for use as a cemetery.

(d) The Commission, after receipt of the investigating report, shall grant or refuse to grant the authority to organize a cemetery based upon the criteria set forth in G.S. 65-55(c).

(e) If the Commission intends to deny an application, it shall give written notice to the applicant of its intention to deny. The notice shall state a time and a place for a hearing before the Commission and a summary statement of the reasons for the proposed denial. The notice of intent shall be mailed by certified mail to the applicant at the address stated in the application at least 15 days prior to the scheduled hearing date. The applicant shall pay the costs of this hearing as assessed by the Commission unless the applicant notifies the Commission by certified mail at least five days prior to the scheduled hearing date that a hearing is waived. Any appeals from the Commission's decision shall be to the court having jurisdiction of the applicant or the Commission.

(f) If the Commission intends to grant the authority, it shall give written notice that the authority to organize a cemetery has been granted and that a license to operate will be issued upon the completion of the following:

(1) Establishment of the care and maintenance trust fund and receipt by the Commission of a certificate from the trust company, certifying receipt of the initial deposit required under this Article.

(2) Full development, ready for burial, of not less than two acres including a completed paved road from a public roadway to said developed section, certified by inspection of the Commission or its representative.

(3) A description, by metes and bounds, of the acreage tract of such proposed cemetery, together with evidence, by title insurance policy or by certificate of an attorney-at-law, certifying that the applicant is the owner in fee simple of such tract of land, which must contain not less than 30 acres, and that the title to not less than 30 acres is free and clear of all encumbrances. In counties with a population of less than 35,000 population according to the latest federal decennial census the tract need be only 15 acres.

(4) A plat of the cemetery showing the number and location of all lots surveyed and permanently staked for sale. (1943, c. 644, s. 9; 1957, c. 529, s. 3; 1967, c. 1009, s. 9; 1975, c. 768, s. 1; 1977, c. 686, s. 8; 1987, c. 488, s. 2; 1991, c. 653, s. 2; 2004-202, s. 2.)

§ 65-56. Existing companies; effect of Article.

Existing cemetery companies at the time of the adoption of this Chapter shall continue in full force and effect and be granted a license but shall hereafter be operated in accordance with the provisions of Article 9 of this Chapter. (1975, c. 768, s. 1.)

§ 65-57. Licenses for sales organizations, management organizations and brokers.

(a) No legal entity shall engage in the business of a cemetery sales organization, a cemetery management organization or a cemetery broker except as authorized by this Article, and without first obtaining a license from the Commission.

(b) Any legal entity wishing to establish and operate the business of a cemetery sales organization, a cemetery management organization or a cemetery broker shall file a written application for authority with the Commission on forms provided by the Commission which must contain such of the following documents and information as may be required by the Commission:

(1) The appointment of a North Carolina resident to receive service of any lawful process in any noncriminal proceedings arising under this Chapter against the applicant, its principal owners, principal stockholders, directors and general manager or their personal representatives.

(2) The states or other jurisdictions in which the applicant presently is conducting the business activity applied for or other similar businesses and any adverse order, judgment or decree entered against the applicant in each jurisdiction or by any court.

(3) The applicant's name, address and the form, date and jurisdiction of the organization and the address of each of its offices within or without this State.

(4) The name, address, principal occupation for the past five years of every director and officer of the applicant or person occupying a similar status or performing similar functions.

(5) Copies of the articles of incorporation or articles of partnership or joint venture agreement or other instrument establishing the legal entity of the applicant.

(c) The application shall be accompanied by an initial filing fee to be set by the Commission in an amount not to exceed one thousand dollars ($1,000) for cemetery sales organization and cemetery management organization and an initial filing fee to be set by the Commission in an amount not to exceed five hundred dollars ($500.00) for a cemetery broker. If ninety percent (90%) or more of the applicant is owned by an existing cemetery company operating under the North Carolina Cemetery Act, then the initial filing fee shall be one half of the sums set out herein. On or before July 1 of each year, each licensed cemetery sales organization, cemetery management organization, or cemetery broker shall pay a license renewal fee to be set by the Commission in an amount not to exceed six hundred dollars ($600.00) per year.

(d) Upon receipt of the application and filing fee, the Commission shall cause an investigation to be made of the legal entity to conduct the business applied for and the qualification of said legal entity to do business in North Carolina.

(e) The Commission, after receipt of the investigation report, shall grant or refuse to grant the authority to organize the organization applied for after it determines that the applicant possesses good character and general fitness or, in the case of a business association, employs and is directed by personnel of good character and general fitness.

(f)　If the Commission intends to deny an application, it shall give written notice to the applicant of its intention to deny. The notice shall state a time and a place for hearing before the Commission and a summary statement of the reasons for the proposed denial. The notice of intent shall be mailed by certified mail to the applicant at the address stated in the application at least 15 days prior to the scheduled hearing date. Any appeals from the Commission's decision shall be to the court having jurisdiction of the applicant, or in the event of an out-of-state applicant, then to the court having jurisdiction of the Commission.

(g)　If the Commission intends to grant the authority, it shall give written notice that the authority to organize the business applied for has been granted and that a license to operate will be issued upon presentment to the Commission of a statement of employment between the applicant and the cemetery or cemeteries to be serviced thereby.

(h)　Any person or any cemetery sales organization or any cemetery management organization or any cemetery broker violating the provisions of this section is guilty of a Class 1 misdemeanor, and shall be subject to revocation of the license to operate. (1975, c. 768, s. 1; 1977, c. 686, ss. 9, 10; 1993, c. 539, s. 500; 1994, Ex. Sess., c. 24, s. 14(c); 2004-202, s. 3.)

§ 65-58. Licenses for persons selling preneed grave space.

(a)　No person shall offer to sell preneed grave spaces, mausoleum crypts, niches, memorials, vaults or any other preneed cemetery merchandise or services under any plan authorized for any cemetery, cemetery sales group, or cemetery management group, before obtaining a license from the Commission.

(b)　Persons wishing to obtain a license shall file a written application with the Commission on forms provided by the Commission. The Commission may require such information and documents as it deems necessary to protect the public interest.

(c) The application shall be accompanied by a filing fee to be set by the Commission in an amount not to exceed one hundred dollars ($100.00) to cover the expenses of processing and investigation. After processing and investigation, the Commission shall grant, or refuse to grant, the license applied for. The license fee for a two-year term shall be set by the Commission but shall not exceed one hundred dollars ($100.00).

(d) If the Commission refuses to grant the license applied for, it shall give written notice to the applicant. The notice shall state a time and a place for hearing before the Commission, and a summary statement of the reasons for the refusal to grant the license. The notice shall be mailed by registered mail or certified mail to the applicant at the address stated in the application at least 30 days prior to the scheduled hearing date.

(e) If the Commission intends to grant the license, it shall give written notice that the license will be issued upon presentment to the Commission of a duly executed statement of employment between the applicant and the cemetery or cemeteries to be serviced thereby.

(f) The provisions of Article 4 of Chapter 150B of the General Statutes of North Carolina relating to "Judicial Review" shall apply to appeals or petitions for judicial review by any person or persons aggrieved by an order or decision of the Commission.

(g) Repealed by Session Laws 1977, c. 686, s. 12. (1943, c. 644, s. 15; 1967, c. 1009, s. 14; 1975, c. 768, s. 1; 1977, c. 686, ss. 11, 12; 1987, c. 827, s. 1; 2004-202, s. 4.)

§ 65-59. Application for a change of control; filing fee.

A person who proposes to acquire control of an existing cemetery company, whether by purchasing the capital stock of the company, purchasing an owner's interest in the company, or otherwise acting to effectively change the control of the company, shall first make application on a form supplied by the Commission for a certificate of approval of the proposed change of control. The application shall contain the name and address of each proposed new owner. The Commission shall issue a certificate of approval only after it determines that the proposed new owners are qualified by character, experience, and financial responsibility to control and operate the cemetery company in a legal and proper manner, and that the interest of the public generally will not be jeopardized by the proposed change in control. An application for approval of a change of control must be completed and accompanied by a filing fee to be set by the Commission in an amount not to exceed one thousand six hundred dollars ($1,600). The Commission shall not approve any change of control until the applicant has provided sufficient evidence that any trust account required under G.S. 65-66(b) and G.S. 65-70(b) is maintained and funded in the required amount. If the cemetery company posted a performance bond in lieu of any trust account required under G.S. 65-66(b) and G.S. 65-70(b), then the Commission shall not approve any change of control until the applicant has provided sufficient evidence that the performance bond is being appropriately maintained and in an amount sufficient to cover all payments made directly or indirectly by or on account of purchasers who have not received the purchased property and services. (1975, c. 768, s. 1; 1987, c. 488, s. 4; 1991, c. 653, s. 4; 2004-202, s. 5; 2010-102, s. 1.)

§ 65-60. Records.

A record shall be kept of every burial in the cemetery of a cemetery company, showing the date of burial, name of the person buried, together with lot, plot, and space in which such burial was made therein. All sales, trust funds, accounting records, and all other records of the licensee shall be available at the licensee's principal place of business in this State and shall be readily available at all reasonable times for examination by an authorized representative of the Commission. (1975, c. 768, s. 1.)

§ 65-60.1. Trustees; qualifications; examination of records; enforcement.

(a) The term "corporate trustee" as used in this Article shall mean a bank, credit union, or trust company authorized to do business in North Carolina under the supervision of the Commissioner of Banks, Credit Union Administrator, or any other corporate entity; provided that any corporate entity other than a bank, credit union, or trust company which acts as trustee under this Article shall first be approved by the Cemetery Commission and shall be subject to supervision by the Cemetery Commission as provided herein.

(b) Any corporate entity, other than a bank, credit union, or trust company, which desires to act as trustee for cemetery funds under this Article shall make application to the Commission for approval. The Commission shall approve the trustee when it has become satisfied that:

(1) The applicant employs and is directed by persons who are qualified by character, experience, and financial responsibility to care for and invest the funds of others.

(2) The applicant will perform its duties in a proper and legal manner and the trust funds and interest of the public generally will not be jeopardized.

(3) The applicant will act as trustee for cemetery funds which will exceed five hundred thousand dollars ($500,000) in the aggregate.

(4) The applicant is authorized to do business in North Carolina and has adequate facilities to perform its duties as trustee.

(c) Any trustee under this Article, other than a bank, credit union, or trust company under the supervision of the Commissioner of Banks, shall maintain records relative to cemetery trust funds as the Commission may by regulation prescribe. The records shall be available at the trustee's place of business in North Carolina and shall be available at all reasonable times for examination by a representative of the Commission. The records shall be audited annually, within 90 days from the end of the trust fund's fiscal year, by an independent certified public accountant, and a copy of the audit report shall be promptly forwarded to the Commission.

(d) Whenever it appears that an officer, director, or employee of a trustee, other than a bank, credit union, or trust company, is dishonest, incompetent, or reckless in the management of a cemetery trust fund, the Commission may bring an action in the courts to remove the trustee and to impound the property and business of the trustee as may be reasonably necessary to protect the trust funds.

(e) Any trustee shall invest and reinvest cemetery trust funds in the same manner as provided by law for the investment of trust funds by the clerk of the superior court; provided, however, that this subsection does not apply to a perpetual trust fund described in G.S. 65-64 or cemetery trust funds held in a fund designated as Trust Fund "A" pursuant to G.S. 65-64(e), which may be invested and reinvested in accordance with G.S. 32-71. (1977, c. 686, s. 15; 1979, c. 888, s. 9; 1995, c. 509, s. 135.3(a); 2010-102, s. 2.)

§ 65-61. Required trust fund for care and maintenance; remedy of Commission for noncompliance.

No cemetery company shall be permitted to establish, or operate if already established, a cemetery unless provision is made for the future care and maintenance of such cemetery by establishing a trust fund and designating a corporate trustee to administer said fund in accordance with a written trust agreement. If any cemetery company refuses or otherwise fails to provide or maintain an adequate care and maintenance trust fund in accordance with the provisions of this Article, the Commission, after reasonable notice, shall proceed to enforce compliance under the powers vested in it under this Article; provided any nonprofit cemetery corporation, incorporated and engaged in the cemetery business continuously since and prior to 1915 and whose current trust assets exceed seven hundred fifty thousand dollars ($750,000) shall not be required to designate a corporate trustee. The trust fund agreement shall contain and include the following: name, location, and address of both the licensee and the trustee showing the date of agreement together with the amounts required deposited as stated in this Article. No person shall withdraw or transfer any portion of the corpus of the care and maintenance trust fund without first obtaining written consent from the Commission. (1943, c. 644, s. 9; 1957, c. 529, s. 3; 1967, c. 1009, s. 9; 1975, c. 768, s. 1; 1977, c. 686, s. 13.)

§ 65-62. Individual contracts for care and maintenance.

At the time of making a sale or receiving the initial deposit hereunder, the cemetery company shall deliver to the person to whom such sale is made, or who makes such deposit, an instrument in writing which shall specifically state that the net income of the care and maintenance trust fund shall be used solely for the care and maintenance of the cemetery, for reasonable costs of administering such care and maintenance and for reasonable costs of administering the trust fund. (1975, c. 768, s. 1.)

§ 65-63. Requirements for perpetual care fund.

A cemetery company may not cause or permit advertising of a perpetual care fund in connection with the sale or offer for sale of its property unless the amount deposited in the fund is at least one hundred dollars ($100.00) or ten percent (10%) of the retail sale price, whichever is greater, per grave space, niche, or mausoleum crypt sold. Nothing may prohibit an individual cemetery from requiring a perpetual care deposit for grave memorial markers to be deposited in the perpetual care fund so long as the same assessment is uniformly applied to all grave memorial markers installed in the cemetery. (1943, c. 644, s. 5; 1957, c. 529, s. 1; 1967, c. 1009, s. 3; 1971, c. 1149, s. 3; 1975, c. 768, s. 1; 1979, c. 888, s. 4; 1987, c. 488, s. 5; 1991, c. 653, s. 5; 2004-202, s. 6.)

§ 65-64. Deposits to perpetual care fund.

(a) Deposits to the care and maintenance trust fund must be made by the cemetery company holding title to the subject cemetery lands on or before the last day of the calendar month following the calendar month in which final payment is received as provided herein; however the entire amount required to be deposited into the fund shall be paid within four years from the date of any contract requiring the payment regardless of whether all amounts have been received by the cemetery company. If the cemetery company fails to make timely deposit, the Commission may levy and collect a late filing fee of one dollar ($1.00) per day for each day the deposit is delinquent on each grave space, niche or mausoleum crypt sold. The care and maintenance trust fund shall be invested and reinvested by the trustee in accordance with G.S. 32-71. Investments may be made through means of a common trust fund as described in G.S. 53-163.5. Cemetery trust funds held in a fund designated as Trust Fund "A" pursuant to G.S. 65-64(e) may be invested and reinvested in accordance with G.S. 32-71. The fees and other expenses of the trust fund shall be paid by the trustee from the net income thereof and may not be paid from the corpus. To the extent that the net income is not sufficient to pay the fees and other expenses, the fees and other expenses shall be paid by the cemetery company.

(b) When a municipal, church-owned or fraternal cemetery converts to a private cemetery as defined in G.S. 65-48, then the cemetery shall establish and maintain a care and maintenance trust fund pursuant to this section; provided, however, the initial deposit for establishment of this trust fund shall be an amount equal to fifty dollars ($50.00) per space for all spaces either previously sold or contracted for sale in the cemetery at the time of conversion or fifty thousand dollars ($50,000), whichever sum is greater.

(c) Repealed by 1991 (Regular Session, 1992), c. 1007, s. 35.

(d) In each sales contract, reservation or agreement wherein burial rights are priced separately, the purchase price of the burial rights shall be the only item subject to care and maintenance trust fund deposits; but if the burial rights are not priced separately therein, the full amount of the contract, reservations or agreement shall be subject to care and maintenance trust fund deposits as provided herein, unless the purchase price of the burial rights can be determined from the accounting records of the cemetery company.

(e) When the amount deposited in the perpetual care fund required by this Article of any cemetery company shall amount to one hundred fifty thousand dollars ($150,000), anything in this Article to the contrary notwithstanding, the cemetery company may make all deposits thereafter either into the original perpetual care trust fund or into a separate fund established as an irrevocable trust, designated as Perpetual Care Trust Fund "A," and invested by the trustee, in accordance with G.S. 32-71. Funds in a trust fund designated as Trust Fund "A" may not be invested in another cemetery company.

(f) For special endowments for a specific lot, grave, or a family mausoleum, memorial, marker, or monument, the cemetery may set aside the full amounts received for this individual special care in a separate trust or by a deposit to a savings account in a bank, credit union, or savings and loan association located within and authorized to do business in the State; provided, however, if the licensee does not set up a separate trust or savings account for the special endowment the full amount thereof shall be deposited in Perpetual Care Trust Fund "A." (1943, c. 644, s. 10; 1957, c. 529, s. 4; 1967, c. 1009, s. 10; 1971, c. 1149, s. 5; 1975, c. 768, s. 1; 1977, c. 686, s. 14; 1979, c. 888, ss. 5, 6; 1987, c. 488, ss. 3, 6; 1991, c. 653, s. 6; 1991 (Reg. Sess., 1992), c. 1007, s. 35; 1995, c. 509, s. 135.3(b), (c); 2004-202, ss. 7, 8; 2010-102, s. 3.)

§ 65-65. Trust fund; financial reports.

Within 60 days after the end of the calendar or fiscal year of the cemetery company, the trustee shall furnish adequate financial reports with respect to the care fund on forms provided by the Commission. However, the Commission may require the trustee to make such additional financial reports as it may deem advisable. (1975, c. 768, s. 1.)

§ 65-66. Receipts from sale of personal property or services; trust account; penalties.

(a)   It shall be deemed contrary to public policy if any person or legal entity receives, holds, controls or manages funds or proceeds received from the sale of, or from a contract to sell, personal property or services which may be used in a cemetery in connection with the burial of or the commemoration of the memory of a deceased human being, where payments for the same are made either outright or on an installment basis prior to the demise of the person or persons so purchasing them or for whom they are so purchased, unless the person or legal entity holds, controls or manages the funds, subject to the limitations and regulations prescribed in this section. This section shall apply to all cemetery companies or other legal entities that offer for sale or sell personal property or services which may be used in a cemetery in connection with the burial of, or the commemoration of the memory of, a deceased human being, but shall exclude persons holding a license under Article 13D of Chapter 90 of the General Statutes.

(b)   Any cemetery company or other entity entering into a contract for the sale of personal property or services, to be used in a cemetery in connection with disposing of, or commemorating the memory of a deceased human being wherein the use of the personal property or the furnishing of services is not immediately requested or required, shall comply with the following requirements and conditions:

(1)   The cemetery company or other entity shall deposit an amount equal to sixty percent (60%) of all proceeds received on the contracts into a trust account, either in the form of an account governed by a trust agreement and handled by a corporate trustee or in the form of a passbook savings account, certificates of deposit for time certificates, or money-market certificates with a licensed and insured bank, credit union, or savings institution located in the State of North Carolina until the amount deposited equals sixty percent (60%) of the actual sale price of the property or services sold. The accounts or deposits or both shall be in the name of the cemetery company or other entity in a form

which will permit withdrawals only with the participation and consent of the Cemetery Commission as required by subdivision (4) of this subsection.

(2)   All funds received on account of a contract for the sale of the personal property or services, whether the funds be received directly from the purchaser or from the sale or assignment of notes entered into by the purchase or otherwise, shall be deposited into the trust account as required by subdivision (1) of this subsection.

(3)   All deposits required herein shall be made into the trust account so established on or before the last day of the month following receipt of the funds by the cemetery company or other entity.

(4)   Withdrawals from a trust account may be made by the depositor, but only with the written approval of the Commission or officer or employee of the Commission authorized to act for the Commission. Withdrawals may be made only upon delivery of the merchandise or services for which the funds were deposited, cancellation of a contract, the presence of excess funds in the trust account, or under other circumstances deemed appropriate by the Commission. The Commission shall promulgate rules and regulations governing withdrawals from trust accounts, including time and frequency of withdrawals, payments that will be made with the withdrawals, notice to the Commission prior to withdrawals, the number and identity of persons other than the owner who are authorized by the owner to make withdrawals, the officers and employees of the Commission authorized to approve withdrawals, and any other matters necessary to implement the provisions of this subdivision. Withdrawals will not be allowed if the amount remaining in the trust account would fall below sixty percent (60%) of all proceeds received on account of contracts for the sale of the personal property or services.

(5)   If for any reason a cemetery company or other entity who has entered into a contract for the sale of personal property or services cannot or does not provide the personal property or perform the services called for by the contract after request in writing to do so, the purchaser or his heirs or assigns or duly authorized representative shall be entitled to receive the entire amount paid on the contract and any income if any, earned thereon by the trust account.

(6)   Every year after September 1, 1975, the cemetery company, the trustee or other entity shall within 75 days after the end of the calendar year, file a financial report of the trust funds with the Commission, setting forth the principal thereof, the investments and payments made, the income earned and

disbursed; provided, however, that the Commission may require the cemetery, trustee, or other entity to make the additional financial reports as it may deem advisable.

(c) Whenever a contract for the sale of personal property or services or both allocates payments to apply to one item at a time under a specific schedule, the contract shall be considered divisible. Title to each item of personal property or the right to each item of services shall pass to the purchaser upon full payment for that item regardless of the remaining balance on other items under the same contract.

(d) Any contract for the sale of personal property or services or both shall state separate costs for each item of personal property, for each act of installation required by the contract, for opening and closing each grave space, and for each other item of services included in the contract.

(e) All contracts for the sale of personal property or services or both must be printed in type size as required by the Truth in Lending Act, 15 U.S.C. § 1601 et seq., and regulations adopted pursuant to that act.

(f) In the event of prepayment, interest charged shall be no more than the interest earned on the unpaid balance computed on a percent per month basis for each month or part of a month up to the date of final payment. Any excess interest which has been paid by the purchaser must be refunded to him, his assigns, or his representative within 30 days after the final payment. No penalty or additional charge for prepayment may be required.

(g) In lieu of the deposits required under subsection (b) of this section, the cemetery company or other entity may post with the Commission a good and sufficient performance bond by surety company licensed to do business in North Carolina and in an amount sufficient to cover all payments made directly or indirectly by or on account of purchasers who have not received the purchased property and services. Money received from the sale or assignment of notes entered into by the purchasers, or otherwise, shall be treated as payments made by the purchasers.

(h) The Commission shall have the power and is required from time to time as it may deem necessary to examine the business of any cemetery company or other entity writing contracts for the sale of the property or services as herein contemplated. The written report of the examination shall be filed in the office of the Commission. Any person or entity being examined shall produce the records of the company needed for the examination.

(i) Any provision of any contract for the sale of the personal property or the performance of services herein contemplated under which the purchaser or beneficiary waives any of the provisions of this section shall be void.

(j) Repealed by Session Laws 1991, c. 653, s. 7.

(k) Nothing in this section shall apply to persons or legal entities holding licenses under Article 13D of Chapter 90 of the General Statutes when engaging in activities for which a license is required under that Article.

(l) If any report is not received within the time stipulated by the Commission or herein, the Commission may levy and collect a late filing fee of twenty-five dollars ($25.00) per month for each month of delinquency.

(m) Within 30 days following the execution of a contract for the sale of personal property or performance of services, a purchaser may cancel his contract by giving written notice to the seller. The seller may cancel the contract, upon default by purchaser, by giving written notice to the purchaser. Within 30 days of notice of cancellation, the cemetery company or other entity shall refund to purchaser the principal amount on deposit in the trust account for his benefit on any undelivered merchandise or services. This amount (no other obligations owed the purchaser by the seller) shall constitute the purchaser's entire entitlements under the contract. The seller may not terminate the contract without complying with this subsection.

(n) A cemetery company shall not require the purchaser or consumer of a grave space, mausoleum, or mausoleum section to purchase a vault from the cemetery company or from any other particular seller of vaults as a condition to the purchase or use of a grave space, mausoleum, or mausoleum section but may require that a casket be enclosed within a vault. A cemetery company may charge a reasonable fee not to exceed twenty dollars ($20.00) for delivery of vaults or inspection of vaults that are purchased from a person other than the cemetery company. (1975, c. 768, s. 1; 1979, c. 888, s. 7; 1987, c. 488, s. 7; 1991, c. 653, s. 7; 1995, c. 509, s. 135.1(j), (k); 2004-202, s. 9; 2010-102, s. 4.)

§ 65-67. Applications for license.

Applications for renewal license must be submitted on or before July 1 each and every year in the case of an existing cemetery company. Before any sale of cemetery property in the case of a new cemetery company or a change of ownership or control as indicated in G.S. 65-59, an application for license must be submitted and license issued. (1975, c. 768, s. 1.)

§ 65-68. License not assignable or transferable.

No license issued under G.S. 65-67 shall be transferable or assignable and no licensee shall develop or operate any cemetery authorized by this Article under any name or at any location other than that contained in the application for such license. (1975, c. 768, s. 1.)

§ 65-69. Minimum acreage; sale or disposition of cemetery lands.

(a)   Each licensee shall set aside a minimum of 30 acres of land for use by said licensee as a cemetery, and shall not sell, mortgage, lease or encumber the same.

(b)   The fee simple title, or lesser estate, in any lands owned by licensee and dedicated for use by it as a cemetery, which are contiguous, adjoining, or adjacent to the minimum of 30 acres described in subsection (a), may be sold, conveyed, or disposed of, or any part thereof, by the licensee, for use by the new owner for other purposes than as a cemetery; provided that no bodies have been previously interred therein; and provided further, that any and all titles, interests, or burial rights which may have been sold or contracted to be sold in such lands which are the subject of such sale shall be conveyed to and revested in the licensee prior to consummation of any such sale, conveyance or disposition.

(c)   Any licensee may convey and transfer to a municipality or county its real and personal property together with moneys deposited with the trustee; provided said municipality or county will accept responsibility for maintenance thereof and prior written approval of the Commission is first obtained.

(d) The provisions of subsections (a) and (b) relating to a requirement for minimum acreage shall not apply to those cemeteries licensed by the Commission on or before July 1, 1967, which own or control a total of less than 30 acres of land; provided that such cemeteries shall not dispose of any of such lands. A nongovernment lien or other interest in land acquired in violation of this section is void. (1975, c. 768, s. 1; 1991, c. 653, s. 8.)

§ 65-70. Construction of mausoleums and belowground crypts; trust fund for receipts from sale of preconstruction crypts; compliance requirements.

(a) A cemetery company shall be required to start construction of that section of a mausoleum or bank of belowground crypts in which sales, contracts for sale, reservations for sales or agreements for sales are being made, within 48 months after the date of the first sale. The construction of the mausoleum section or bank of belowground crypts shall be completed within five years after the date of the first sale made; provided, however, extensions for completion, not to exceed three years, may be granted by the Commission for good reasons shown.

(b) A cemetery company which plans to offer for sale space in a section of a mausoleum or bank of underground crypts prior to its construction shall establish a preconstruction trust account. The trust account shall be administered and operated in the same manner as the merchandise trust account provided for in G.S. 65-66 and shall be exclusive of the merchandise trust account or the other trust accounts or funds that may be required by law. The personal representative of any purchaser of the space who dies before completion of construction shall be entitled to a refund of all moneys paid for the space including any income earned thereon.

(c) Before a sale, contract for sale, reservation for sale or agreement for sale in the first mausoleum section or bank of underground crypts in each cemetery may be made the funds (one hundred twenty percent (120%) of construction cost) to be deposited to the preconstruction trust account shall be computed as to the section or bank of crypts and the trust account payments must be made on or before the last day of the calendar month following receipt by the cemetery company or its agent of each payment. The trust account portion of each payment shall be computed by dividing the cost of the project plus twenty percent (20%) of the cost, as computed by a licensed contractor, engineer or architect by the number of crypts in the section or bank of crypts to ascertain the cost per unit. The unit cost shall be divided by the contract sales price of each unit to obtain a percentage which shall be multiplied by the amount of each payment. The formula shall be computed as follows:

Cost plus twenty percent (20%) divided by number of crypts = cost per unit

Cost per unit divided by contract sales price = percentage

Percentage x payment received = deposit required to preconstruction trust account.

(d) The cemetery company shall be entitled to withdraw the funds from the preconstruction trust account only after the Commission has become satisfied that construction has been completed; provided, however, that during construction of the mausoleum or bank of belowground crypts the Commission may, in its discretion, authorize a specific percentage of the funds to be withdrawn when it appears that at least an equivalent percentage of construction has been completed.

(e) If a mausoleum section or bank of underground crypts is not completed within the time limits set out in this section the corporate trustee, if any, shall contract for and cause the project to be completed and paid therefor from the trust account funds deposited to the project's account paying any balance, less cost and expenses, to the cemetery company. In the event there is no corporate trustee, the Commission shall appoint a committee to serve as trustees to contract for and cause the project to be completed and paid therefor from the trust account funds deposited to the project's account paying any balance, less cost and expenses, to the cemetery company.

(f) In lieu of the payments outlined hereunder to the preconstruction trust account the cemetery company may deliver to the Commission a good and sufficient completion or performance bond in an amount and by surety companies acceptable to the Commission. (1975, c. 768, s. 1; 1977, c. 686, ss. 16, 17; 1979, c. 888, s. 8; 2010-102, s. 5.)

§ 65-71. Penalties.

(a) Except as provided in this subsection, a person violating any provisions of this Article, of any order or rule promulgated under this Article, or of any license issued by the Commission is guilty of a Class 1 misdemeanor. Each failure to deposit funds in a trust fund in accordance with this Article is a separate offense. A person who has failed to deposit funds in a trust fund in accordance with this Article and whose delinquent deposits equal or exceed twenty thousand dollars ($20,000) is guilty of a Class I felony.

(b) The officers and directors or persons occupying similar status or performing similar functions of any cemetery company, cemetery sales organization, cemetery management organization or cemetery broker, as defined in this Chapter, failing to make required contributions to the care and maintenance trust fund and any other trust fund or escrow account shall be liable for any offense based on the failure and upon conviction for the offense shall be punished in the manner prescribed by law. (1943, c. 644, s. 14; 1967, c. 1009, s. 13; 1975, c. 768, s. 1; 1991, c. 653, s. 9; 1993, c. 539, ss. 501, 1281; 1994, Ex. Sess., c. 24, s. 14(c).)

§ 65-72. Burial without regard to race or color.

(a) It shall be the public policy of the State that all cemetery companies or other legal entities conducting or maintaining public or private cemeteries shall sell to all applicants and bury all deceased human beings on equal terms without regard to race or color. Anything contrary hereto is void and of no legal effect. Bylaws, rules and regulations, contracts, deeds, etc., may permit designation of parts of cemeteries or burial grounds for the specific use of persons whose religious code required isolation. Any program offering free burial rights to veterans or any other person or group of persons shall not be conditioned by any requirement to purchase additional burial rights or merchandise.

(b) Any cemetery company or other legal entity violating the provisions of this section shall be guilty of a Class 1 misdemeanor, and each violation of this section shall constitute a separate offense. (1975, c. 768, s. 1; 1993, c. 539, s. 502; 1994, Ex. Sess., c. 24, s. 14(c).)

§ 65-73. Validation of certain deeds for cemetery lots executed by suspended corporations.

Any deed for a cemetery lot or lots which was executed prior to January 1, 1979, and which would have been valid if the charter of the grantor corporation had not been suspended at the time the deed was executed, is hereby validated. (1979, c. 225, s. 1.)

Article 10.

Access to and Maintenance of Private Graves and Abandoned Public Cemeteries.

§ 65-74: Repealed by Session Laws 2007-118, s. 6, effective July 1, 2007, and applicable to all trusts created on or after that date.

§ 65-75: Repealed by Session Laws 2007-118, s. 6, effective July 1, 2007, and applicable to all trusts created on or after that date.

§ 65-76: Reserved for future codification purposes.

Article 11.

Minimum Burial Depth.

§ 65-77. Minimum burial depth.

When final disposition of a human body entails interment, the top of the uppermost part of the burial vault or other encasement shall be a minimum of 18 inches below the ground surface. This section does not apply to:

(1) Burials where no part of the burial vault or other encasement containing the body is touching the ground.

(2) Burials where the land is located in a family owned cemetery that was established by deed recorded prior to January 1, 1989, and the individual to be buried is to be buried in a surface burial vault in a manner similar to that of the individual's deceased spouse who was buried prior to January 1, 1981. (1995, c. 123, s. 16; 1999-425, s. 4; 2003-420, s. 8(b).)

§ 65-78: Reserved for future codification purposes.

§ 65-79: Reserved for future codification purposes.

§ 65-80: Reserved for future codification purposes.

§ 65-81: Reserved for future codification purposes.

§ 65-82: Reserved for future codification purposes.

§ 65-83: Reserved for future codification purposes.

§ 65-84: Reserved for future codification purposes.

Article 12.

Abandoned and Neglected Cemeteries.

Part 1. General.

§ 65-85. Definitions.

As used in this Article, the following terms mean:

(1) Abandoned. - Ceased from maintenance or use by the person with legal right to the real property with the intent of not again maintaining the real property in the foreseeable future.

(2) Cemetery. - A tract of land used for burial of multiple graves.

(3) Department. - The Department of Cultural Resources.

(4) Grave. - A place of burial for a single decedent.

(5) Neglected. - Left unattended or uncared for through carelessness or intention and lacking a caretaker.

(6) Public cemetery. - A cemetery for which there is no qualification to purchase, own, or come into possession of a grave in that cemetery. (2007-118, s. 1.)

§ 65-86: Reserved for future codification purposes.

§ 65-87: Reserved for future codification purposes.

§ 65-88: Reserved for future codification purposes.

§ 65-89: Reserved for future codification purposes.

§ 65-90: Reserved for future codification purposes.

Part 2. Trust Funds for Care of Cemeteries.

§ 65-91. Money deposited with the clerk of superior court.

For the maintenance and preservation of abandoned or neglected graves or abandoned or neglected cemeteries, any person, firm, or corporation may, by will or otherwise, place in the hands of the clerk of the superior court of any county in the State where such grave or lot is located any sum of money not less than five thousand dollars ($5,000), the income from which is to be used for keeping in good condition the abandoned or neglected grave or the abandoned or neglected cemetery with specific instructions as to the use of the fund. (1917, c. 155, s. 1; C.S., s. 5024; 1979, c. 38; 2007-118, s. 1.)

§ 65-92. Separate record of accounts to be kept.

It shall be the duty of the clerk of the superior court to keep a separate record for keeping account of the money deposited as provided in G.S. 65-91, to keep a perpetual account of the same therein, and to record therein the specific instructions about the use of the income on such money. The clerk shall see that the income is spent according to such specific instructions and shall place a copy of the accounting in the estate file. (1917, c. 155, s. 1; C.S., s. 5025; 2007-118, s. 1.)

§ 65-93. Funds to be kept perpetually.

All money placed in the office of the superior court clerk in accordance with this Part shall be held perpetually, or until such time as the balance of the trust corpus falls below one hundred dollars ($100.00), at which time the trust shall terminate, and the clerk shall disburse the remaining balance as provided in G.S. 36A-147(c). Except as otherwise provided herein, no one shall have authority to withdraw or change the direction of the income on same. (1917, c. 155, s. 2; C.S., s. 5026; 1995, c. 225, s. 2; 2007-118, s. 1.)

§ 65-94. Investment of funds.

Money placed in the office of the superior court clerk in accordance with this Part shall be invested in the same manner as is provided by law for the investment of other trust funds by the clerk of the superior court. (1917, c. 155, s. 3; C.S., s. 5027; 1943, c. 97, s. 1; 2007-118, s. 1.)

§ 65-95. Clerk's bond; substitution of bank or trust company as trustee.

The official bond of the clerk of the superior court shall be liable for all such sums as shall be paid over to the clerk in accordance with the provisions of this Part. In lieu of the provisions of this section, the clerk may appoint any bank or trust company authorized to do business in this State as trustee for the funds authorized to be paid into his office by virtue of this Part; provided, that no bank or trust company shall be appointed as such trustee unless such bank or trust company is authorized and licensed to act as fiduciary under the laws of this State.

Before any clerk shall turn over such funds to the trustee so appointed, the clerk shall require that the trustee so named qualify before the clerk as such trustee in the same way and manner and to the same extent as guardians are by law required to so qualify. After such trustee has qualified as herein provided, all such funds coming into the clerk's hands may be invested by the trustee only in the securities set out in G.S. 7A-112 and the income therefrom invested for the purposes and in the manner heretofore set out in this Part. All trustees appointed under the provisions of this Part shall render and file in the office of the clerk of the superior court all reports that are now required by law of guardians. (1917, c. 155, ss. 3, 4; C.S., s. 5028; 1939, c. 18; 1943, c. 97, s. 2; 2007-118, s. 1.)

§ 65-96. Funds exempt from taxation.

All money referred to in the preceding sections of this Part shall be exempt from all State, county, township, town, and city taxes. (1917, c. 155, s. 4; C.S., s. 5029; 2007-118, s. 1.)

§ 65-97: Reserved for future codification purposes.

§ 65-98: Reserved for future codification purposes.

§ 65-99: Reserved for future codification purposes.

§ 65-100: Reserved for future codification purposes.

Part 3. Access to and Maintenance of Abandoned or Neglected Cemeteries.

§ 65-101. Entering public or private property to maintain or visit with consent.

Any of the following persons, with the consent of the public or private landowner, may enter the property of another to discover, restore, maintain, or visit a grave or abandoned public cemetery:

(1)   A descendant of the person whose remains are reasonably believed to be interred in the grave or abandoned public cemetery.

(2)   A descendant's designee.

(3)   Any other person who has a special personal interest in the grave or abandoned public cemetery. (1987, c. 686, s. 1; 1991, c. 36, s. 1; 2007-118, s. 1.)

§ 65-102. Entering public or private property to maintain or visit without consent.

(a) If the consent of the landowner cannot be obtained, any person listed in G.S. 65-101(1), (2), or (3) may commence a special proceeding by petitioning the clerk of superior court of the county in which the petitioner has reasonable grounds to believe the grave or abandoned public cemetery is located for an order allowing the petitioner to enter the property to discover, restore, maintain, or visit the grave or abandoned public cemetery. The petition shall be verified. The special proceeding shall be in accordance with the provisions of Articles 27A and 33 of Chapter 1 of the General Statutes. The clerk shall issue an order allowing the petitioner to enter the property if the clerk finds all of the following:

(1) There are reasonable grounds to believe that the grave or abandoned public cemetery is located on the property or it is reasonably necessary to enter or cross the landowner's property to reach the grave or abandoned public cemetery.

(2) The petitioner, or the petitioner's designee, is a descendant of the deceased, or the petitioner has a legitimate historical, genealogical, or governmental interest in the grave or abandoned public cemetery.

(3) The entry on the property would not unreasonably interfere with the enjoyment of the property by the landowner.

(b) The clerk's order may state one or more of the following:

(1) Specify the dates and the daylight hours that the petitioner may enter and remain on the property.

(2) Grant the petitioner the right to enter the landowner's property periodically, as specified in the order, after the time needed for initial restoration of the grave or abandoned public cemetery.

(3) Specify a reasonable route from which the petitioner may not deviate in all entries and exits from the property. (1987, c. 686, s. 1; 1991, c. 36, s. 1; 1999-216, s. 12; 2007-118, s. 1.)

§ 65-103: Reserved for future codification purposes.

§ 65-104: Reserved for future codification purposes.

§ 65-105: Reserved for future codification purposes.

Part 4. Removal of Graves.

§ 65-106. Removal of graves; who may disinter, move, and reinter; notice; certificate filed; reinterment expenses; due care required.

(a) The State of North Carolina and any of its agencies, public institutions, or political subdivisions, the United States of America or any agency thereof, any church, electric power or lighting company, or any person, firm, or corporation may effect the disinterment, removal, and reinterment of graves as follows:

(1) By the State of North Carolina or any of its agencies, public institutions, or political subdivisions, the United States of America or any agency thereof, when it shall determine and certify to the board of county commissioners in the county from which the bodies are to be disinterred that such removal is reasonably necessary to perform its governmental functions and the duties delegated to it by law.

(2) By any church authority in order to erect a new church, parish house, parsonage, or any other facility owned and operated exclusively by such church; in order to expand or enlarge an existing church facility; or better to care for and maintain graves not located in a regular cemetery for which such church has assumed responsibility of care and custody.

(3) By an electric power or lighting company when it owns land on which graves are located, and the land is to be used as a reservoir.

(4) By any person, firm, or corporation who owns land on which an abandoned cemetery is located after first securing the consent of the governing body of the municipality or county in which the abandoned cemetery is located.

(b) The party effecting the disinterment, removal, and reinterment of a grave containing a decedent's remains under the provisions of this Part shall, before disinterment, give 30 days' written notice of such intention to the next of kin of the decedent, if known or subject to being ascertained by reasonable search and inquiry, and shall cause notice of such disinterment, removal, and reinterment to be published at least once per week for four successive weeks in a newspaper of general circulation in the county where such grave is located, and the first publication shall be not less than 30 days before disinterment. Any remains disinterred and removed hereunder shall be reinterred in a suitable cemetery.

(c) The party removing or causing the removal of all such graves shall, within 30 days after completion of the removal and reinterment, file with the register of deeds of the county from which the graves were removed and with the register of deeds of the county in which reinterment is made, a written certificate of the removal facts. Such certificate shall contain the full name, if known or reasonably ascertainable, of each decedent whose grave is moved, a precise description of the site from which such grave was removed, a precise description of the site and specific location where the decedent's remains have been reinterred, the full and correct name of the party effecting the removal, and a brief description of the statutory basis or bases upon which such removal or reinterment was effected. If the full name of any decedent cannot reasonably be ascertained, the removing party shall set forth all additional reasonably ascertainable facts about the decedent including birth date, death date, and family name.

The fee for recording instruments in general, as provided in G.S. 161-10(a)(1), for registering a certificate of removal facts shall be paid to the register of deeds of each county in which such certificate is filed for registration.

(d) All expenses of disinterment, removal, and acquisition of the new burial site and reinterment shall be borne by the party effecting such disinterment, removal, and reinterment, including the actual reasonable expense of one of the next of kin incurred in attending the same, not to exceed the sum of two hundred dollars ($200.00).

(e) The Office of Vital Records of North Carolina shall promulgate regulations affecting the registration and indexing of the written certificate of the removal facts, including the form of that certificate.

(f) The party effecting the disinterment, removal, and reinterment of a decedent's remains under the provisions of this Part shall ensure that the site in which reinterment is accomplished shall be of such suitable dimensions to accommodate the remains of that decedent only and that such site shall be reasonably accessible to all relatives of that decedent, provided that the remains may be reinterred in a common grave where written consent is obtained from the next of kin. If under the authority of this Part, disinterment, removal, and reinterment are effected by the State of North Carolina or any of its agencies, public institutions, or political subdivisions, the United States of America or any agency thereof, any electric power or lighting company, then such disinterment, removal, and reinterment shall be performed by a funeral director duly licensed as a "funeral director" or a "funeral service licensee" under the provisions of Article 13A of Chapter 90 of the General Statutes.

(g) All disinterment, removal, and reinterment under the provisions of this Part shall be made under the supervision and direction of the county board of commissioners or other appropriate official, including the local health director, appointed by such board for the county where the disinterment, removal, and reinterment take place. If reinterment is effected in a county different from the county of disinterment with the consent of the next of kin of the deceased whose remains are disinterred, then the disinterment and removal shall be made under the supervision and direction of the county board of commissioners or other appropriate official, including the local health director, appointed by such board for the county of the disinterment, and the reinterment shall be made under the supervision and direction of the county board of commissioners or other appropriate official, including the local health director, appointed by such board for the county of reinterment.

Due care shall be taken to do said work in a proper and decent manner, and, if necessary, to furnish suitable coffins or boxes for reinterring such remains. Due care shall also be taken to remove, protect, and replace all tombstones or other markers, so as to leave such tombstones or other markers in as good condition as that prior to disinterment. Provided that in cases where the remains are to be moved to a perpetual care cemetery or other cemetery where upright tombstones are not permitted, a suitable replacement marker shall be provided.

(h) Nothing contained in this Part shall be construed to grant or confer the power or authority of eminent domain, or to impair the right of the next of kin of a decedent to remove or cause the removal, at his or their expense, of the remains or grave of such decedent. (1919, c. 245; C.S., ss. 5030, 5030(a); Ex. Sess. 1920, c. 46; 1927, c. 23, s. 1; c. 175, s. 1; 1937, c. 3; 1947, cc. 168, 576; 1961, c. 457; 1963, c. 915, s. 1; 1965, c. 71; 1971, c. 797, s. 1; 1977, c. 311, s. 1; 2001-390, s. 3; 2007-118, s. 1.)

§ 65-107: Reserved for future codification purposes.

§ 65-108: Reserved for future codification purposes.

§ 65-109: Reserved for future codification purposes.

§ 65-110: Reserved for future codification purposes.

Part 5. County Care of Rural Cemeteries.

§ 65-111. County commissioners to provide list of public and abandoned cemeteries.

Each board of county commissioners shall have the following duties and responsibilities:

(1)   To prepare and keep on record in the office of the register of deeds a list of all public cemeteries in the county outside the limits of incorporated municipalities, and not established and maintained for the use of an incorporated municipality, including the names and addresses of the persons in possession and control of those public cemeteries.

(2)   To prepare and keep on record in the office of the register of deeds a list of all abandoned public cemeteries.

(3)   To furnish to the Department and the Publications Division in the Department of the Secretary of State copies of the lists of such public and abandoned cemeteries, to the end that it may furnish to the boards of county commissioners, for the use of the persons in control of such cemeteries, suitable literature, suggesting methods of taking care of such places. (1917, c. 101, s. 1; C.S., s. 5019; 1939, c. 316; 2007-118, s. 1.)

§ 65-112. Appropriations by county commissioners.

To encourage the persons in possession and control of the public cemeteries referred to in G.S. 65-111 to take proper care of and to beautify such cemeteries, to mark distinctly their boundary lines with evergreen hedges or rows of suitable trees, and otherwise to lay out the grounds in an orderly manner, the board of county commissioners of any county, upon being notified that two-thirds of the expense necessary for so marking and beautifying any cemetery has been raised by the local governing body of the institution which owns the cemetery, and is actually in hand, is hereby authorized to appropriate from the general fund of the county one-third of the expense necessary to pay for such work, the amount appropriated by the board of commissioners in no case to exceed fifty dollars ($50.00) for each cemetery. (1917, c. 101, s. 2; C.S., s. 5020; 1979, c. 735; 2007-118, s. 1.)

§ 65-113. County commissioners to have control of abandoned public cemeteries; trustees.

The county commissioners of the various counties are authorized to oversee all abandoned public cemeteries in their respective counties, to see that the boundaries and lines are clearly laid out, defined, and marked, and to take proper steps to preserve them from encroachment, and they are hereby authorized to appropriate from the general fund of the county whatever sums may be necessary from time to time for the above purposes.

The boards of county commissioners of the various counties may appoint a board of trustees not to exceed five in number and to serve at the will of the board, and may impose upon such trustees the duties required of the board of commissioners by this Article; and such trustees may accept gifts and donations for the purpose of upkeep and beautification of such cemeteries. (1917, c. 101, s. 3; C.S., s. 5021; 1947, c. 236; 2007-118, s. 1.)

§ 65-114: Reserved for future codification purposes.

§ 65-115: Reserved for future codification purposes.

§ 65-116: Reserved for future codification purposes.

§ 65-117: Reserved for future codification purposes.

§ 65-118: Reserved for future codification purposes.

§ 65-119: Reserved for future codification purposes.

§ 65-120: Reserved for future codification purposes.

§ 65-121: Reserved for future codification purposes.

§ 65-122: Reserved for future codification purposes.

§ 65-123: Reserved for future codification purposes.

§ 65-124: Reserved for future codification purposes.

§ 65-125: Reserved for future codification purposes.

Vision Books Order Form

Fax Orders: 1-980-299-5965

Phone Orders: 1-704-898-0770

E-mail Orders: www.visionbooks.org

Mail Orders: Vision Books, LLC
P.O. Box 42406
Charlotte, NC 28215

Shipp To:
Name_____
Address_____
City_____State_____Zip_____
Phone_____Fax_____
Email_____@_____

Bill To: We can bill a third party on your behalf.
Name_____
Address_____
City_____State_____Zip_____
Phone____(_____)_____Fax_____
Email_____@_____

Pamphlet Number ($15.00 Each)	Qty	Total Cost
_____	_____	_____
_____	_____	_____
_____	_____	_____
_____	_____	_____
_____	_____	_____
_____	_____	_____
_____	_____	_____
_____	_____	_____
Full Volume Set 1-92	**92 Pamphlets**	**1,380.00**

Free Shipping Shipping & Handling on Full Volume Orders
Add $1.00 Shipping & Handling per pamphlet $_____

Total Cost $_____

Thank you for your order. Management!

DID YOU ENJOY THIS BOOK?

Vision Books, LLC would like to hear from you! If you or someone you know has been fasely imprisoned, we would like to hear your story. If the 'North Carolina Criminal Law and Procedure' has had an effect in your life or if you have suggestions, we would like to hear from you. Send your letters to:

Vision Books, LLC
Attn: Staff Writers
P.O. Box 42406
Charlotte, NC 28215
Email: staff@visionbooks.org

Order Additional Copies:

Fax Orders: 1-980-299-5965

Phone Orders: 1-704-898-0770

E-mail Orders: www.visionbooks.org

Mail Orders: Vision Books, LLC
                       P.O. Box 42406
                       Charlotte, NC 28215

www.ingramcontent.com/pod-product-compliance
Lightning Source LLC
Chambersburg PA
CBHW051634170526
45167CB00001B/181